The

RELATIONSHIP

Sexual

SECRETS

Education

FROM THE

of a

TRENCHES

Beauty

TAYLOR MARSH

Queen

OPEN ROAD

INTEGRATED MEDIA

NEW YORK

Cover and interior design by designSimple

Back cover photo by Robert Evans

ISBN 978-1-4976-6316-9

Published in 2014 by Open Road Integrated Media, Inc.
345 Hudson Street
New York, NY 10014
www.openroadmedia.com

Always, for Mark

"How do women still go out with guys, when you consider the fact that there is no greater threat to women than men? We're the number one threat to women."

—Louis C.K.,
from the HBO special Oh My God

"Analysis is no substitute for guts."

—Naomi Shields,
from The Chapman Report,
Screenplay by Wyatt Cooper and Don Mankiewicz

Contents

Introduction

Everyone remembers where they were on 9/11, the day nineteen hijackers flew planes into the World Trade Center towers. I was sitting at home in Beverly Hills, California, getting ready for my early morning shift as a phone sex actress.

It was the latest escapade in my sexual education that began when I discovered my father's dog-eared edition of *Candy* in our garage attic, when I was around nine. Terry Southern's raunchy erotica blew my mind and began a journey that landed me in the most outrageous places, especially for a former beauty queen.

A goody two-shoes, Miss Missouri from the Show-Me State, I grew up during the modern feminist revolution that secured my interest in politics and eventually landed me as a national political writer living in the Beltway area of Virginia, just outside of Washington, D.C.

How a Miss America contestant, not to mention a Miss Friendship in the Miss Teenage America Pageant, and homecoming queen, ended up as editor-in-chief of the first female-run soft-core website to make money on the web is only part of the story, but it did get my picture on the pages of *USA Today* at the time.

Wait. *But...*

How in God's name could a former Miss Missouri also be a liberated feminist, especially if she chose to delve into the sex trade and adult entertainment worlds? She couldn't possibly believe she could solve the questions of her own life by asking strangers looking for love, marriage and sex, questions about why they wanted what they wanted, let alone figure out what it all meant for others.

When first the *Washington Post* and then the *New Republic* sent reporters to interview me for profiles during the height of the 2008 presidential election cycle, I described myself as "the Hugh Hefner of politics," which became the title to TNR's article. At the time I was excavating the adult industry, I intended to write about politics on the female-owned, soft-core website for which I worked, like Hugh Hefner did for *Playboy*, giving my political analysis of events, while offering the female-dominated site a social and political consciousness in an industry run by men. Hefner had been at the epicenter of the sexual revolution itself. When all hell broke loose in the early 1970s, I was part of the feminist generation that rose up and began changing what it meant to be a woman in America.

In the mid-'90s, the web offered females in the sex industry their first glimpse at the possibilities for economic and creative independence, a prospect that fascinated me. Conservatives and feminists rail against the sex industry for good reasons, but I wasn't there to judge women whose choices were theirs to make. I jumped at the chance to have a front-row seat at the history they were making in a man's industry.

But being Relationship Consultant at the *LA Weekly* in 1992 was my first foray into finding out what men and women want and how they go about getting it. When my column moved to the web in 1996, I became one of the first people writing about relationships, men, women and the politics of sex online. From helping love-seekers write mainstream personal ads to starting the first alternative personal ads in the *LA Weekly*, I helped people find fun, love and "special arrangements." My trademarked relationship column was titled "What Do You Want?" The answer to that question is where it all begins for each of us.

Online dating has now evolved into a multi-billion dollar business.

The Pill made women's liberation a reality, just as the modern feminist revolution made the next advances possible and relationships much more complex. The trajectory my life and writing career were taking as the web took off matched the arc of women's freedom, sexual power and political ascension.

Why I picked the family I did to drop into from oblivion I'll never know for sure. So, no sins of omission or confessions here, just a simple explanation for the road I chose. My adventures were fueled by the crazy combustion of family life at the moment the feminine mystique collided with sexual liberation, leading to the birth of the modern feminist revolution.

I'm also not a believer in dragging people through a tiresome chronicle about a screwed-up family. Abusive beginnings don't make a life. And if I'm certain of one thing, whether I can explain it all or not, it's that as sure as I was Miss Missouri, every exhilarating, unbounded experience and drama of my story has set me on the ride of a lifetime that I've authored myself. I wouldn't change any of it. Without my family, I would not have found and tapped the bravery of kin to venture into places I was told a lady never went, and wouldn't have come to understand my own humanity, let alone get a glimpse of others', so I could relate to them and relay the stories of those who dared to tell their tales of love and lust to me.

The heroine of my life is my mother, Marjorie, who almost 100 years ago blasted onto earth and dared to never give up so that I'd be here today. It wasn't until April of 2013 that we finally pieced the rest of her story together and I learned she was originally named Phyllis. Born in 1916, she would learn she'd been adopted *twice*, was left by her father when her adoptive mother was killed, and had been told her wrong birthday, which she didn't learn until she applied for Social Security. As she told it to me (but few others), the woman she thought was her birth mother, Eva, had stuffed herself out to appear pregnant when she was not.

Then, when my mother was still a baby, the gas stove blew up, engulfing the house and killing Mom's first adoptive mother, Eva Gaynell McKain Cloughley. Her adoptive father Robert promptly turned tail and ran for the hills, never to be seen again. That is, until she took us on a visit when I was in my early teens to Wichita, Kansas, and he appeared out of nowhere at the front door of the person we were visiting, decades after running out on my mother when single-fatherhood came calling. Just the thought of him being at the front door sent my mother into hair-raising panic. She bolted from the house, dragging me out the back door, and drove immediately back to Missouri without staying one night in Kansas, talking a blue streak about her crazy life as we drove along. She forever awakened my wide-eyed consciousness, as she told me what she knew of her beginnings, how she entered the world.

My mother's second adoptive mother, Lily M. McKain, became my great grandmother, whom I never knew, but who is legend in our tiny surviving family. In this part of her story, my mother got lucky, because the McKains had some money, as their living on the north side of Joplin, Missouri at the time signified. This is how Mom landed in college, the University of Arkansas, pledging Tri Delta. In the early twentieth century, going to college was unheard of for a girl raised near the Boot Heel area of Missouri.

In the middle of my mother's dramatic entrance, throw in a handsome rapscallion dandy of a man, my father Floyd. He was a smooth-talking shoe salesman, popular with the ladies, and a bastard of a man from start to finish. This is the relationship that everyone goes back to for any girl, especially one who takes close to a ten-year detour to excavate the worlds of sex and men, women, dating and relationships. The first male relationship seals a girl's destiny on the road to understanding men and even finding love for daddy's little girl, or so the shrinks tell it. Ours was a short, strange and unhealthy relationship, and that's all you're going to get from me on it.

Hurricane Floyd tore through our lives and left carnage across the family landscape. But it's not like he planned it. His mother, grandma Marshall to me, was a witch of a woman, with my life's embedded memory of her simply a picture in my mind: Grandma Marshall standing over my beloved grandpa as he sat at his desk, hissing at him in a voice that sent chills down my spine as I watched from the stairs. My daddy simply labeled it "black Irish," which for our family meant a vicious strain of temperament that seemed to wreak havoc through evil.

Before Floyd showed up at the University of Arkansas and my mother climbed out the sorority window to elope with him, Daddy had plenty of troubles of his own. One moment that seemingly haunted him was the time he was driving and ended up in an accident that left his date dead and him still alive. The girl riding shotgun had been named Marjorie, the same as the woman he would marry, my mother. But after Daddy married Mom, he always called her *Duchess*, the name *Marjorie* never spoken from his lips.

Floyd and Marjorie were beautiful people, epic partiers and big drinkers. Not that I was there to see it, because they had me late, so by that time Daddy spent most of his time in the hospital, and I in front of the TV. But the pictures left behind show it, the happier chapters of their lives unfolding frame by frame on the flip side of the carnage-riddled drama their partnership organically caused. Happy times turned to dramatic soap opera events at a time in the twentieth century when roles for men and women were starting to implode, and late-entry kids like myself watched it all unravel.

The next generations, including my brother, sister and me, were all forged through this emotional volcano and not only survived it, but thrived as a result of being made stronger and smarter as a result of it, making ours a quintessentially American story. This isn't a whine, but the truth, the foundation and the proof of the inevitability of the modern women's revolution and just one of the stories that helped shake it loose from America's gut. Our family was a microcosm of the foundation that came before what continues to play out in our culture, though today's families have more outside forces invading, while ours came from internal thunder.

It's just that nobody talked about what was happening openly when it was happening. We never processed anything; we pushed the struggles and the secrets down. Life played out on top, while underneath was a landscape of cultural convulsion and societal fracking, a precursor of what's going on today in the great information giveaway, as parents melt away and controls disappear. It was back during the 1950s and '60s when the traditional notion of relationships started falling apart, because women had begun to rebel on the way to being set free to walk away from the setup.

Mom and Dad were smokers, caught in the cloud of advertised glamour in the *Mad Men* era. My Aunt Maxine and Uncle Dick were part of the cast of the musical of my family life, which always had a soundtrack playing in the background. It began with Frank Sinatra, but included all things cool and male and libidinous. A smoldering track was always playing at our family record store, Marshall's Record Rendezvous. Maxine was a bombshell of a broad who, while my Uncle Dick was off flying way too many missions in WWII (and ending up with battle fatigue for his heroism), was trying her hand at modeling, which was quite the scandal for the midwestern norm. The scuttlebutt was she was too much woman for him, because she wasn't the housewife type.

While Uncle Dick was off fighting the enemy for his country, my dad was at Boeing Aircraft in Wichita, Kansas doing his part for the war efforts in an essential industry that meant he couldn't be spared for combat. However, what isn't known is whether he ever had a choice to fight in combat instead, which was an option given to many men of draft age, while women were taking their places in factories so the men could fight.

Since I was so young when all this played out, I relied on parts of my story's validation from my older brother Larry, the only real father I've ever known. The man who became my sister's rock, but also rescued my mother and me, too, when Daddy died. He would also become the mentor of my political life, because of the impact John F. Kennedy had on him, something I chronicled in my one-woman show, *Weeping for JFK*. Whatever a father is supposed to mean to a little girl growing up, Larry was that for my sister and me.

When my father died my mother didn't even know where the checkbook was kept. That's the way it was. It hardly mattered, because there was nothing in it. Daddy had left a financial black hole behind. Mom also had to get her head around working for a living again at midlife, while learning to cope with a young, ambitious hell-on-wheels little girl with dreams of Broadway and changing the world. It was an all-hands-on-deck moment, and as usual, there stood Larry to help guide me on a path, which I blasted into on a trajectory that no one quite understood.

Making sense of a gang of disparate misfits, otherwise known as my family, wasn't easy, but that's what I did. Eventually. So I chose my mother as heroine and cast my dad as a character fitting a Hemingway novel, which gave his life some grace and allowed me to face my family, understand and forgive. It was far more satisfying than the psychobabble alternative that didn't fit the grand sweep of the life I intended to manifest, which had no place in it anywhere for moping victimology. Our story was as American as anyone else's, it being hardly original that my father left me with more than the usual share of daddy issues, even if the details diverged.

All of this was the story of my family, the drama of the woman who gave birth to me in her late thirties at a time in the 1950s when few women that age were having children. Mom told me the event of her pregnancy made the papers, though that may have just become part of her myth on the way to surviving it all.

Marjorie's life was all so unbelievable for its force of insanity and unfairness, particularly when you look at the burden she carried so much of the time in a moment in America when men were king. It's part of the inheritance feminists are still fighting to change. The woman who sent me on my journey was born in the second decade of the twentieth century. Now, as we travel through the second decade a hundred years later, telling her tale is part of the book on the road to women's independence. The rest of this story represents our struggle for equality, especially in our relationships.

Watching my mother fight for us at midlife, our secret celebrations when she'd get a nickel raise per hour, her generosity when she'd send me five dollars one month at college, and then leaving me that final payment to finish off my school loan in a tiny life insurance policy that might as well have been a million dollars to me, stays with me, because of what it meant about her life and ours.

Before it was over, my mother got yet another shock. When applying for Social Security, she couldn't locate a birth certificate. There was a call to my big brother, the curious story shared, letters back and forth to the Social Security Administration, and then, she finally was told that the birthday we'd always celebrated wasn't the actual date of her birth. She wasn't born in July 1916, but in June 1916. It was a weird moment in a life that had its start tumultuously, with her birth mother, Catherine, handing her off to someone who thought that adoption wasn't proper and had to be kept secret, so she had pretended to be pregnant when she wasn't. You simply didn't openly adopt in those days. But also the shame of not being able to conceive, a woman's primary value at that time, was too much.

If I'd been born in my mother's age, I would have been swallowed up whole and never allowed to rebel and discover. If I'd listened to my sisters in the modern-girl revolution, I wouldn't have had the gall to dare to venture into the man's world and find answers to questions women had been asking for years about men, sex and relationships. These were questions from women who couldn't figure out what they wanted or how to get it when they knew.

It's also the reason beauty pageants came into the picture. They offered scholarships and money, leading to industrials and other gigs that paid better for a beauty queen, who was also a dancer and actress, all of which made me more marketable. It was a way to college at a time when everyone was determined to get me there, especially me. There was no money from Daddy and no loan options, so I would have to get my degree by whatever means necessary, which I did, a semester early.

But coming at the moment when women's liberation was front and center, modern judgments abounded for beauty pageants and their queens. Like when I was in Atlantic City, New Jersey competing in the Miss America Pageant. I came out of the Chalfonte-Haddon Hall Hotel one day, where I was staying, to find N.O.W. picketing the pageant. One female protester confronted me, asking, "How can you demean yourself like this?" That was easy, so I simply replied: "You want to pay for my college tuition?"

Mine was a journey in the Age of Gloria. Steinem, of course. She was that gorgeous girl who commanded attention and rocked America's comfy, traditional world. She even took it to Hugh Hefner, exposing his business practices and how he treated women who worked for him, who weren't the chosen top models. People don't talk about it much today, but feminism in the Age of Gloria was S.E.X.Y., caps required. But it would forever be for me a complex juggling of societal expectations and my own renegade vision for myself that included no boundaries on what I could explore.

It's all Gloria's fault that freedom and my own hell-bent passion to live my life exactly as I wanted became a wild, unexpected adventure, where curiosity and exploration replaced security. I write that with gratitude and a smile. What I owe her and the women who came before is something I can never repay, beginning with my mother who sacrificed everything so I would never doubt I could do anything, even if she watched through half-opened eyes.

What I can do for you is share what I've learned in a life that has taken me to places where most people never tread, while educating me on the most fascinating journey of all, the dance between women and men. Including the societal pressures that have compounded the challenges between the sexes exponentially in the modern era, sex, love and relationships, however they manifest, the stuff that is the beating pulse of a life.

The time when I grew up also cemented the fact that politics was in my DNA. Not the petulant stuff of Democratic versus Republican, but the gooey drama that is men and women, sex, love, a decent relationship if you're lucky, and marriage *if you choose*. It's the politics of sex. As in what happens in a modern relationship between a woman and a man, where roles sometimes are switched and traditionalism of the

1950s not only doesn't apply but has been blown to smithereens. Where women no longer need men, but still want them very much. Where men no longer control women in relationships, because we make our own money and choose our own future, instead of looking for an "MRS. degree" in college in order to keep from starving or becoming homeless. A time when girls could call boys, though whether it worked for us was a different story, and saying yes to sex was possible without worrying about getting pregnant, though no plan is perfect, as I found out myself. But still, we were sexually free and on our way to economic independence, if not equality.

Between personal ads, working as a phone sex actress, and being at the center when the blastoff of the Internet happened economically, I learned about sex, dating and relationships from people all over the country, even people around the world. Distance and anonymity — not speaking to them or looking them in the eye — offered a chance at candor and transparency that a personal interview rarely achieves. Get enough responses of the same type and gripe, and you can cull through the questionable to find consensus.

The social media era has blasted away the foundation and left few remnants of what dating used to mean when I first began digging around and dishing the dirt with hundreds of men and women. The convoluted redefining of what men and women are supposed to mean to each other today, notions of a "post-dating" era, have only served to confuse women, while once again allowing men to define the dating game, which won't end any better than it did the first time around.

Being online when it all began, following the trends that take us to today, all the avenues I've traversed have evolved into research, into understanding what was happening between the sexes and to our relationships that you can't get from any courses.

I don't pretend to have definitive answers that you can only get for yourself, but I've ventured into places that have provided me insight into relationships, women and men that few others have. I have discovered more information about sex, men, love and relationships than most; played matchmaker to both sexes; and listened to the fantasies of hundreds of men.

This is simply a tale of discovery and education through one woman's liberated excursion into worlds that had finally opened up and allowed women, and men, to explore sex, love, dating and relationships in a wholly new way, at a time when traditional walls had crumbled. It includes sharing the places I've been — some where good girls weren't supposed to go — in a world where the politics of sex between women and men had set the United States ablaze.

I now find it humorous to remember my talent number from the Miss America

Pageant — "If They Could See Me Now" from the musical *Sweet Charity*, the lead role I played in college. No song title ever pegged the eye-popping reaction I would get from people once they learned I'd gone from beauty queen to Broadway to digging into what women and men want as a Relationship Consultant, which led to a sexual education few "experts" can claim.

Making sense of it all is something each of us must do for ourselves. But when you've heard and seen as much as I have, let's just say I may not have definitive answers for you, but I've certainly learned a lot along the way that you would benefit from knowing, too.

1

What Do You Want?

A *New York Post* article making the rounds and getting a fair amount of attention on the web had a titillating title: "More City Co-eds Turning to Sugar Daddies for School Support."

It caught my attention for a number of reasons, not the least of which was that the article and the website at the center of the report were talking about a subject I'd become an expert on back in the mid-'90s. The *Post* story may have appeared on January 15, 2013, but it jettisoned me back to another era, before social media took off, and when the web was just revving up.

Once upon a time, I was the Relationship Consultant — my actual title — for the nation's largest newsweekly, the *LA Weekly*, second only in circulation to the *Village Voice*. Dating, love and helping people find long-term relationships through personal ads was my job, and I loved it. The romance business through personal ads was wonderful fun and a booming business back in the '90s.

It was always a challenge, because the art of matchmaking through word combinations in ads, having morphed into the $3-4 billion online dating business today, according to the *Economist*, isn't easy. But when it works, it's magic. An online ad is just the beginning, because after the language, the logistics of dating gets complicated pretty quickly. Love is the part that hasn't changed so much, though it, too, has gotten more complicated. So I also helped women, and even men, navigate the minefields of dating and manifesting relationships in the age of hooking up and keeping your independence.

Back when AOL first started Digital City, I was the featured guest in "live chat" events that were advertised like this: "Learn how you can be your own matchmaker." That's exactly what I helped people do, and it's precisely what the online dating industry continues to do.

I also did "For Women Only" events, where we'd have dish-sessions about feminism, relationships and even flirting, highlighted by the best way to attract the right guy in an ad, with a followup of what you do once you've got him interested. Questionnaires helped me find out who the women were and what they wanted in a relationship, also asking them their greatest frustrations with men.

It was a long way from the original advice columnist "Dear Abby," aka Pauline Phillips, who got her start in 1956, putting relationship advice on the map. When I was giving advice, "Dear Abby" still wouldn't advise women and men to live together, even if cohabitation is now a modern-day reality. Phillips' twin sister was the advice columnist Ann Landers. The two sisters were so competitive at one point that they didn't speak to one another for five years.

"Dear Abby" got its start when Mrs. Phillips called the *San Francisco Chronicle* to confront the paper, telling an editor she could do better than the current columnist, whereupon they dared her to try. She did, and ended up with a syndicated column and more than a million readers. When she died in January 2013, the *New York Times* characterized her style like this: "If Damon Runyon and Groucho Marx had gone jointly into the advice business, their column would have read much like Dear Abby's. With her comic and flinty yet fundamentally sympathetic voice, Mrs. Phillips helped wrestle the advice column from its weepy Victorian past into a hard-nosed twentieth-century present."

The full name used for "Dear Abby" was Abigail van Buren, a composite of a name pulled from the Bible and Phillips' favorite president.

I took the name Taylor when interviewing prostitutes in Amsterdam, simply to separate my work from my personal life and to get some anonymity. It was also one of my favorite names for a woman, because it was gender neutral. Marsh was a lopped-off version of my given name, Michelle Marshall, which I added once I was at the *LA Weekly*, officially taking a writing pseudonym.

My guide as Relationship Consultant began with my instincts, but also the reading and research I'd already done on sex, dating and relationships, including interviews with people. The language of attraction turned out to be a natural for me.

Online ads remain a practical way to meet someone, though few clients look anything like the way they were represented on the big screen in *This Means War*, the Hollywood movie starring Reese Witherspoon, Chris Pine and Tom Hardy. Cultural movies continually serve up weird scenarios that have no resemblance to reality, but are great fun to watch. One thing that one did get right is that online dating offers an opportunity to find someone when you're busy and want a way to screen people that can be effective. The difference is that before online dating, personal ads offered a degree of distance and worked a lot slower.

As Relationship Consultant, I also had a trademarked advice column titled "What Do You Want?" The first online writing I did at the *LA Weekly* debuted in 1996. This is also where my first political writing appeared, covering topics including feminism and dating, and RU486, known more commonly today as mifepristone, which allows a woman to end a pregnancy within seven weeks of conception. I also wrote on the Telecommunications Act of 1996, and took on Dr. Laura Schlessinger over her homophobic rants when she was attempting to blast onto TV. But the main topics of conversation between me and my readers were dating, relationships and personal ads.

There wasn't much interaction at first. Beyond my relationship column and my advice on placing a personal ad, I also received letters from readers that evolved into Q&A Dear Abby-style advice sessions. Back before email and social media, in the mid-1990s, everything between women and men placing and responding to ads was negotiated through voicemail accounts.

Some of my column titles included "Privacy, Public Figures and Reality," "Adultery and the Armed Services," "The Battle of the Sexes Has Climaxed," "Creating a Game Plan that Works" and "Redefining Feminism." Sadly, none of this is online today, as it all predated common use of the Internet. But knowing I intended to write more about relationships in the future, I kept some select copies of my "What Do You Want?" advice column in my files, along with several choice interactions with readers and those seeking relationship help. Some of the topics include "Cyber Fantasy or Infidelity," "His Fantasies Aren't Mine," "A Sexless Marriage," "Living Together Isn't Marriage!" and "Unfaithful With Children."

What I call the politics of sex was the whole of what I covered, including what a woman should do to get exactly what she wants in an era where she has a lot more control. After sexual liberation exploded in the 1960s, the dynamic between women and men changed dramatically, and women could assert themselves more, and ask for and expect to get what they wanted to be delivered.

Birth control, sex before marriage, and women's equality of satisfaction in the bedroom, not to mention our ability to pay our own bills, set the world of dating, relationships and marriage on its head. It's what brought the debate back about what rules women should follow when dating men in the modern era, because being able to be the driver didn't mean you could get men on board.

Carol Hanisch catalyzed it all in her 1969 essay "The Personal Is Political," which was a feminist cry, but it's exactly what is still happening in our relationships *now*. Women's personal freedoms, which include making money professionally, and how that affects our relationships at home, including something as small as dividing chores and asking men to share responsibilities, are all very political things inside our personal lives. It's the politics of sex, and of gender.

Nothing could have represented this reality more perfectly than when Yahoo CEO Marissa Mayer revoked the company's longtime work-from-home policy through a memo leaked to the press in February 2013. Mayer got blasted across the media for giving Yahoo employees until June 2013 to get adjusted to their new reality, with one *Forbes* headline blaring, "Back to the Stone Age? New Yahoo CEO Marissa Mayer Bans Working From Home." After Yahoo's stock performance sky-rocketed, in October 2013 AllThingsD reported that Hewlett-Packard CEO Meg Whitman began implementing it at HP. This is the very definition of the personal becoming political that applies in the twenty-first century as much as ever before.

The flip side to the way we work and make money, sexual interaction, is the second most important dynamic between two people in a relationship. That money and sex are often the two most frequently cited reasons for a relationship blowing up isn't surprising.

Like men, women go through changes in our lives that make our sex drive ebb and flow, but a woman's sexual appetite can be equal to any man's and just as easy to ignite, though women can always fake it and men can't. It's a pressure point we can't possibly understand fully.

The questions coming in to me back in the '90s could easily be asked today.

Dear Taylor: I've been married for just three years and I'm dying to have an affair. There's a guy I see all the time at a place the girls and I stop at after work. All I really want to do is f*#! him, you know. He's gorgeous and I'm really bored with my husband. Don't get me wrong, I love him and all, it's just that it's always the same old thing and we only do it about twice a week. Believe me, that's not enough! He works late a lot and is tired when he gets home. What should I do? I need an answer quick! —Horny Married Gal

This is a great example of the sexual ego of women that just about everyone underestimates.

Dear Horny Married Gal: You are acting like a coward, someone who should have never gotten married in the first place. Three years?! Are you kidding me? You've given your word to this man, you've got responsibilities to him and to yourself. What's wrong with you? Talk to him. Tell him what you're feeling, what you want; even say that if things don't change something serious is going to happen. My guess is he doesn't know how you feel. Also, get off your tush. Make the first move: Seduce him when he walks in... Then, after you've tried every single method possible, and if your husband still isn't responding, kick him out of bed. That's right. If he chooses not to give you what you want, he loses his privileges.

Guys wrote in to me, too. Though most of the columns I saved don't have a visible date, this one is from Christmastime, 1995.

Dear Taylor: My girlfriend and I broke up about three months ago, after being together for about two years. I really love her and have tried to get back with her, but she won't listen to me. She wants to get married and I don't. At least I don't right now. I was willing to live with her, but the marriage thing was just too much for me. Now she's gone and I'm really hurting. I can't get her out of my mind and really believe that she's the one. Christmas was always a fun time for us. We'd drive around and look at lights, drink wine, then make love all night. Now, everything in my life is suffering. What the hell am I going to do? —Heartbroken at Christmas

That's a reminder that if a woman keeps giving and doesn't ask for what she wants in return, doing so early and honestly, she just might find herself giving everything and not getting what she wants, because some men will take and take and take. Make it easy on a man and he'll let you until you wise up.

Dear Heartbroken: I certainly hope your girlfriend reads this because I have something to say to her: "Good for you." As for you... What's wrong with you?! What you're asking her to do is unacceptable. This lady knows what she wants and you aren't willing to give it to her. She's a very smart woman for moving on and not accepting less than she deserves. Too many people waste too much time waiting for what they'll never get. Also, if cohabiting is as far as you're willing to go with a woman, tell her so at the very beginning of the relationship. ...But let me tell you something. You just let a good woman go. Of that I am certain.

The above exchange remains a perfect example of why my column was titled "What Do You Want?" It's an obvious question that requires specific answers. It doesn't matter if you're talking about your relationship or getting a job or deciding about how to create a family. In fact, it applies triple when contemplating a relationship with someone, or even if you've just decided it's time to seek one.

A young woman I helped to figure this out, coaching her on how to get exactly what she wanted, had been living with a man whom she loved dearly and wanted to marry. However, he wouldn't commit beyond cohabitating. Jennifer was beautiful and accomplished, had a great job and was a devout Christian. She also wanted children and was heading past thirty-five, when a woman's body can begin to betray her dreams. The man she lived with didn't say he wouldn't marry her, just that he wasn't ready. So, she waited... and waited... for years. She truly believed he'd finally see the light, because they had it all — great sex, loads of fun, years of shared experience, and he had no intention of leaving her. But when, if ever, would he pop the question and commit to marriage? The clock was ticking.

After leaving and then giving in and coming back to him repeatedly, she finally allowed me to coach her through leaving for the last time. We talked for hours and hours, at all times for days, as she stayed this course. Screaming fights ensued with her ex, as he begged her to return. It took her a while before she realized that nothing would make him ask her to marry him. She got busy with her career and concentrated on healing from a relationship she had given herself to for years and now believed was time wasted. It wasn't, but we all know the feeling. It was a while before she could date again, but eventually she was ready.

The first thing I suggested was to start looking for a man inside her church circle or in spots men who are spiritual, too, can be found. Finding a man of deep faith mattered a great deal to her, yet she wasn't scoping out places where they can be found. By the time Jennifer answered the question "What Do You Want?" the list was very specific and seemed a tough sell. She was in her mid-thirties, wanted a spiritual man who attended church and respected her career, but she also wanted to have children and stay home to raise them, too. It was traditionalism with a modern twist, something some women still want if they can swing it.

As hard as it may seem to manifest, Jennifer ended up with the whole package. We discussed many times the uncompromising standards she had set for the man she wanted, but they were *her* rules based on exactly what *she* wanted and expected out of a long-term relationship that would lead to marriage. Compromise would come later, because it's inevitable if you want a marriage to work.

That's quite different from taking guidelines put together from someone else and applying them. One honors who you are as a woman; the other sets up arbitrary rules predicated on how you must perform to attract someone who expects a certain behavior pattern, whether it's who you are or not. There's a big difference.

It's one thing to want a traditional relationship in the old-fashioned sense of the word. That type of traditional relationship often doesn't make room for a woman who has her own life and career going for her, too. If you're self-employed, you have a better chance of juggling everything, but if not, some careers are very competitive, and women have to sacrifice a lot to have them, including time with their children. It's also not like the workplace is a friendly place for women who still have most of the responsibilities at home. This can often mean the man has to pick up the slack and be graceful while doing it. The woman still sacrifices a lot for her choice to have a marriage, children and a career, which some people describe as "having it all."

In the PBS documentary *Makers: Women Who Make America*, which aired in late February 2013, the network's Judy Woodruff asked Gloria Steinem in an interview if women can have it all. Her answer was classic Steinem: "It's a ridiculous question. …No, of course women can't have it all, as long as we have to do it all, until — I mean, we have realized, and the majority of Americans fully agree — that women can do what men can do. But we haven't yet realized that men can do what women do."

It should be noted before we go any further that men can't have it all either; it just seems like they can because they run everything *and* get out of household chores. That's a retort that women can rightly feel is apt. However, there is real heartbreak, guilt and loss on all sides when a man sacrifices himself to make money, while his kids speed through their lives without him being there to share their growth. Men never complain about it, because it's an ingrained, primal responsibility. They're unaccustomed to having the freedom to fight for their fatherhood role, their place as husbands in families that need them present, so they suck it up and pay the price, which has no relationship to having it all.

Now, having my feminism forged in the age of Gloria, I never was told that it was about having it all, and I was certainly never promised that was what the pot at the end of the rainbow contained. In my world growing up in Missouri, I learned that I had a lot more options from which to choose, a galaxy compared to my mother's, but that I needed to select what I wanted wisely and then take responsibility for what I'd decided, because no one was forcing me in a particular direction anymore. You could bitch about what you'd picked, but why anyone should listen was a mystery. At least I had choices, and women in the twenty-first century have even more. That's progress, but it's not the end of the story.

So when Anne-Marie Slaughter wrote a piece for the *Atlantic Monthly* in August 2012 titled "Why Women Can't Have It All," it was understandable that all hell broke loose. Living in the Washington, D.C. area and covering national politics and women as I do, I considered Ms. Slaughter to be a well-known and respected woman in a privileged position she had earned. Former Secretary of State Hillary Clinton had appointed her the first-ever woman Director of Policy Planning at the State Department.

Ms. Slaughter's husband is a willing participant in supporting her high-profile career, doing the parenting of two teenage boys, with Ms. Slaughter returning home on weekends to Princeton, New Jersey while she worked at the State Department. When her two-year leave from Princeton University was up, as her *Atlantic Monthly* article revealed, she "hurried home as fast as I could." She'd once been talked out of writing in a column that women can't have it all, but now, having safely parachuted out of the State Department and back at Princeton, she unloaded.

Slaughter believes women *can* have it all and "have it all at the same time," just not today. In an article in *New York Magazine*'s "The Cut," published in December 2012, after following her lecture tour, Slaughter said she had wanted to title the *Atlantic Monthly* article "You Can't Have It All *Yet*," and the final title was about selling magazines. What "The Cut" also learned is "millennials love her." Slaughter told "The Cut": "Pretty much anybody under thirty-five is almost uniformly positive. They are grateful, they are positive, they want to have this debate." She went on to say that women over thirty-five gave her a "very different response. ...Their jaws tighten."

This is an important debate, one I gladly engage in, and I say that with a loose jaw.

The American economy and corporations aren't structured yet to make having it all easy for women or even possible, and neither are our relationships or American society in general. However, it also means defining what having it all means to you, as well as admitting this can change as you live your life.

For Slaughter, having it all depended on what job she had, which turned out to have changed and was not the dream job she'd worked her entire life to earn and finally nabbed at the State Department. She also had to admit: "I am writing for my demographic — highly educated, well-off women who are privileged enough to have choices in the first place.... But I realized that I didn't just need to go home. Deep down, I wanted to go home." In April 2013, Slaughter became President of the New America Foundation, a public policy institute.

Wealthy women have many options that middle-class women do not, so having it all is going to depend on who you are and the economic strata in which you live. Having it all can mean grabbing what you can while planning and dreaming about a better job, as you juggle marriage, family and career, at the same time you're maintaining your sanity, which isn't easy when you and your significant other are barely paying your bills.

Not only had Ms. Slaughter gotten everything she'd planned, translated by many women as having it all — a top spot in the most elite club in the world, the foreign policy establishment of the State Department — but she made history as she did it. She has two beautiful boys, and a supportive husband who helped make it possible. However, the demands she placed on herself, including her own judgments and feelings about what she should be required to give each aspect of her life, blew out all expectations of what was possible without blowing a gasket.

Answering the question "What do you want?" is predicated on also coming to grips with what happens when you get it.

Slaughter never anticipated the fury her column would unleash on the web when it landed. Twitter exploded, and the new-media world lit up, every website trying to take advantage of the latest feminist to declare that women still can't have it all.

Men can't have it all either, just ask them, but that's never up for discussion. We never talk about how they juggle life, or sacrifice time with their kids, because it's always been a given. Of course, men don't have to do the grocery shopping and many other chores around the house when their job is taking all their time, while women are still expected to pick up the slack no matter what their job demands. This is the unsettled conflict in middle-class life when a family needs two incomes.

This debate is central to a woman's life today, but it's not just about having it all, because the choice to change your mind and go in a different direction and leave your job isn't one many women even have, which Ms. Slaughter made clear she knows.

However, the real issue is that having it all was never promised by the feminist revolution in the first place.

Somewhere, at some point, women conjured this up out of whole cloth and heaped the promise onto feminism, which was always and simply about having options equal to what men have. What we're seeing shake out and brought into the light now is the demand women have placed on themselves to be *equally* engaged in *all* the facets of their lives, in all areas at once, with the same attention and care to each. It's nuts *and* impossible.

Try doing this in the middle of a relationship, and you can bet it's going to fall apart along with everything else in your life.

Secretary Hillary Clinton, in an interview with Ayelet Waldman for *Marie Claire* which came out in October 2012 after Slaughter's piece, addressed the issue of women and work/life balance, saying: "I can't stand whining. I can't stand the kind of paralysis that some people fall into because they're not happy with the choices they've made. You live in a time when there are endless choices. …Money certainly helps, and having that kind of financial privilege goes a long way, but you don't even have to have money for it. But you have to work on yourself. …Do something! Some women are not comfortable working at the pace and intensity you have to work at in these jobs. …Other women don't break a sweat. They have four or five, six kids. They're highly organized, they have very supportive networks."

In Facebook COO Sheryl Sandberg's book, *Lean In: Women, Work, and the Will to Lead*, Sandberg quotes Judith Rodin, president of the Rockefeller Foundation and the first woman to serve as president of an Ivy League university, who was talking to a group of women the age of Sandberg, who is 43 today: "My generation fought so hard to give all of you choices. We believe in choices. But choosing to leave the workforce was not the choice we thought so many of you would make."

Believe it or not, this directly relates to the type of relationship you create, starting with the man you choose, especially if marriage is your goal. It's never before been put as succinctly as is done in Sandberg's book, and because it's something my whole life has revolved around, I related to it in an intensely personal way, which I'll talk about later.

Having it all, when I began embracing feminism, never meant anything other than women having the same choices as men. We would have the same freedoms as men, including the important aspect of making the same money for the same job, which, unbelievably, is still being debated. Let's all agree that until this is fixed, having it all is a mirage.

We can have families *and* careers now. Being a mother is a tremendously important and fulfilling role, an aspect of womanhood that most women would never choose to live without, but for the same majority of women it isn't all they want for themselves either. Many have no choice, because of the economic realities today. Being able to choose to have a family and a career never came with any guarantees that you could juggle it all easily, gracefully or without coming to the conclusion that the amount of discipline it required could very well drive you nuts. You had to learn to accept that you could only give a hundred percent of yourself to one thing at a time.

If, after you get everything you want, you decide it's no longer what you want, it doesn't mean a thing for anyone else. It means you might have outgrown your choices, even that you are about to embark on a new adventure. It's okay to change your mind, but it's not some eternal message for the masses, especially if you're the one privileged to be in the income bracket that allowed you to orchestrate having it all, and you're unable to deal with that gift. Just say, I've got it all and it's not what it's cracked up to be, because I miss my kids, so I'm going to take advantage of what my lifestyle affords and bail from the rat race. Oh, and by the way, I feel for the women who wish they could make this choice but can't.

That was always the beauty of feminism as I saw it. There are as many examples of it as there are women, though bucking traditional gender expectations is essential, including equality in child-rearing, household duties and financial contribution. Each of us gets to decide what works for us, and we can even change our minds midstream. Unfortunately, feminism inevitably gets the blame, even if it's what has made the multiple-choice lives women lead today possible.

The most important thing about feminism for me is that it doesn't stop with my own life. It's why I laughed out loud at the notion of "post-feminism." The feminist revolution that lit up my life might have begun as a movement meant to advance American women one step up the ladder. But after it took hold in my heart and mind, it became clear the core of the feminist *revolution* had the potential to affect women everywhere. The hopes for my life, your life and other generations of American women isn't all it was about, at least not for me. Feminism had at its core a universal call for women everywhere, and that was long before we knew women and girls in Afghanistan were getting acid thrown in their faces just for wanting to be educated. Long before we learned about so-called honor killings. Feminism in the twenty-first century is a collective, global cry for female equality, even as we each work to manifest the life we personally want.

How we go about getting what it is we want is as individual as we are, though that's not how it's seen by some who insist on a universal roadmap.

Two other columns I wrote back in the '90s that were featured online were titled "Debating *The Rules*" and "*The Rules* Strikes Again." *The Rules*, written by Ellen Fein and Sherrie Schneider, became the hottest-selling publishing phenomenon in decades and the most disastrous list of dos and don'ts for women since the 1950s. First published by Warner Books in 1995, it exploded and became a best seller and all the rage, taking the oxygen out of the relationship-equality discussion and packing old-school rules from a girl's grandmother in 1917 into a nice, sweet list of what women should do to snare a man.

The Rules starts off like this: "The purpose of *The Rules* is to make Mr. Right obsessed with having you as his by making yourself seem unattainable." Oh, but it gets worse. "Remember that you're dressing for men, not other women, so always strive to look feminine," page 17. It was followed by *The Rules II, The Rules for Marriage, The Rules for Online Dating* and *All the Rules*.

Unfortunately for Ellen Fein, her own rules didn't work in her first marriage, which ended after sixteen years in 2000, and just as the sequel to the first book, titled *The Rules for Marriage: Time-Tested Secrets for Making Your Marriage Work*, was hitting bookstores. Writing online at the time, I watched as the media went wild over the irony. Nobody is immune to heartbreak, including experts. Covered in the *New York Times,* Fein claimed abandonment and then tried to sue her cosmetic dentist for, as the *Times* put it, "accusing him of ruining her teeth and her marriage."

See, in the land of *The Rules*, it's never the woman's fault, even when she loads the courtship up with all sorts of fakery and pretense, hiding behind a bundle of nerves that actually foreshadows the trouble to come once the man strips away the facade, or the woman explodes in anger and blames the man for causing it all when he didn't know what was happening in the first place.

When Fein met her new husband, Lance — good for her, by the way — he offered her his business card, which she refused to take. "I wasn't going to call him! I knew I liked him but if he didn't call me, I was perfectly capable of losing interest in him," she was quoted saying in the *Times,* in August 2008. He asked her out two days later, the *Times* reported, but she was ready with a plan. "He asked me out for the next Saturday night. And I counted to four — it doesn't look so desperate — before I said yes."

Just in case you're wondering, it's unlikely Lance even noticed whether she counted to four or not. It's hard to imagine this type of tape playing in your head, cuing you to wait — three…two…one…time to answer *now*. It's the perfect example of the unnatural woman. This type of game-playing would be exhausting even if it "worked."

In January 2013, as ridiculous as this nonsense is and after all the progress women have made, Anderson Cooper featured Fein and Schneider on his ABC daytime show *Anderson Live*. The authors have now updated *The Rules* for the cyber era in *Not Your Mother's Rules: The Secrets for Dating*, which has thirty-one new rules for women. Unsurprisingly, Fein and Schneider "run a dating and consultation service," according to their Amazon profile at the time of the book's release. Cooper picked out a couple of Not Your Mother's Rules to talk about.

Rule number six: "Wait at least four hours to answer a guy's first text and a minimum of thirty minutes thereafter." Another "new" rule is to stay away from the guy's Facebook page. If that's not groundbreaking enough for you, try this one: "Don't sext."

Fein claims women "begged us for the updated version." Because, obviously, women don't know what to do in the twenty-first century with all the new ways to interact with men.

The *New York Daily News* covered the publishing news of *Not Your Mother's Rules*, too. "There's no app for love," ladies, went the report, and that's true. Just in case you don't get what's going on here, there are also different rules depending on your age, your tribe and your culture. Fein and Schneider have dedicated an entire chapter, "complete with text-back time chart," which is predicated on age. Whereas young women should wait thirty minutes before texting a guy back, older women need to wait "at least four hours — longer if possible."

Let's unpack what they're selling.

Fein and Schneider are perpetuating the nonsense that a woman's love life depends on what the man expects out of her, not what she wants. What will drive the man off? Their answer: It's going to be something you do the first time you meet, so you better choreograph everything down to waiting four hours to respond to a text. The entire scenario is predicated on arbitrary rules that won't do any good at all, if all the woman is thinking about is how to act to get the guy's approval. It also perpetuates the notion that when a guy doesn't call you or isn't interested, it's automatically something you did.

Now I'm thinking about the 2009 smash hit movie *He's Just Not That Into You*. Based on the book by comedian Greg Behrendt, who also was involved as a script consultant on the TV series *Sex and the City*, the material was like a slap upside the head for women. Imagine the concept that if a guy's into you, he'll call, and if he isn't, it's likely not going to matter what rules you follow. It's not anything *you* did, it's something that just didn't click when you met. It might even be about *him*. Imagine that.

Chances are, when Ms. Fein met her dreamboat Lance, who became her husband, he was simply into *her*, the chemistry was right and it worked. There is nothing that can keep a guy away from you if it's right. He'll beat a path to your door no matter what, if he feels it.

What this should mean to every woman looking for a relationship is monumental, regardless of your age.

Most women today are perfectly capable of making their own rules for their own life without the help of strangers who are concocting arbitrary guidelines, complete with timetables, out of thin air. If you're one of those girls who's unsure about what to do in the new-media era, first take a moment to think about all of this for a second.

Very few writers have been online as long as I have. Even fewer were snooping around in the dating game at the moment personals and online dating went viral. So, let me take you through this.

What's the point of social media, Facebook, texting, Instagram or, taking it even further, sexting? Immediate intimacy, an oxymoron if ever there was one.

That didn't keep iPhone from developing Tinder in February 2013. As featured on NBC's *Today*, Tinder is an iPhone app that, by April 2013, had led to Tinderitis, which Huffington Post described as "the sensation of having a sore thumb from swiping to approve or reject the faces of people offered up as potential date material." One sophomore at Cornell University reviewed it this way: "People don't think of [Tinder] as online dating; they think of it as a game."

The excitement value is clear, but anything that happens this quickly and spikes your attention and emotional engagement can easily bring you down just as fast.

In February 2013, new research by psychologists at the University of Kansas revealed through three different studies that being transparent on Facebook about your relationship can cause you big romantic problems. Here's a clue: Just because there are social media trends and everyone's doing it, doesn't mean it's a good idea or will get you what you want. Some things *never* change, starting with the fact that if you want intimacy between you and a guy, keep personal details to yourself, and then, eventually, share them solely between the two of you.

From the article on the study, which was posted at News.Ku.edu just before Valentine's Day in 2013: "KU researchers created two mock Facebook walls, one of which featured a circumspect user — who briefly mentioned sports and weather and linked to items of interest on the Internet — the other of which had a user who let it all hang out, bemoaning parents, classes, weight problems and posting a plethora of party pictures. 'We asked participants to imagine that these were the Facebook walls of their romantic partner,' Lee said. 'We found that people who were given the high-disclosure wall felt less intimacy with the user than people who were given the low-disclosure wall.' The researchers predicted their results in advance, based on previous studies of Facebook and real-world romance, including one that found Facebook was mentioned in a third of divorce filings in the United Kingdom.'"

People twenty-five and under have figured this out, as they begin to assess their own privacy, including that Facebook has now become the primary place where parents and "grey-haired ones" troll. In November 2013, Facebook admitted they'd seen a "decrease in daily users, specifically among teens," which was the lead in to an article in the *Guardian* by Parmy Olson, a technology writer for Forbes magazine and the author of *We Are Anonymous*. Ms. Olson reported a "gradual exodus" away from Facebook and that "the fun stuff is happening elsewhere. On their mobiles." Messenger apps like WhatsApp, WeChat and KakaoTalk allow people to have more privacy, because the groups consist of "real-life friends," people who already have each other's mobile numbers. According to Olson, "about 90% of the population of Brazil uses messaging apps, three-quarters of Russians, and half of Britons, according to mobile consultancy Tyntec. WhatsApp alone is on more than 95% of all smartphones in Spain."

According to MobileYouth, cited by Olson, 61% of teens sleep with their mobiles. The messenger app shift toward more privacy, less Facebook, hints that the online fetish for public oversharing with strangers is less interesting to younger generations. Real connections are slowly encroaching on virtual intimacy, with 78% of teens and younger generations preferring "mobile messengers to plan a meet-up with friends," according to Olson, citing MobileYouth. Her *Guardian* report also reveals why there is a move away from Facebook. Apps aren't just apps anymore when it comes to mobile messaging; they're social networks, the holy grail of modern personal connection, which Facebook began.

Women have never had greater ability to control the whole meeting and dating cycle, but are choosing to relinquish much of it. This is because of how men have reacted to the ease of social media, with girls opting to following the boys' lead. I'll cover this as we go along, but what women really need to know is that technology hasn't changed the basic human instincts and predilections of men. So, don't be seduced by ease of communication and group outings, because men will lap up easy connection as long as women play that game and allow them to get away with it.

Of course, if you like group dates instead of intimate, one-on-one dates, go for it, but just remember *you* made the choice to embrace a "post-dating" philosophy. Many men will appreciate it, because it makes things easier for *them*.

Technology is terrific. I've been using it since it took off. However, Facebook and texting are there to make communication between people easier and quicker. Dating isn't about ease, and relationships don't develop quickly. Attraction can be instant, but it doesn't make a relationship.

If you've just met someone, you're not even friends yet, so quick virtual banter is something that isn't going to facilitate anything but setting up a false sense of familiarity. To become friends you have to establish in-person communications over a shared interest, cocktails or coffee. An online relationship alone is for people who want cheap, immediate thrills, which are great, but you need to make sure this is what you want, and all you want. If it's a long-term relationship you're setting up, your entire online persona and footprint must be different.

In the February 2013 issue of *Psychology Today*, the column "Love on the Internet," by Hara Estroff Marano, made a very important point that has been the truth about Internet connections since even before Facebook and other social media took off. If you've jumped into an online relationship, understand that "very little personal investment is required to initiate or respond" to someone who catches your eye online, Marano wrote.

The person you are instantly put into contact with may not have any intention of following through beyond what's convenient, so it comes down to how much discipline you have in the moment. Because if you let yourself get sucked in before you've established that you both are willing to put in equal amounts of energy toward what it is you both want, you're likely headed onto a one-way road to frustration and disappointment, and a colossal waste of time.

Dating is about setting up a foundation of communication to see if you like each other and are compatible. Immediate intimacy is a booty call, which can just as easily be virtual, too. A relationship is something that is meant to develop over time as you get to know someone. Facebook, texting and other social media don't foster this, and waiting thirty minutes before returning a man's text won't help.

If you're out of high school or college, or over that age, you shouldn't be texting *anyone* but friends, unless for example you have to let a person you're dating know you have to work late and will not make a date on time. Texting should be used for basic information, not conversation, at least not until things are established. It is casual communication between people who have already established a relationship. Unless you have, don't do it. Texting is also an easy rush for guys that allows them to juggle girls without really investing anything of value. Once you open that gate, it's impossible to set boundaries that work in your favor. Texting creates a fake intimacy between people where shortcuts and quick banter rule. It also drains anticipation and energy away, while making longer phone conversations moot.

Facebook presents a real dilemma today for daters. I've never understood why women put so much personal information about themselves on Facebook. You've got to have some great shots of yourself, as well as your interests, but divulging too much publicly is a mistake. In some instances it can also be dangerous.

Online discipline requires so much more energy than before virtual matchmaking existed. It starts with stopping yourself from thinking an immediate text or tweet from a guy means anything. It also involves keeping your eyes off his Facebook page and including some mystery on your own page. Not designing it as if it's a promo for what you offer as a potential partner, and not saying everything that's on your mind on a public web page. Refusing to be confused by the temptations of text and an instant relationship that is all manufactured in your head takes personal discipline. Indulging yourself can bring easy, quick satisfaction, but will eventually deliver frustration if he doesn't virtually react every day as quickly as he did the day before.

Romantic predators aren't just physical and emotional, they're also quick-fix, virtual-love junkies who get bored quickly and move on to the next thrill just as fast. One day's rapid-fire, fun and romantic banter can lead to quick burnout and the next virtual conquest hunt for him. This can all turn into a roller coaster ride that's fun and fleeting but never gets you much for your time and energy, if you're not methodically disciplined. Cheap thrills are great, if that's what you want. Just make sure it is.

As the article in *Psychology Today* warns, if things start off fast, but begin "downtrending" just as quickly, you've got yourself what I call a quick-thrill, virtual Casanova.

Also remember that the compressed time in the online dating world results in distorted expectations. It doesn't allow for life lived in real time, so the obsessed clock-watcher can interrupt what may be developing by making demands on someone to answer in a specific timeframe, when their prior obligations, job commitments and basic living don't always allow it. Virtual demands, before an in-person connection has been firmly established, are a budding-relationship killer.

Dating and setting up a relationship require a commitment of time. Both are natural components needed until you know someone, especially if you're intending to manifest a romantic connection. I assume women aren't giving just anyone their phone number, so why would you invite someone to text you when you don't really know him? If you're lost or late, or are dispensing basic information, like the location of the restaurant where you're meeting, perhaps so he can make reservations, that's one thing.

Here's another idea: Trust yourself, and listen to that little voice you sometimes hear speaking out when you least expect it. That's the sound of your heart, which will break through if you let it. It's different from the tape in your head, because that never-ending lecture running in a constant loop composed of other people's words is a lot like the rules that come from "experts." It keeps you from hearing and then listening to when your heart speaks out, which can only surface if there's enough space for it to squeeze through amid the cacophony of advice or rules you're getting from the outside. If you can't hear that voice inside yourself, maybe the last thing you need is a relationship, and the first thing you might want to consider is finding out what it sounds like, so you can hear what it's saying to you, because it's never wrong, even if you don't want to listen.

If you're not sure about texting, rules aren't the answer. Maybe you just shouldn't be doing it, and if he doesn't think that's cool, tough. Make sure you know who you are first. What you want comes next, before you start listening to someone else's rules about how to get it, especially when they don't know or you haven't decided what it is you want.

Not everyone wants the same things either.

This brings me back to the article I quoted in the *New York Post* at the top of this chapter about college students turning to sugar daddies for financial support. It got my attention because I started the first alternative personal ad section in the *LA Weekly* back in the '90s.

Relationships aren't easy, but one basic feature is sexual compatibility. It may seem strange to consider that in the mid-'90s the premier newsweekly out of Los Angeles didn't have an alternative personal ad section. The *LA Weekly* had a very successful personal ad section that was going gangbusters before I arrived, but there are a lot of people looking for something else beyond traditional dating, love and marriage. This aspect of dating and love was part of my sexual education that took me way beyond my strait-laced, beauty queen roots.

The alternative personal ad game was a lot trickier for a mainstream newsweekly. The paper that lived off of advertising did huge business with Hollywood and had mainstream corporations spending significant money to place advertising, the paper's bread and butter. One of the big selling points to convincing the publisher that alternative personals was worth a try was that I created code words to use in the alternative personals. The publisher at the time was leery about the whole operation, so it was the only way to make it fly.

Knowing Los Angeles as I did, I knew that "special arrangement" ads would definitely get women's attention, but also bring in the high-caliber businessmen, some who travel to Los Angeles, as well as Hollywood types, which were a natural.

The website the *Post* article focused on was called SeekingArrangements.com. The article reported that three hundred NYU co-eds had joined the site in 2012 seeking a "mutually beneficial" relationship with "rich older gentlemen." This was reportedly a 154% jump over 2011. Hundreds more co-eds from Syracuse, Columbia and Cornell had also joined up to try the special-arrangement path to pay for college tuition, someone from SeekingArrangement.com told the *New York Post*:

"Alex Cranshaw, 22, who graduated from NYU last year, said three of his female classmates had sugar daddies — including a woman whose benefactor financed a whole semester in Madrid. 'He funded her tuition, paid for her housing, gave her spending money and paid for her airfare,' Cranshaw said."

Jennifer Gwynn, a spokesperson for SeekingArrangements.com, told the *Post* that the average "sugar baby," as she called the co-eds, receives approximately $3,000 in allowances and gifts per month from her benefactor.

This is hardly a new thing. Back in the 1990s, women in Los Angeles wanted fun and games, too, and wanted to financially benefit from it as well. "Benefactor" is one of the code words for "sugar daddy," which is a bit dated and ignores that it can include younger men. The women I worked with as Relationship Consultant had many choices, and some of them picked an "arrangement," because it suited their lifestyle and was exactly what they wanted.

Clearly, a young woman from NYU or Cornell has more choices than a sugar daddy ad implies. Female college co-eds were choosing the relationships because they were easier than struggling with back-breaking student loans, in their estimation. Such an arrangement didn't require much maintenance or demand emotional entanglements, though that can happen. Obviously, the women were attracted to the guys, though any feminist can argue against this choice. Ultimately it was up for each to decide. Was it good for the girl?

That has never been my role, to decide what's right for someone else. It's not up to me to judge another woman, even if I disagree. I reminded women to keep asking themselves what they want and to make sure they're taking care of themselves while they're getting it.

Any girl seeking an arrangement, whether she's twenty-two or forty-two, is looking for something quite different from someone seeking a romantic relationship in the hopes of manifesting marriage. Emotional ties in a special arrangement shouldn't be deep, and the relationship will last until the day it doesn't, so women beware.

I'd often get asked what the difference is between being in a special arrangement and being a hooker. The woman is accepting money to date a man she might not be attracted to if she wasn't benefiting financially. A special arrangement is a sort of contract between two people who like each other but want the convenience and disposability of the arrangement, without the risk of seeking out an illegal relationship that involves money for sex. You seldom take a hooker to dinner, but a special arrangement can include travel, dinner and even mixing with friends. Judgment about the notion of special arrangements, as well as their morality, makes the real difference.

The alternative ads I created had a glossary that had to be followed. The usual terms for S&M, sadomasochism, became *commanding* and *passive*. Boy, did that piss people off! At least at first. It meant people who were used to the usual lifestyle lingo had to smooth off edges they preferred. It was the price of having alternative ads, I told them. I tried to get people placing ads to think of it like a word game. Bondage was turned into *knotty* adventures, as well as *rope play*. It was all so ridiculous, but I'd learned from many years of reading and researching the sex world that there was a whole other world out there beyond vanilla sex, and many people were enjoying themselves engaging in it.

This wasn't my thing and might not be yours, but as long as people are consenting adults, why should anyone care?

Flashing on to *Fifty Shades of Grey* right now, the sexy trilogy series by E.L. James? It's quite different, because of how the male character, Christian, became a dominant, but also because he was set "free."

Another part of alternative ads when they first began was an introduction into lifestyles that were always around, but not out in the open in the personals. These included threesomes, couples looking for a partner, women looking for a couple, swingers who enjoyed partying with other couples. Some of this was explored on *Sex and the City*, when Miranda, played by Cynthia Nixon, started doubting her attractiveness. Miranda answered a couples ad, with the female in the couple wanting to give her boyfriend a birthday present. Miranda was simply exploring and seeking validation that she could be wanted in that way by a couple. So, when she found out she could be, she bailed. However, some people enjoy the threesome lifestyle.

Threesomes can be tricky things, however. Jealousy can flare up between people in a monogamous relationship, where none previously existed, if the exploration being sought isn't fully discussed and the partners aren't totally honest with one another about how they feel, their doubts and their trepidations.

Alternative ads landing at the *LA Weekly* also finally acknowledged the sexual smorgasbord that exists in life. Transgender ads were available, acknowledging individuals who are constantly battling sexual inequality and harassment. Transgender people are born one sex, but identify in every way that's important with the opposite gender. It may seem like something small — after all, it's only personal ads, but sexual equality matters. Inclusion matters, too. It's not easy to find love, no matter who you are, but especially when basic services open to others are out of bounds.

One person who put transgender individuals in the headlines and in the news is Chaz Bono, the son of Cher and the late Sonny Bono, who rocketed into the American consciousness through his heroic performances on *Dancing With the Stars*. Jenna Talackova, who competed for Miss Universe Canada in 2012, was the first transgender contestant ever to be in the pageant. Jenna was born a boy but always self-identified as a girl. Chaz and Jenna want to live lives as they choose, without being discriminated against, just like anyone else.

It's also why Amanda Simpson was so important. Ms. Simpson became the first-ever openly transgender person and political appointee, President Barack Obama giving her the nod as special assistant to the secretary of the United States Army for acquisition, logistics and technology. Legitimization matters, and in the structure of our society is critical, even if you never heard of Ms. Simpson before. If her inclusion, as with Chaz Bono and Jenna Talackova, creates even a tiny ripple of acceptance, it's important.

It's not just about surgery, looking beautiful and personal acceptance, because we all live in a connected society. It's also about discrimination laws in employment, housing and all sorts of avenues remaining closed because of bigotry and belief that a trans person doesn't deserve the same respect as anyone else. It's another moment when the personal becomes political. You don't have to understand it. It's about basic civil rights for any individual, which shouldn't be predicated on sexuality.

Alternative ads were our one small step in favor of sexual inclusiveness. It was exciting to open it up and let everyone in. It was also a never-ending sexual education class for me.

Then there were the dominatrixes I talked to. We gradually got to know one another, because they placed ads every week on the phone and preferred dealing with me, once I arrived. The details of their lives were fascinating, and I realized quickly that this was another avenue for alternatives. It wasn't that it was new to me, because I'd done enough reading to know the landscape, but being able to have a dialogue was important. The doms I talked to all said they made from high five- to six-figure incomes and had a diverse clientele, from businessmen to lawyers to the TV and movie industries to truck drivers.

One of the things I learned over the years was that high-powered men enjoy being submissive with the doms they pay to treat them in humiliating fashion. Crawling on the floor, getting whipped is how some bad-boy executives get off, while the dom made out like any thriving entrepreneur.

I felt like a voyeur being led through a world I could only imagine in my head. What I knew about dominatrixes and spanking men now went beyond my Kinsey, Masters and Johnson and *Playboy* research. It would be continued with men during my stint as one of the first female online editors-in-chief in the soft-core adult industry, which we'll talk about later, and was an education like no other. It taught me how men think and what they say about women when we're not around, including what sex means to them in real terms.

Human sexuality is a fascinating subject, and the technological era provided me with a roadmap to learn all about it through an education I couldn't get in any school. I didn't label myself an investigative journalist, but that's part of the role I played, as I dipped in and out of industries that mined the secrets of dating, relationship, sex and love, also learning the pitfalls and prurient traps that lay embedded in the new technologies. For any unsuspecting or trusting soul, there would be a world of hurt waiting.

Judgment and my feminist notions were put on a shelf. Perhaps my strait-laced life and Missouri sensibilities were also seduced by hearing wild stories and living vicariously through them. Human sexuality has always fascinated me, and over a ten-year period, from around 1992-2001, I learned more talking to all sorts of people — hundreds of men and women — than I could ever have learned anywhere else. It was a lot more fun than school, with the phone, email and online conversations offering people anonymity that provided a shield and gave me a broad canvas on which to view the American appetite. I had to then decide if I was hearing fakery or honesty. People talking in extraordinary candor about the one thing that makes us feel more alive than anything else in human grasp, a loving relationship and sexual communion with another person.

The job of Relationship Consultant at the *LA Weekly* was one of the best jobs I have ever had. I once had a large box of thank-you notes from people, all of whom found love and even marriage through the work we did together. There was nothing better than working with women and men, helping them craft personal and later online ads to attract someone to date that could become the lasting relationship of their life.

The hardest thing I had to sell the single women on, as they looked for lasting love in the personals, was that putting their sensuality up first was the key to getting the attention of the most eligible bachelors. At first, no one believed what I was telling them. In a personal ad, the best way for a good-looking single woman with a great job to attract the man she wanted was to first sell herself as a hot commodity physically, then seal it with her smarts, education and what made her unique.

Remember Melanie Griffith in *Working Girl*? "I have a head for business and a bod for sin," is what she said to Harrison Ford, which left his jaw on the floor and his mind reeling at the possibilities. But she said it in a dress worth thousands of dollars and her hair perfectly coiffed, never mind that she was parading around as someone she wasn't, at a high-profile investment event. The point is that the foundation of her statement was absolutely true and delivered by the woman she was in person. The trick in an online ad is to get this combination in their mind.

Everyone knows that men are visual, so that's what you had to serve up first in personal ads, before the social media era. You may not even be able to relate to personal ads in newspapers now, but it's exactly what works today online only better, because a picture is out there somewhere, likely on Facebook, for someone curious about you to find. I bring personals up for context to show you how we've fast-forwarded, but that fundamentals stay the same.

For a guy's profile, the biggest thing in early 2013 was a picture showing him holding a guitar. For a woman, there's nothing that beats a sexy shot where you can tell the girl's eyes are saying something; she's thinking something, but you can't tell what. Mystery sells the sexy, confident woman you are, because in the new-media speed dating era, people know way too much about each other way too soon, which isn't conducive to the slow burn that builds feelings and emotional ties with one another.

A sexy shot on Facebook or in your online dating profile is the visual version of what you would have described in your personal ad, before online dating. We're now into an era that requires a completely different type of game plan. It's your choice, but slowing the pace down is a coveted thing today, because dating and finding a long-term relationship requires simmering.

We're in a completely different era from the '90s, when personal ads blasted onto the scene and turned the dating world upside down yet again, just like the era of the sexual revolution did in the '60s. But someone else's rules are still dogging women, offering a fake foundation on which girls can plan the perfect move, including nonsense like "don't talk to a man first," which is on the back of the paperback version of *The Rules*.

When chemistry between two people collides, nothing can stop what evolves, except the fear of falling in love and getting exactly what you want, provided that you know what that is.

What is very different now is the freedom women have and the perception of who we are as sexual creatures, coupled with the work lives we've created for ourselves, which often demand equal time.

The culture in which we live and what's seen in our mainstream media, online communication, Facebook and other social media, including Twitter, Tumblr, texting and sexting, instantly viral photographs, Instagram and videos, but also the movies, broadcast and cable TV, and even advertising, all make up a gigantic mirror in which to see women's lives, forcing pressure down on us all. Once we got the opportunity to unleash our individual sexuality that we now safely control, and the real-life economic choices that came with it, the stress became even more intense for women.

It's now all on display for everyone to witness.

Our lives in the rapidly churning modern era now include being bombarded by social media and cultural expectations that heap pressure on women at younger ages. These pressures often reemerge when we're older in second-chance relationships. We're taking it all on, crafting lives of once-unimaginable possibilities, no matter our ages.

Alicia Keys' "Girl on Fire" comes to mind. When she was interviewed in the *New York Times* Sunday magazine in September 2012, the award-winning singer explained what she was saying in the song. "A girl on fire is loud and obnoxious and destructive and... free," and *she's not backing down.*

2

Hollywood to Sexy Baby and Girls

The door broke wide open for modern women on what came to be known as K-Day, August 20, 1953. More than sixty reports in publications such as *Life, Time, Newsweek, Modern Bride, Collier's, Reader's Digest, Redbook* and *U.S. News & World Report*, according to the Kinsey Institute website, teased Dr. Alfred Kinsey's upcoming landmark book, *Sexual Behavior in the Human Female*, offering excerpts of Kinsey's research. The revelations would change the conversation about sex forever. It was Kinsey who revealed through meticulous research that women were sexual beings, capable of orgasm and all sorts of libidinous thoughts, which started a lot younger than anyone wanted to think about. Seven years before the Pill, his book primed the public consciousness for the inevitable overturning of American social norms.

Kinsey had published a preceding report on the human male in 1948, but nothing compared to the response from critics on daring to mine and report the sexual proclivities of women. Coming after Freud's "anatomy is destiny" moralistic paternalism and ridiculous "penis envy," Kinsey landed like a crashing wave in the post-Freud era, when women were waking up in very tight cultural corsets. Rev. Billy Graham, the evangelical preacher to presidents, was quoted as saying Alfred Kinsey "certainly could not have interviewed any of the millions of born-again Christian women in this country, who put the highest price on virtue, decency and modesty."

The Kinsey Reports rocked traditionally religious America to its core, freaking out the faithful over the thought that women's sexuality was even being discussed out in the open. *"It's impossible to estimate the damage this book will do to the already deteriorating morals of America,"* Rev. Graham opined. Kinsey was unlikely surprised. His own hyper-religious upbringing was an oversized influence in the shakeup he unleashed, when he dared to challenge America's notion of female sexuality during the manufactured suburban bliss of the 1950s.

When the film *Kinsey* debuted, starring Liam Neeson in the title role and Laura Linney as his wife, conservative groups reacted much the same way they did in the 1950s. *"Instead of being lionized, Kinsey's proper place is with Nazi Dr. Josef Mengele or your average Hollywood horror flick mad scientist,"* was the overwrought reaction of Robert Knight, director of Concerned Women of America's Culture & Family Institute, as the Associated Press reported. It was a rehashing of the old characterization of Kinsey as the "American Mengele," which he was commonly called when his findings on women were first released.

Perhaps the real grudge conservatives groups, including Focus on the Family, had against Alfred Kinsey was that he opened the gateway to sexual education in public schools, taking the teaching of biology and the science of reproduction out of the hands of parents, but more importantly, away from the church. So powerful was Kinsey's reach thought to be by the American right, that blame for abortion, high divorce rates, pornography and even AIDS was laid at his feet. It was the same beef cited by conservative outlets like Morality and Media, which Newsmax reported when the film *Kinsey* hit the big screen.

Whatever Alfred Kinsey was in people's minds, or whether people agree with his studies or methods, the impact of his work is unquestionable. Once the subject of female sexuality could be discussed not only openly, but seriously, the change in American culture worked like a contagion. That's what mattered.

Masters and Johnson took what Kinsey unleashed and quantified it. The audacious research and historic scientific witness to women's sexuality provided through the work of Dr. William Masters and Virginia Johnson would finally and thoroughly question and then silence the misogynistic presumptions of Dr. Sigmund Freud. Burying the purely ideological notion that a woman's orgasm came in legitimate and illegitimate forms that depended on a man, instead of her own personal needs and physiological experiences.

Virginia Johnson's ability to talk with women and easily engage them in the most private conversations resulted in convincing them to take part. Through his medical reputation and scientific expertise, Masters legitimized the risks to the work they were doing. Virginia Johnson offering the human touch, because Masters was too standoffish to have ever convinced women to reveal themselves sexually.

At St. Louis, Missouri's Washington University's Maternity Hospital, Masters and Johnson turned the science of human sexuality into liquid gold by chronicling an estimated 14,000 orgasms, from 1956 until their book *Human Sexual Response* was released in 1966, as reported in *Newsweek*. Their story is chronicled by Thomas Maier in his book, *Masters of Sex: The Life and Times of William Masters and Virginia Johnson, the Couple Who Taught America How to Love*, which is the basis for the Showtime series and was updated for the show. *Masters of Sex* has turned the St. Louis team's liberating sexual cry into a deliciously satisfying and emotionally grounding romp, starring Michael Sheen as Dr. Masters, Lizzy Caplan as Virginia Johnson and Caitlin Fitzgerald as Libby Masters.

Sigmund Freud's ridiculous ruminations on female pleasure included the notion that a clitoral orgasm was a sign of emotional immaturity, but also that pleasure is best found through the more "mature" experience of vaginal intercourse. After Kinsey, Masters and Johnson reduced Freud's psychological babble to a footnote on the way to providing facts through witnessing women's sexual satisfaction in a lab setting.

As someone who grew up in St. Louis, Missouri, it's astounding that such break-through sexuality studies on women could have come from the same state that still produces politicians like Republican Representative Todd Akin, in the second decade of the twenty-first century, no less, who in 2012 ran a failed Senate campaign claiming a women's body can protect her from pregnancy after a "legitimate" rape.

Not only did Masters and Johnson prove Freud wrong, but through the wonders of using a giant dildo, their sexual studies proved that women don't need men to climax. Not to mention that if a man ignores a woman's clitoris he may even prevent her from enjoying an orgasm altogether. A whopping 75% of women require clitoral stimulation to climax, the figure most often cited, though I'd suggest it could be even higher. Masters and Johnson also discovering that women can have multiple orgasms, with the second and even third sometimes being more powerful than the first.

To punctuate the hold Freud had on human sexuality in the 1950s, the sequence of *Masters of Sex* scenes with Allison Janney, who plays Margaret Scully, the wife of Dr. Masters' boss, is painfully illustrative. Janney and her husband, Barton Scully, played by Beau Bridges, don't sleep together. Bridges' character is a closet homosexual who has been exposed to Dr. Masters by one of his male prostitute subjects, allowing Masters to blackmail his boss into financially backing his research.

In what launches a contagion of evocative scenes, Janney is playing bridge with her girlfriends, when one of them reveals she has signed up for Dr. Masters' study, which she tells the girls revolves around sex. That gets Margaret Scully's attention, whose marriage is lacking any deeply physical sexual enjoyment. It leads Janney to seek out Virginia Johnson. But when Janney meets with both Masters and Johnson together so they can compile data before she's hooked up to the machinery and the dials start evaluating her physical reactions to pleasure, in answers to questions about her own sexual experiences, the very married Margaret Scully is led to admit she has never had an orgasm, a prerequisite for being part of their sexual research. Janney talks about feeling "pressure" during sex, but never the "release," as Virginia Masters describes it to her. The shock of her own admission seems to stun and deeply embarrass Mrs. Scully, and is felt by both Virginia Johnson and Dr. Masters. How could a married woman of thirty years never have experienced an orgasm?

When Dr. Scully returns home after a secret homosexual tryst in one scene, he finds Margaret reading *Peyton Place* in bed. Written by housewife Grace Metalious, who had her own frustrations in 1956, it was a loud cry against the hypocrisy of 1950s morality and dramatically written to shock. Seen as scandalous, it sold 100,000 copies in the first month and eventually sold 12 million, according to *Vanity Fair*, and it was turned into a big screen soap opera in 1957. Dr. Scully has no interest in seeing the film, so his wife decides to see it alone.

At the theatre, Mrs. Scully meets the dashing Dr. Austin Langham, played by Teddy Sears, who happens to be participating in the Masters and Johnson study, but has suddenly experienced what we know of today as erectile dysfunction. The minute the two meet after the movie the foreshadowing of what's about to happen is as rich as what an odd couple these two make. But their sexual hunger, angst and awkwardness binds them and leads to an improbable and wholly liberating sexual adventure between a woman and a man desperate to find connection, touch and release with someone who understands what it's like to be frustrated and marooned while married.

So long Freud, hello Kinsey, thank you Masters and Johnson. Women weren't just daughters and mothers anymore. We were sexual and now there's proof. Dr. Spock supposedly once said, "Everything is about sex." After Masters and Johnson it was no longer just about cocksmen and the sexual prowess of males, but also about whether women got off, too.

This shouldn't have been news after the roaring 1920s, when women were free and flaunted it. But believers in American puritanism tend to continually work to reassert themselves over our culture. It's why, borrowing from Alicia Keys again, we're not going to back down again — because we can't afford to. We've seen the results when we relax. It's called the 1950s.

The religious right is never more fearful than when independent, liberated females are exercising personal freedoms and women start expressing themselves in a way that challenges traditional norms. They will never grasp that they lost the argument, beginning in 1960, when biology began shifting to no longer being our destiny.

As Showtime's *Masters of Sex* illustrates through Allison Janney's character, during the era of the feminine mystique, committed relationships often left the women in them feeling nothing but frigid.

The Pill took the findings of Kinsey, and Masters and Johnson, personalizing them further for females. In the book *The Aesthetic Brain* by Anjan Chatterjee, which was excerpted on Salon.com in November 2013, Chatterjee writes how neuroscience explains why sex feels so good, including that orgasm releases "beta-endorphins, prolactin, and oxytocin, …a hormone associated with trust and a sense of affiliation."

I'm a lifelong devotee of film and TV, both of which became an escape for a midwestern girl intent on fleeing the traditional, moralistic Missouri confines that didn't fit my independent nature. It's a beautiful state to be from, but once I came of age, the lack of respect for modern women's quest for equality was stifling.

The stuff coming at me as a girl was blinding, especially since I spent much of my childhood in front of the TV, though it's nothing compared to the onslaught coming at girls today through social media and the web. The big box in front of me was my babysitter, and I was a passenger captivated by this dream machine. The ramp up to what became the reality for new generations of liberated women was amazing to watch once it blasted into American living rooms. There is nothing that impacted me more growing up than the images of women I saw on the screen, big and small.

I simply was *That Girl,* the character Ann Marie, in ABC's epic television series, or at least I wanted to be. The show starred the indomitable Marlo Thomas as an aspiring actress who moved to New York City to make it big. From 1966 to 1971, girls like me watched the single-girl life play out on TV, dreaming, visualizing that we could be that girl, however we each defined her, because not everyone wanted to be an actress. I honestly don't know what I would have done if Ann's engagement at the end of the sitcom's run would have manifested in marriage. It would have been a disaster, but it would not have been surprising, because TV was run by men, just as advertising was in the 1950s, so it would have been their version of what's best for us. But Marlo Thomas and others on the show were ahead of the curve and knew things had already started changing.

Still, I got sucked up in the whole engagement-ring ritual so many college females fell into in the 1970s. It was an escape from struggles at home and from working too hard, though I was a statistic just as quickly as I said "I do," because I really never wanted to. That I thought marriage would be an escape shows you just how naive I was, though I was hardly alone. We've all learned a lot since the 1970s, but *That Girl* had it right all along, earlier than American society.

In 1970, the *Mary Tyler Moore Show* picked up the slack and then some, with Mary Tyler Moore playing TV's first never-married career girl, Mary Richards, who was paying her own way without money from a husband or ex-husband, and without a steady boyfriend. By the time the show was off the air, I was well on my way to being long gone from Missouri.

These two TV shows validated my existence and the fact that being different wasn't weird. I rarely saw women outside these shows I could relate to, which is why *That Girl* and *Mary Tyler Moore* mattered so much. Everything else started with finding a husband, marrying said man, having children, then never wanting for more or even considering there was more. In fact, thinking differently about dating and men got you classified as less — not feminine, not sufficiently womanly. To say I was in mortal conflict with myself is an understatement.

When *Sex and the City* hit, created for HBO by Darren Star, and based on the book by Candace Bushnell, nobody had ever excavated the gritty intimacy terrain this show tread. Sure, it was about fashion, glamour and how the girls all made it happen for themselves in New York City, but this show went where *That Girl* and *Mary Tyler Moore* never did. The episode "Evolution," in Season Two, when Carrie Bradshaw, portrayed by Sarah Jessica Parker, dropped the news that for the first time she "did a #2" at Mr. Big's place, what can go through a girl's mind when she's in close quarters with a man and one bathroom was still a very private hassle. As Charlotte howled it was "the end of romance," Miranda confessed she'd gone an entire relationship "never doing that," including during a trip to Bermuda where she traipsed down to the lobby the whole weekend, rather than let him know she "did a #2." The logistics alone of hiding a basic bodily function boggles the mind! Samantha's answer was dating only rich men where money meant there was enough space to "distance yourself from the #2." There was nothing in a girl's life that was off limits to Carrie, Charlotte (Kristin Davis), Miranda (Cynthia Nixon) and Samantha (Kim Cattrall), with women the better for their often-profane frankness.

In Season Three, the episode "Attack of the Five-Foot-Ten Woman," the show took on a current topic in 2000, long before Sheryl Sandberg's *Lean In*. The woman in the title is Natasha, played by Bridget Moynahan, the new wife of Mr. Big, made famous by Chris Noth. As Charlotte reads from the Weddings/Celebrations section of the Sunday *New York Times*, referred to by Carrie as the "single woman's sports pages," which includes her ex in this particular issue, it seems that every caption starts with "Until recently, the bride...." What comes after is the career or job "the bride" had "until recently," implying that once a woman gets engaged and decides to marry, whatever she was once interested in suddenly vanishes. This passage sets Miranda off and mocking this notion, with Samantha joining in, saying, "Until recently, the bride had a life of her own." Women continue to struggle for marriage not to change their initial dreams and hijack their life that began centered on what makes them tick.

Hopscotching across Hollywood filmland, because I could never name all of the films that mattered and cemented the politics of sex in American culture, let's go back to Garbo's *Flesh and the Devil* in pre-censorship 1927. Some films grabbed me stronger than others, even when I unearthed them years after they were made, because of how Hollywood manipulated women through them.

The Chapman Report was a minor blip in 1962, the subject it tackled taking it off the map of what was considered appropriate at the time. George Cukor was the king of directors for females, but not even he could survive the Hollywood censors once they got a hold of this film. The movie is based on Irving Wallace's novel, which is based on Kinsey's research on women's sexuality. The quote at the beginning of this book, "Analysis is no substitute for guts," comes from *The Chapman Report* and registered immediately with me when I finally saw the film on TCM, Turner Classic Movies. Anyone who has ever been in therapy, and I have, no matter how valuable it is, recognizes this truth.

It was said in the film by Naomi Shields, played by Claire Bloom, whose nymphomaniac character ends up getting gang-raped, which you never see, though you do get the picture, when after a night out with the boys, she's dumped on the curb. Of course, she ends up committing suicide. Unbridled female sexuality is a killer. She's one of four women featured in *The Chapman Report*. Jane Fonda plays a frigid, pent-up wife; Shelley Winters portrays the perfect, hopeless, idiot female, who falls for a married man who delights in serial infidelity at her expense. A married, flighty Glynis Johns runs around after a hunky, athletic jock.

The characters and storyline were butchered through censorship, the depictions of the women in the film coming out weirdly contorted. Virtue and sexuality collided in this film, as they did in other releases at the beginning of the modern sexual and feminist revolutions. A mass-marketed movie industry just wasn't allowed to cover what was going on with women honestly.

Treating women in a way that could be absorbed by the movie masses wasn't the goal of *The Chapman Report*, because it dealt with what was considered taboo, as if the very notion of women's sexual power was dangerous if not properly contained and compartmentalized. Cukor had chosen a subject considered cultural dynamite, and it seemed as if Hollywood ruined his movie to get even and send a message. The director of the 1939 all-female cast of *The Women* couldn't get any respect for his 1962 film on female sexuality as liberation was hitting.

The Chapman Report made the Production Code Administration files, with wardrobe photographs only part of what passed through that office. The Supreme Court case *Mutual Film Corporation v. Industrial Commission of Ohio*, which was a unanimous decision, said that films weren't the press so weren't protected under the First Amendment. This is obvious, but the unintended results were a disaster for women. The images girls would see on the screen of women were male-approved and sanitized. The rest is history, and for women that meant our sexuality on screen would be monitored, shaped and contorted by the men who ran the entertainment industry. It was a long way from the pre-censored days of the movies, when girls were as free as men.

Women couldn't pay their own bills at the time. Ah, but female actors and performers could, so is it any wonder they have always been considered a little dangerous? A woman paying her own way, especially if she's not married, is just a little suspect, and so is the role she's portraying on the screen for all of America to see.

It already had been decided that men's sexuality was dangerous, which was shrugged off as men being men. Through the pages of *Playboy* that came paper-wrapped to your doorstep to protect the wife, men's visual expressions of sex have always been seen as pornographic, something too risqué for women. Smut is banished from sight whenever possible, kept secret. It now hides behind passwords and subscription memberships, where only the lost are seen to traverse. Sexual curiosity through visual gratification is a sin by itself for many, even if it's harmless voyeurism in the privacy of your own home. We must all be protected, especially women, as if we don't lust equally to men. This is the American setup that has led to the alienation of affections and the segregation of sexual romping, as well as the myth that women aren't carnally inclined to "kinky fuckery" too, to quote E.L. James, the author of *Fifty Shades of Grey*.

When I think about all those Kindles or iPads being read and women privately enjoying *Fifty Shades of Grey* and keeping it to themselves, I wonder. How in the world can a long-term relationship or marriage survive without individual privacy? I don't think it can. I'm not talking about illicit secrets that create a separate life outside your relationship which, given oxygen, can take your attention and focus away from your partnership, even harm it. But there's been an effort to suggest that we have to spill everything to our mates. It's preposterous. Of course a man engaging a woman not his wife is wrong. But there's got to be privacy, so men and women can have a little breathing room to discover their own curiosities without having to share that we're looking at men's penises, because we like hot, naked hunks, just like men do with women.

Also in 1962 was *Lolita*, which was directed by the audacious Stanley Kubrick. Based on the classic novel by Vladimir Nabokov, it unpacks the forbidden, illegal attraction of middle-aged men to young girls, making any fantasy in porn magazines like *Barely Legal* come to life on screen or at least in your mind. Imagination was the guide in Kubrick's *Lolita*, which starred James Mason as Humbert Humbert and Sue Lyon as the adolescent nymphet. Censorship neutered Nabokov's classic novel, with Kubrick forced to change Lolita's age from twelve in Nabokov's book to about fifteen on screen (the character's precise age is never mentioned in the film). The maverick director was later rumored to have said that if he'd known what was going to happen to his film he likely wouldn't have made it, but that couldn't eradicate the truth it depicted. When the remake with Jeremy Irons as Humbert was filming, the Child Pornography Act was signed by President Bill Clinton, which rightly banned computer-generated child pornography. It provoked discussions that the film should be banned as well, even if you can't ban the perversion itself. Just don't discuss.

Sexual education is worth the scandal if it informs.

Breakfast at Tiffanys in 1961, starring Audrey Hepburn and George Peppard, is a film adaptation of Truman Capote's short story that has no resemblance to it.

The character of society girl Holly Golightly is vapid and ridiculous, though Hepburn is spellbinding, which is why she earned the Oscar. But the Hollywood Holly shares nothing with Capote's darker, deeply sexual and profane, post-WWII vamp. At least Hepburn's Holly found love, though Capote's Fred is hardly a love interest who would be into her, because it's implied he's homosexual. The signature cigarette holder and her little black dress cemented Hepburn's image, Hollywood contorting the real, live character from Capote's imagination, which was in no way suitable to show on screen at the time. The theme song sung by Andy Williams, "Moon River," talked about "two drifters off to see the world. There's such a lot of world to see. We're after the same rainbow's end. Waiting 'round the bend..." It's surreal compared to Capote's vision, which was a lot more honest and is likely why it scared Hollywood into sanitizing it.

Hepburn's Holly was a long way from the 1940s, when the Howard Hughes western *The Outlaw* was unleashed, with a movie poster that made Jane Russell a star and sent the Hays Office, the Motion Picture Producers and Distributors of America's censorship office, to DefCon1. Breaking "decency" codes, the poster in 1946 allegedly revealed part of Russell's nipple. It's quintessentially American that Hughes kept fighting, and when the film was released, it was a blockbuster hit, making Russell a household name that later got her paired with Marilyn Monroe, both on film and with their handprints immortalized together in cement outside Grauman's Chinese Theater.

In pre-Code, Depression-era Hollywood, women were free, very strong and, unapologetically, scantily clad. Ruth Chatteron, whom I bet most have never heard of, played Alison Drake, the title character in *Female*, a CEO "who's used to buying love...," says AltFG.com, a blog about alternative films. Norma Shearer was the title character in 1930s *The Divorcee*. In 1932, Jean Harlow was *The Red Headed Woman*, sleeping her way to the top.

The Roman Catholic Church had a fit and launched a campaign that finally brought Hollywood to heel, bringing the Hays Code to life and creating a monster at the same time. Before the Coding, which began in earnest around 1934, films were mostly governed by local laws. Men who rule organized religion have been at the heart of corralling women since the dawn of time. Today they can only succeed when women help them.

Alfred Hitchcock's *Psycho* landed in 1960 and was an obvious must-see when I came of age, but it haunted me for days and still does when I see it. After watching HBO's *The Girl*, the story of how Hitchcock terrorized, raped and ruined the career of Tippi Hedren because she wouldn't reward his tortured obsession, it's no wonder *Psycho* freaked me out. It was meant to. Subliminally terrorizing and questioning women's sanity through the camera lens was a Hitchcock trademark, as he targeted women — even Mother — in spectacular films, creating masterpiece after masterpiece. But look at the female characters he created in his films. More importantly, look at the relationships they have with the men.

The foreshadowing of women's PR troubles in the modern visual era is Academy Award-winning actress Ingrid Bergman, who was also a Tony- and Emmy-winner. She went from playing a nun in *The Bells of St. Mary's* to being called out on the Senate floor by Senator Edwin C. Johnson for being a "free-love cultist..., a horrible example of womanhood and a powerful influence for evil." While married to one man, she had the child of another. It was sacrilege.

An online story by the *National Enquirer* keeps alive Bergman's exile by chronicling and highlighting the gory details from the 1950s, a time which some people actually glorify today. Gossip mean-girls of the era, Hedda Hopper and Louella Parsons, were only too happy to dissect Bergman's dissent into wanton womanhood, which resulted in her films being banned for several years, as fans turned on the former screen-nun, now that she was seen as libidinous, sexual and, even worse, an adulterer. Men would be men and take a mistress, but for a woman to make a man a cuckold? For American society, Bergman had committed the worst societal sin.

In 1942, Errol Flynn was tried for statutory rape of two girls. Not only did he get off, but he enjoyed widespread support, with the likes of William F. Buckley, a conservative icon, reportedly joining the American Boys Club for the Defense of Errol Flynn (ABCDEF).

The 2013 *Enquirer* piece on Bergman quotes her daughter, Pia Lindstrom, telling Larry King that Bergman was forbidden to enter the country: "There was a vote in Congress, where she was made persona non grata."

Bergman herself was quoted as saying, "I have no regrets. I wouldn't have lived my life the way I did if I was going to worry about what people were going to say."

A lot can be said for having guts.

When I discovered Bette Davis, it was a revelation. Ms. Davis chewed up plots that featured brazen females and spit them out in the audience's eye, daring us to disapprove. Her imprint stuck. In life, she took on Warner Bros. and demanded better roles and more money. When asked about her life and marriages, she said she "loved being a wife," but that if she had married "much, much, much later and maybe found the right person," it might have worked. In a 1981 *Good Morning America* interview,

Davis said, "The big romance of my life was this work I do."

There's real evidence today that getting married later matters even more, and it goes beyond the importance of finding the right person to make sure it lasts. The Knot Yet Report in 2013, sponsored by the National Campaign to Prevent Teen and Unplanned Pregnancy, the Relate Institute, and the National Marriage Project at the University of Virginia, reveals why waiting matters to modern women: "Women enjoy an annual income premium if they wait until thirty or later to marry. For college-educated women in their mid-thirties, this premium amounts to $18,152. Delayed marriage has helped to bring down the divorce rate in the U.S. since the early 1980s, because couples who marry in their early twenties and especially their teens are more likely to divorce than couples who marry later."

Like Ms. Davis, Joan Crawford had four marriages. Her image in "Mildred Pierce" is seared into film lovers' memories but was shattered by the horror story in *Mommie Dearest*, told by her daughter. That she ended up Mrs. Pepsi-Cola seems weirdly incongruent, but I'll never forget the image of her as Mildred Pierce, the mother doing everything for a daughter who is determined to ruin her life. It's the ultimate warning for any parent who thinks they can control how a child turns out.

In 1971, Jane Fonda landed in *Klute*, the bookend to her role in *The Chapman Report*. Ten years after *Butterfield 8*, but also *Breakfast at Tiffany's*, Fonda's Bree Daniels is stalked, but escapes. Like Elizabeth Taylor and Audrey Hepburn, Fonda, too, won the Oscar for best actress. Over a decade of time, Hollywood still marveled at a woman playing the role of hooker, but to my eyes, it seemed like a message that a sexual woman was always doomed.

Katharine Hepburn was one of the strongest female actresses on screen. But she was the opposite in the one relationship that threaded throughout her life, the one with Spencer Tracy. By all reports, she chose obedience and subservience to Tracy, a married alcoholic and religiously chained man who refused to acknowledge their relationship. Ms. Hepburn acknowledged as much, with Scott Berg being one of those recounting the incident. "She did admit to falling asleep one night in the hallway outside the Beverly Hills Hotel room in which he had passed out and from which he had thrown her out," Berg wrote in his biography of Hepburn, *Kate Remembered*.

When James Bond hit in 1962 with *Dr. No*, 007 didn't come alone. Ursula Andress as Honey Ryder introduced the Bond girl and exposed the cinema sex symbol as something well beyond the fragile sensuality that Marilyn Monroe created. All I knew is that I couldn't relate to Ursula or Marilyn. I envisioned myself the opposite of the sexy bombshell, relating more to the stuff of the girl next door that most guys knew was a virgin.

I culled through the screen characters, taking stock of each woman, each character's persona, wondering where I fit in, because no one in my immediate vicinity represented anything to which I could relate.

It was *Gone With the Wind*'s Scarlett O'Hara and her romantic drama that really hooked me, grabbed my attention and fixated my imagination on her reckless fearlessness. Scarlett lived a tortured existence inside an impossible infatuation with Ashley Wilkes that was capable of destroying her own happiness with a man who worshipped her (Rhett Butler) though she didn't deserve it. Oh, and she didn't find out she wanted Rhett until he left. It was all so volatile, so exciting, so *romantic*; but actually, it was the ultimate soap opera.

If ever there was a synopsis that encapsulated the person I was fighting not to be but was hopelessly drawn to, it was the Scarlett-Rhett scenario. I was spellbound watching Scarlett refuse to surrender to the virile Rhett, whom she obviously feared might be everything Ashley Wilkes wasn't. Scarlett embodied the age-old story of chasing what you can't have, while convincing yourself that this emotional and physical feeling of torment was actually the ultimate romantic swoon. It's Shakespearean to love a man who denies you. The drama, the notion that love hurts, is a narcotic that girls and women have been feeding off of for centuries. What else did women have to do? Yet even when we became serious people, we still succumbed to this torture.

Scarlett taunts Rhett, the man she could have but who would expect her to deliver on the physical passion she pretends to feel toward Ashley, who allows her to play only safe, romantic head-games instead. Ashley is unattainable and way too cool to ever make her happy.

It's what makes the brief alignment and calm surrounding Rhett and Scarlett's ultimate consummation so satiating. We know it's only a matter of time before the emotional brawls resume and the physical tug of power escalates again inside a marriage where it's always a test of wills.

The drama, lust and friction, the stuff of pure passion, was all ambrosia for a girl who wouldn't permit herself to let go and experience anything sexual without overarching angst and guilt. Mentally, I was consumed by an overwrought sense of self-possession and self-importance that were choking the life out of any personal happiness meant to be enjoyed in what I was being told were my carefree years.

But I was never carefree. I was possessed by the fear, anxiety and danger of never finding a way to live that didn't depend on what women were supposed to do. Somewhere along the line, I knew I'd step off the discipline merry-go-round I'd gladly chosen when I was a kid and earn the right to explain that there were women out there who were determined to experience things outside what was considered normal and traditional — women who wanted to organize their lives as the mood struck them, which had nothing to do with biology, let alone the setup American culture ordained.

Inside the beauty-queen persona lived an emotional volcano.

While sunbathing at my boyfriend Brian's elite country club, along with his mother and several other mothers of the next generation of pampered pricks, I rebelled at these women railing against the Equal Rights Amendment. Still in high school at the time, Brian was the man with whom I'd have a fly-by marriage and one of the many men I tortured who put up with my mood swings of on-again, off-again courtship.

After listening to these women pitch first-class fits over feminism and how the ERA would ruin everything, I got so annoyed, I walked off the sun deck on more than one occasion, and out of the club entirely. That my big brother Larry was in the Missouri Senate and was one of the many co-sponsors supporting the Equal Rights Amendment meant I actually knew what the key twenty-four words meant and could do. The women married to elite St. Louis men were sure it meant they'd have to squat in cubicles next to men peeing at urinals, which would bring the end of polite society as they knew it. That this visual in no way represented the point of the ERA didn't matter, because they had a tape of Phyllis Schlafly on a loop in their heads.

Enemy Number One back then was anything liberated, which certainly started with sex and the purveyors of such insane notions that good girls liked it, too.

Hugh Hefner called himself "Kinsey's pamphleteer" for a reason. Publishing the first issue of *Playboy* in 1953, the same year Kinsey told America that women were sexual, Marilyn Monroe on the cover codified the Kinsey Reports in our culture. Celebrating fifty years of the magazine in 2013, *Playboy* once again put Monroe on the cover. Magazines were slowly being edged out and replaced with online smut and video memberships for voyeurs. It made the commotion Marilyn's nudes in print once caused seem quaint.

Author Margaret Mitchell's Scarlett, played on film by Vivien Leigh, who also won an Oscar for best actress, was made of much tougher, more determined stuff than Liza Minnelli's character in *Cabaret*, or Jane Fonda's Bree Daniels in *Klute*, never mind *The Chapman Report* or Audrey Hepburn and Elizabeth Taylor. Scarlett represented women before Freud got to us, as she blew through husbands and became a ruthlessly unemotional capitalist who partnered with carpetbaggers. She is someone who lives her life separate from the men whom she needs to accept her. At the same time, she can be practical and do business with the enemy to survive.

"What a woman," says Rhett Butler, as she heads off to shantytown with a gun in her lap, a testament to the hellcat spirit of liberated women, which fell silent in the 1950s. Contrary to the "men may flirt with girls like that but they don't marry them," comment in the film, Scarlett got to do both, repeatedly, while working in a man's world in the post-Civil War South.

Now, in the second decade of the twenty-first century, we find ourselves smack in the middle of an unbounded visual extravaganza, while still trying to cement the fearlessness that came without guilt for the businesswoman Scarlett, no matter what she did. In the last twenty years, beginning in the early 1990s, the image of women in movies has whipsawed from *Pretty Woman* one year to *Thelma and Louise* the next. Today we have *Zero Dark Thirty*'s Maya (Jessica Chastain), the woman who got Osama bin Laden, not to mention Rooney Mara's Lisbeth Salander in *Girl with the Dragon Tattoo*, who tortures her rapist. Then there is Cameron Diaz, who comes close to melting the screen, and the windshield of a Ferrari, as the wicked and sexually carnivorous Malkina, in Ridley Scott's *The Counselor*, who manages to also best the men in the category of wits while she's at it. There's not a hooker in sight, while *Lovelace* is a reminder how seventeen days of sex can change a girl's world.

On top of it all comes a barrage of images, stories and new confrontations that assault us all so quickly in a variety of platforms that few can digest it fast enough to help women, whatever the age, put it all into context.

When *Sexy Baby* hit Showtime, the web lit up. Billed as a documentary about "how pornography, social media and pop culture affect women and girls," it chronicled the sexual education I'd mined over many years. The film follows the lives of a hip twelve-year-old girl, a twenty-two-year-old looking for a "normal" vagina, like what guys watching porn expect to see, and an ex-adult film actress who's now on the production side of things and longing for her first child with her husband. The girls have nothing in common but the exploding visuals of women in the media they see everyday and the impact these images have on their lives. These images now aren't just found in magazines, movies and on TV, but are part of our visual day through billboards and other advertising, which we see any time we log onto the web or our smartphones, via social media platforms like Facebook, Tumblr and Twitter, which is where people today hang out.

One of the first lines in the documentary is "Sex, sex, sex everywhere."

A screen-shot from a web page: "Has Pubic Hair in America Gone Extinct?"

flashes across the TV. The caption below it reads, "Carrie Bradshaw, Hugh Hefner and Barbie have all helped construct a new generation's ideal woman, who is athletic, alluring..., and waxed."

No doubt Carrie Bradshaw and *Sex and the City* changed the perception of women, but it's doubtful that a waxed bush was the nut of it.

It's been politically incorrect to like Barbie for a while now. That's someone else's rule that didn't compute in my world. Barbie wasn't made to be held, fed or rocked. Hallelujah. She came with a baby as an accessory. Sure, you could have a baby — most girls want to — but it wasn't all of what you were as a woman. Barbie's perfect body and her erect tits weren't what I saw. Barbie had a Dream House. She had a hot car and lots of clothes. But best of all, Barbie had a career choice. It meant someone understood that girls didn't have to check the wife-and-mother box unless we wanted to, but also that there was something beyond it, too. So, Barbie was a heroine to me.

I didn't even notice she didn't have a vagina. Most of the adults around me didn't think girls under eighteen had a vagina either. In fact, lingerie for Barbie wasn't introduced for decades. She was sexy, but sexless. If you're not married, that is America's idea of the perfect girl.

The alternative to Barbie when I was a kid was a baby doll called Thumbelina. She was a crushing bore. Holding, feeding and rocking a baby doll didn't require any imagination. I saw mothers everywhere with babies, so I knew the drill. It was a constant picture in my life, the norm, traditional and expected. I wanted to see alternatives. What else was out there?

There was a waist-high talking doll called Chatty Cathy. The name said it all.

Culture doesn't happen in a vacuum, as *Sexy Baby* proves. But Kinsey had now left the conversation. There was someone new to blame.

At the top of *Sexy Baby*, it shows three teenage boys hanging out. A woman asks them whether they've "ever seen a bush on a girl." One guy says, "No bush, none," and the other guy says, "Once, but I didn't ever talk to her again."

I immediately wondered if this is setting up an expectation that matters. Guys talking smack, sending a message girls should heed, or whether girls should be reminded they don't need guys like this in their lives. It did remind me of when I was that age and not having sex when everyone else seemed to be. One time in high school I trusted a guy to go down on me, though when he began, I wasn't sure where he was going or what he was about to do. It was glorious. It was also the first and last time I allowed it until I was long gone from high school, because the next day everyone informed me they knew I had a "big bush." Did I really?

The best defense for the onslaught of peer pressure and judgment is having something to do in your life that matters to you more than what's being said about you. Finding that can be a lifelong search, or it can hit you when you're a kid; it can also change with age. It's where everything starts. It's where your uniqueness takes hold or is reinvented. Over a lifetime, it's what will ground you, no matter the combustible, changing nature of events.

Cut to a little four-year-old girl in *Sexy Baby*, watching a web video of Lady Gaga. Asked her favorite artist, she says "Britney, bitch." Not much later, she's humping the floor and giggling, before her mother stops her and tells her she doesn't want to see that type of dancing.

When I was that age and already addicted to dancing school, I didn't even know that type of dancing existed, because it wasn't in my face.

"We're like the first generation to have what we have," says Winnifred, the twelve-year-old, who's one of the three female stories being chronicled and documented in *Sexy Baby*. "We are the pioneers."

Next shot is Winnifred performing with her acting troupe. On stage, Winnifred proclaims, "What we're saying is, people know more about Paris Hilton and Lindsay Lohan than Susan B. Anthony and Ruth Bader Ginsburg, and that's gotta change."

It's enough to make you believe that everything is happening as it should. Transparently, openly, young girls speaking out amid the barrage of sex, sex, sex coming at them.

Until twenty-two year-old Laura introduces the *Sexy Baby* audience to "meat curtain," meaning part of the girl's labia is hanging down so long, well, you get the picture. She's readying to get a labiaplasty. Laura is an assistant teacher with kindergartners. She's determined to get genital cosmetic surgery so she'll feel better about herself, because she's heard what guys have said about other women's vaginas. She says she has nightmares about her labia, but also admits that her first serious boyfriend, who watched X-rated movies, commented to her, "Oh, it's bigger than most girls', what's wrong?"

"I just feel it would be a huge turn-on to a guy to look like a porn star," Laura continued.

Are you wondering if Laura was risking her teaching assistant position for sharing her labiaplasty story in the documentary? That's the way things work today.

One of my serious relationships, after leaving New York, lasted four years and was among several serial monogamous partnerships I had over the years. Jeffrey, a handsome lawyer in a Beverly Hill's law firm, couldn't get it up, though I didn't discover his real issue until much later. It was before Viagra became widely available, but again, that wouldn't have mattered either. It was the '80s, and we were big partiers and enjoyed the L.A. club scene, which I threw myself into once I left performing. We'd go clubbing and drinking, getting into all sorts of mischief, then come back home where we were living together. It would get hot and heavy... then... stop. Cold.

We weren't having sex, but were in love, and he was so hot it was driving me crazy. We slept together every night, but nothing was happening. I was losing my mind. Then I found out what his deal was: getting off on porn magazines. He kept them in his briefcase, which I found one frustrating night. He liked to masturbate to all different types. I honestly didn't care about that, as long as he didn't throw it in my face, but I cared a lot that he wasn't having sex with me.

Miss Missouri couldn't get laid. How hilarious.

I wasn't laughing.

So I know some of what Laura is feeling when she talks about the guy she's in a serious relationship with loving X-rated porn and asking what's wrong with her labia. In my situation, we weren't having sex because he was either impotent and didn't know what to do about it or because he was masturbating enough to satisfy himself and didn't really care about me. The bottom line is that he was spending all of his sexual energy on porn to get off, leaving me in a sexless relationship.

I knew that if the guy I was living with preferred pornography to me, knowing he was faithful in every other way, it's likely I'm not the only woman experiencing this with a man. Getting him to talk about our problem on any level was impossible. This became a personal hell for me, but unlike Laura, an operation wouldn't fix it. Jeffrey fueled my curiosity to find out more about the secret sex lives of men, which was obviously a very real thing, and learn a lot more about pornography.

Years later, watching Charlotte in *Sex and the City* catch her first husband Trey MacDougal masturbating to pornographic magazines, it wasn't just a scene in an HBO sitcom to me. It could have been a scene starring Jeffrey and me, minus being married.

Jeffrey was no Don Jon, the name of the lead character in the film *Don Jon's Addiction,* Joseph Gordon-Levitt's wildly entertaining romp about porn addiction. Gordon-Levitt's character loves porn more than pussy, as it's put in the movie, because porn makes him forget everything else. One difference between Jeffrey and Don Jon is that while my guy wasn't having sex with me, Don Jon was having lots of sex with lots of girls. They were both porn junkies, but Don Jon delivered in the sack, while Jeffrey wasn't interested in trying.

The beauty of *Don Jon* is where the lead character starts and where he finishes.

When Don Jon meets Barbara Sugarman, played flawlessly by the gorgeous Scarlett Johansson, she won't have sex with him, expecting courtship done all her way. Then she finds out he's a porn "junky," and explodes. When he can't keep his promise to stay away from it, she catches him after snooping through his browser history. It's over. Screw her! Back he goes to his faithful porn, masturbating ten times a day again and loving it, complete with a contagion of Catholic confessions that soothe his guilt.

It's all good, until Don Jon starts talking to Esther, played by Julianne Moore, who caught him watching porn in their night class. She offers him an adult video, which he thinks is weird. It's a lot better than the trash he's watching on the web, she tells him. Eventually, Esther asks him if he can go one day without watching porn. Don Jon says, "I lose myself" in porn, so why should he? They've had sex by now, so she calls him out, saying that's the way he fucks her, like she's not even there. It's a two-way thing… get lost together, Esther suggests. It turns Don Jon's idea of sex upside down.

Suddenly Don Jon's insatiable lust for pornography, which is never quenched, shifts. Without porn, he suddenly finds sex with Esther more satisfying than whacking off. He starts singing when he drives, instead of screaming at people in cars. Hilariously, the priests in his Catholic confession sessions never take into account he's now monogamous, porn free, and being a very good boy.

The best sex is about orgasm, as much as it is how you get there. It's also why some porn fans get attached to the girls they watch when they masturbate. Connection is key in mind-blowing sex, so your average porn junky's problem isn't the visual extravaganza. It's an emotional issue, which cannot be explored as long as smut is keeping a guy absorbed and alone in his very own secret sex world that cuts him off from engaged intimacy.

The scenes with Laura in *Sexy Baby* and the other stories, as well as reports about cybersex, sexting and social media, prove the pornification impact in our culture has widened. At least now documentaries are being made that include the voices of young teens.

My reaction to my problem with Jeffrey was different than Laura's in *Sexy Baby*: Dump the jerk. But it sure didn't happen quickly. First, I had to go through the gauntlet of figuring out that my sex drive wasn't abnormally voracious. Guys are the ones who enjoy sex so much, I'd been told, only to find out in other relationships that I was any man's sexual equal. After a relatively normal start with Jeffrey, it was a year before I went looking for a reason why we weren't having sex, and I found out about his porn obsession. That's also when I finally figured out it wasn't about me; it was his problem, not mine.

I was obviously choosing guys that didn't deserve me. The important question was why had I chosen him in the first place? I wasn't going to change myself. The object was to change the guys I was dating. I did prove Kinsey's theory, however, that women are sexual, and sex matters to us a great deal, though how much can differ between girls. We also have healthy sexual egos that can be crushed just like a man's, which is rarely discussed.

Jeffrey never considered my sexual needs or my ego or pride. At one point, since this went on for years, I demanded we have sex-dates once a week. We'd put on Barry White and get comfy in the living room and he'd take care of me or I'd take care of myself while he... Honest to Christ, I have no idea what he did. My head was flipping through naked males, with beautifully erect penises and all I cared about was that one brief release, which kept me from becoming a pent-up, raving bitch. Because going without sex is bad for your health. Anyone who does it is certifiable. When it's not great, finding a way to at least make it better is the only alternative, because what sex does for your self-esteem, mood and general happiness is undeniable.

Even as embarrassing as it was at first, confronting my boyfriend, it was a whole lot easier solving my problem with a guy obsessed with porn magazines than Laura's problem was for her.

But getting a labiaplasty? Surgery on external female genitalia to make it prettier is one issue; if it's surgically needed because of pain during sex, that's another. Both are legit, but we're into new territory here. Check out labiaplasty on Wikipedia, the web's free, group-sourced encyclopedia. The definition comes with four pictures of different labias for you to compare, or you can watch a web video to educate yourself.

In January 2013, VH1's *Best Week Ever* highlighted a reality show *Plastic Wives*, on TLC. The show, getting coverage from TMZ to the *New York Daily News* to Fox News, starred Veronica Matlock, Dayna Devon, Alana Sands and Frances Marques, who are all married to successful Los Angeles plastic surgeons who also appear on the show. The plot develops from there. One wife sits down in front of the camera holding a tray, takes the jar that's sitting on it and pronounces, "This is my labia. You know, I think she looks better in the jar than hanging down there."

Words fail.

"We're seeing more and more requests from teens under the age eighteen even, because of a heightened sexual awareness, because of magazines, because of porn, because of the Internet," says Dr. Bernard Stern, a labiaplasty surgeon interviewed in *Sexy Baby*.

As Beyoncé sings in "Pretty Hurts," from her 2013 record-shattering iTunes release on her self-titled album, "perfection is the disease of a nation." In the video released with this song, Beyoncé is competing in a beauty pageant, but the content of the lyrics revolves around seeking the approval and applause of others, which goes well beyond the pageant scene. "Nobody frees you from your own body," is something all girls know. "It's the soul that needs surgery," sings Beyoncé.

Nikita Kash, the ex-stripper in the documentary, who also became a porn actress, not to mention a contestant on *America's Got Talent*, makes the point that the "adult entertainment world has completely infiltrated the mainstream." She blames the digital age for helping make it all possible. She's right when she talks about women mimicking strippers in nightclubs. She also says guys are now doing moves in bed from adult movies. Think about sleeping with Dirk Diggler, the fictional porn star made famous by Mark Wahlberg in *Boogie Nights*.

The mainstreaming of the adult industry was also facilitated by some of the top five hundred companies in the country, including Marriott, which streamed pornography into their hotel rooms until 2011. Why shouldn't they, if it makes money? As long as children don't have access, adults can play, and it can even help your sex life.

Sexy Baby makes an important distinction beyond the obvious, between the twelve-year-old and the ex-stripper and porn star. Nakita admits that she wishes her mother would have encouraged her dancing, because it might have made a difference. Winnifred's parents are divorced, but both her mother and father are involved with her on screen, questioning her and talking to her about what's coming at her on Facebook and in the world.

"You can either be part of the conversation, be part of their thinking, or you can let them figure it out on their own. I sort of would rather be part of the conversation... I get blown off a lot," Winnifred's mom Jeni offers.

It reveals a relationship with her daughter that I couldn't have dreamed of having with my mother. Not in a million years.

It's not the access, it's the judgment people apply to their situations, to the things that infiltrate their daily lives and assault their relationships. This is nothing new, even if the situations are wildly different and the subjects far wider to tackle than they were in Kinsey's era, when he was just introducing America to the sexualized female who has always existed.

Winnifred's dad lies to her, by his own admission, telling his girls that it doesn't matter what you look like. They'll learn the truth soon enough, that it's easier for a girl who is pretty, and maybe even combat it through having more to offer than looks that change through age. Right now their dad is pumping up their confidence. As Sarah Jessica Parker, aka Carrie Bradshaw, has proven conclusively, if you have audacity, confidence and brains, it can more than make up for not being what's considered a classic beauty.

The conversation *Sexy Baby* joins is that girls now focus as much on what they want to do as what they look like. It strengthens self-confidence and makes you less dependent on a man for approval, which will relax the whole relationship situation. It's become more about how the girl or woman sees herself, not how she's seen through a man's eyes or through anyone else's eyes. The self-possession obsession is replaced by something inside that drives her.

The overexposure of sexy images and pornography has led to the mainstreaming of soft-core visuals on broadcast and cable TV. The *Victoria's Secret Fashion Show* has become a lingerie-model extravaganza that now includes major entertainers in a production that is now a musical fashion show each Christmas.

But look at Marilyn Monroe, then look at the Victoria's Secret model. It's an example of just how much our visual standards have changed for women. Could Monroe get cast today in any major role? With her voluptuousness, you wonder if it would be possible. The skinny-girl perfection of the Victoria's Secret models is challenging for any girl watching. The abnormally small waists, super-skinny legs and skin perfection are enough to make any girl give up or run to the nearest plastic surgeon.

What else do the Victoria's Secret models have, and what are we getting besides an hour of eye candy? It doesn't really matter, unless you consider how the image of these models blankets our culture in other forms beyond the lingerie store. Then there is what it takes to be a Victoria's Secret model, which is endemic across our culture.

It's one thing to be beautiful and have the right body type and height, but has anyone thought about the "training"? In an interview with the UK *Telegraph*, the model Adriana Lima talks about her eating habits beginning nine days before the show, when "she will drink only protein shakes — 'no solids.'" Lima worked with a nutritionist and a trainer, jumping rope, boxing and working out twice a day. She did this just months after giving birth, showing up at the December 2012 Victoria's Secret show looking spectacular.

The American Decency Association, whose name alone is enough to make any woman wince, has boycotted Victoria's Secret, because it "sells lingerie in an inappropriate and immoral manner and therefore contributes to the sexual objectification of women and the desensitization of moral sensibilities." They raised a ruckus when the first show was scheduled to air, but the public decided that the viewer could always turn the channel if the sight of vamping lingerie models wearing angel's wings was too shocking.

I'm not trying to make light of the images we all see every day, with the supposedly perfect woman being pictured as thin, beautiful and without a mark on her skin or any extra fat anywhere, or saying it isn't overwhelming at times. Remember that the photos are retouched.

This is the twenty-first century, and with the onslaught coming at girls and women, we're all going to have to buck up. Objectification is real, and the only antidote is to address it straight on, not simply react to it. It also depends when it occurs. In a professional setting, combat it with what you have to offer that really matters and make it known. We can't stop it, but we can challenge it by addressing the appropriateness of any comment, depending on the situation.

Being in the pageants was a means to an end for me. I was never the prettiest girl there, but seeing the most beautiful made me look at who I was and what I had that was unique that they didn't. It also teaches you that what you're looking at on the surface doesn't tell the whole story. It reminds you that the hardest work of all is not impressing someone else; it's crafting your own narrative that takes you where you long to go. Don't get distracted.

I watch the Victoria's Secret show and I enjoy it, especially with the added productions and the musical extravaganza it has become, which is a hint to a shifting reality. After the novelty of the first year, it simply wasn't enough to see the girls strutting around in extravagant costumes, no matter their beauty. Naked or half-clothed girls are everywhere today.

Even the famous swimsuit issue of *Sports Illustrated* has become supersized. To keep people interested they need to give readers more bikinied beauties than ever before. It's the only way to keep up with the onslaught of sensory bombardment the web offers that also desensitizes.

Now think about the *Sexy Baby* profile of Nikita Kash. She traded on her looks as a major part of her career, which now becomes about booking other strippers in clubs. Strippers and adult actresses make fantasies come true in people's minds for differing types of pleasure and profit. It's a brave, new, creatively capitalistic world for all liberated ladies, no matter how you define the terms or whether society approves of what we're doing or not.

No one has begun to work what's happening to women today more uniquely, while redefining the territory, than Lena Dunham and the show she created for HBO, *Girls*. Dunham puts a whole new meaning to the words *sex and the city*, because she doesn't look, act or sound like anything close to what came before or what popular culture shows us non-stop today. What Dunham is doing is revolutionary, but the pilot episode included a nod to *Sex and the City*, with Shoshanna, played by Zosia Mamet, breaking down her own personality in terms of the *Sex and the City* girls who came before. The image Dunham's presenting is groundbreaking, her material worthy of acknowledging as the earthquake it is in modern American culture. Dunham's healthy body image blasts a message, whether intended or not, just like the lives of the "girls" on the show. Live out loud any way you choose, and make it up as you go along.

It didn't take long at all before the twenty-six-year old Dunham pissed everyone off for being so brilliant at such a young age. Funny how our culture never freaks when a man does it young. I can relate to *Girls*, because at the very same age, I was living in New York City making my way on Broadway after college, experiencing it all as it came my way.

The first observations and reviews about the show didn't focus on the fact that it obliterated every Marilyn-Monroe-to-Victoria's-Secret-to-*Sexy-Baby* image of women with a realistic view of ordinary females not in the *Sex and the City* glamour loop. The critics instead commented that the whole thing was just too "bleached." Where were the people of color? After all, it was taking place in New York City.

So, in season two, Dunham began by bedding a hot African-American guy. Asked and answered.

Co-executive producer Judd Apatow explained after the backlash landed. "We wanted it," the Huffington Post's Crystal Bell quoted him saying enthusiastically. "That's the point of it, really. It's supposed to be a comedy about women in New York who are really smart, but their lives are a mess. They know they should be doing great things, but they don't know what it is, and they have kind of a feeling of self-entitlement about it. That's the joke of the show."

Girls is about a slice of the female population. But it's a section that is anything but put together, perfectly coiffed and worried about designer anything. The characters are fairly certain they should be on their way to doing something great. They just haven't a clue what it is.

After *The Devil Wears Prada* and Anne Hathaway's perceived perfection, Lena Dunham's *Girls* competes with no glamour icon or vision of visual perfection. It's more in the style of Jennifer Lawrence, though with a twist. It informs why Anne Hathaway is irrationally disliked and mocked in the social media universe. The disdain for any hint of trying to measure up, which begins with maintaining an aura of behavior that screams, "I'm doing what's expected."

For her classic moment in the 2013 Oscar spotlight, Jennifer Lawrence felt no similar compunction. She literally tripped and stumbled on her way to accept the Best Actress award. Her reaction to this public screw-up was not only charming, but refreshing in a way that made all girls exhale. You can trip and fall in couture at the Oscars, no less, and it doesn't mean a thing. That's revelatory. After it happened, the website Jezebel.com published, "11 Reasons Why Jennifer Lawrence is Your BFF in Your Head." They nailed it with Number 11: "Basically she's perfect. Mostly because she's not."

Lawrence also didn't try to act cool when she lost it over meeting Jack Nicholson. She's simply unafraid of being who she is, which at that moment meant reacting like an average fan when meeting one of the great cinematic icons of Hollywood royalty.

After her own Oscar acceptance speech, Anne Hathaway unleashed deafening Twitterverse noise from the "Hathahaters," complete with #hathahaters hashtag. "It came true," Hathaway said in her speech, referring to her lifelong dream of Hollywood success, but the emotional intent was way too cool for the words. In today's social media atmosphere, people react when canned word-salads sound perfunctory or insincere. We want to hear Hathaway speak from her heart when her dream comes true without worrying about being sloppy or sentimental at a moment that requires just that.

One reason we not only crave the unscripted but also expect it is because reality shows, social media and our 24/7, new-media, *American Idol* existence has made everyone a star — at least in their own minds. Women put intensely personal observations on Facebook for anyone to see. Men tweet and email comments they'd rarely claim one-on-one. A person's fifteen minutes of fame may be one YouTube, tweet, Instagram away. So, when someone says something that doesn't include the human, real-time reaction that matches the words, we reach for a virtual rotten tomato.

Lawrence caught the social media zeitgeist perfectly. Hathaway blundered into it with an old stereotype of what women should say and do, the irrelevance of her efforts seemingly punctuated by Lena Dunham's *Girls*. Ironically, regardless of their differences, Lawrence and Hathaway both still share the *Girls* universe, which is made up of women struggling to live amid a world commenting and critiquing our lives. These two very public women both do so with quite a lot of grace, while the entire global audience discusses them.

It's a cataclysmic collision that remains a rolling crash. There's never been anything like it for girls, regardless of age. Anyone stopping to ponder what strength of character this demands of these particular public women would be as duly impressed as I am.

I relate to both Anne Hathaway and Jennifer Lawrence, thanks to an incident that, while it's not remotely the same magnitude as the Oscars, for me personally, it was. I had my own horrifying, public, near-catastrophe when I was competing in the swimsuit portion of the Miss Missouri Pageant and found a large, deep brown splotch of foundation makeup on the butt of my canary yellow one-piece. I had just been announced as one of the top ten finalists, so I had mere moments to get dressed before I had to flounce back on stage. Girls gathered as someone grabbed the suit to wash out the makeup, which otherwise would have looked like I'd sat in poop backstage. When it was handed back to me, rung out but still very wet, the names of the top ten contestants being introduced in the background, I pulled it on and had seconds before "Miss Gateway" was called (I had won the local St. Louis pageant to qualify for Miss Missouri). I went strutting out on what seemed like an endless ramp.

Now, it's bad enough to be judged in a one-piece swimsuit with heels to match. With the crotch wet from back to front, I was praying to the pageant gods that there wouldn't be excess water leaving a dripping trail as I walked away from the audience and back up the runway! All I could do was grin ear-to-ear and look straight at the judges, then the audience, acting as if nothing in the world was wrong. To see, then hear the girls cheer when I got backstage was the biggest charge I could have gotten. They would top it later that night by TP'ing my room after I was crowned Miss Missouri, something that makes me smile thinking about to this day.

In the second episode of *Girls*, Lena Dunham's character, Hannah Horwath, shares a modern-day trauma for most sexually active females at one time or another in our lives. Why, she's going to get an STD test. That's preceded by an afternoon of Googling what the possibilities are of a condom not protecting her during sex, not to mention discussing the horror of the scary stuff found around the condom's rim, all the while inspecting her vagina. "…And then when they pull out, it's fucking mayhem. I've been diagramming it in my head all afternoon. And no one speaks about this," Hannah shrieks.

The Catholic League will need something strong for this HBO show, and it's only a matter of time before Bill O'Reilly's head explodes.

But this is the ultimate gift for women who watch.

It's identity combat.

In the doctor's office for her exam, later in the same episode, Hannah just starts babbling. Hannah's response to the pelvic exam begins where we all did way back when: "Ow."

"Is that painful?" asks the doctor.

"Yeah, but only in the way it's supposed to be," Hannah responds.

It's the twenty-first century version of, "Only a man could have come up with the idea of stirrups and that cold steel vagina scoop"— the ultimate *Girls* joke.

If the HBO show does one thing, I only hope it can energize the usage of the word *girls* for us all, no matter our age. Because it has become clear to me the older I get that deep inside me that thing that keeps me going no matter what comes is my very *girl*-ness. The energy at my core that doesn't change, no matter the life assaults and the injurious physical indignities that begin once you're out of your twenties, which isn't my womanness, but the unflagging force of my inner, raging GIRL.

Lena Dunham's writing for her character is one thing, but her presence as a brilliant, average girl with anything but a Victoria's Secret-model image is especially stirring. And there's certainly no discussion on whether Hannah or any of her girlfriends have the perfect labia or not. The notion that Hannah would consider a labiaplasty seems outlandish, but the conversation about it would be one for the books. If Hannah did it, can anyone doubt that the reason would be to write about it? The post-operation labiaplasty ouch factor would be gut-splitting comedy, and one can only imagine what the back-and-forth about "meat curtain" would sound like.

You cannot deny the statistics that show a lot of women are turning to "designer vaginas." The pornification of modern culture is one reason, but it would happen even if women were supremely confident about themselves, because the accessibility and medical affordability of cosmetic surgery from face to foot makes it possible.

From the UK *Guardian* in February 2011: A study published in the *British Journal of Obstetrics and Gynaecology* in 2009 revealed that there had been an almost 70% increase in the number of women having labiaplasty through Britain's National Health Service over the previous year. The *Guardian* reports there were 404 such operations in 2006, rising to 669 in 2007, and jumping to 1,118 in 2008.

Then there is RealSelf.com, billed as "the world's largest consumer review and information site for plastic surgery," which found that in 2012 the hottest trend in plastic surgery was a laser-based treatment for cellulose. The website reported 1.25 million searches on the site in 2012. It was followed, believe it or not, by "butt augmentation," with the most popular such method being the "Brazilian Butt Lift," which takes fat from "unwanted areas of the body and injects it into the buttocks." Talk and blog gossip have surrounded hip hop artist Lil' Kim and rapper/singer Nikki Minaj, who are said to have these Brazilian Butt Lifts. If you're also flashing on Samantha, played by Kim Cattrall, in *Sex and the City*, you've got it.

Labiaplasty by the way, came in third, but was up 22% in 2012.

Body image follows us all. To be able to change the body parts that have become your nemeses through procedures that won't break you, and sometimes won't even break your bones, means we're now into a whole new world for girls, especially since we're all living longer.

When you're over forty, it's harder for women to find positive face and body images in the media, not to mention sexual role models. That's finally beginning to change. The 85th Academy Awards, televised in February 2013, featured sumptuous women in their seventies, including Shirley Bassey, seventy-six, Jane Fonda, seventy-five, and Barbra Streisand, seventy, all looking radiant and ready for their close-ups at an age when men are seen as "distinguished," but women have rarely been seen at all, especially not in Hollywood.

Meryl Streep stepped up in the movie *Hope Springs*, demanding that her husband, played by Tommy Lee Jones, offer a full marriage — aka they need to start making love and touching one another — or she was going to end it. No sex sucks, Meryl's character declares, and she's not going to take it anymore. It's an unheard of demand from women in the movies, especially a character willing to walk if her man won't satisfy her. That Streep plays a sixty-three-year-old in a marriage demanding more or else is something we haven't seen before.

Why would you let that happen? How do you let that happen? Those are my first questions. Well, it creeps up on you, I've been told. Then women start telling themselves it doesn't matter, marriage is a friendship, too. That is true, but what makes marriage different from friendship is it also comes with the benefits of sex, as Steve Harvey labels it in his book *Act Like a Lady, Think Like a Man*. Well, Streep sets out to fix what's broken and does, with the help of Steve Carell, who plays a marriage counselor.

Long before we get to be sixty-three, women hit a huge age-and-sex speed bump. It's one of the least talked about issues, but it's not by accident that a man's midlife crisis often comes at the same time as a woman's hormones are turning her sexuality upside down. Women can lose their libido, as well as their orgasm, the cruelest blow by nature of all. When men are feeling age hit and want a reminder of their once-youthful virility, women are often feeling their most dowdy and asexual. Today we can do something about it, or at least read Suzanne Somers and go from there.

A popular video made by safersex4seniors.org has attracted more than 1.2 million hits as of 2013 and shows clothed seniors doing Kama Sutra poses. I'm still waiting for eighty-six-year-old Hugh Hefner and his twenty-sex-year-old wife Crystal Harris to do their own video. On another subject, can anyone imagine the ages being reversed and equally celebrated? You'd have to go back to the 1971 film *Harold and Maude*, which became a cult classic partly because the age role-reversal of its two title characters was so groundbreaking.

One of the most iconic film actors of the twentieth century, Jane Fonda, who is getting deserved praise for her role in HBO's *Newsroom*, not only looks great at seventy-five, but she says she's having the best sex of her life. She told Britain's *The Sun* that she was experiencing "true intimacy" and was more confident about her desires than ever before.

"The only thing I have never known is true intimacy with a man. I absolutely wanted to discover that before dying. It has happened with Richard," she told *The Sun*, of her relationship with music producer Richard Perry. "I feel totally secure with him. Often, when we make love, I see him as he was thirty years ago."

The story came tumbling out when Fonda was doing promotional work for her movie *Peace, Love and Misunderstanding* in July 2012. Having been married to Tom Hayden, French director Roger Vadim, as well as CNN founder Ted Turner, Fonda's candor about sex at the age of seventy-four was phenomenal. I can't name another woman so forthcoming about being libidinously satisfied at that age. She's the girls' answer to Hugh Hefner, and looks a hell of a lot better, too.

Fonda went even further in Britain's *Hello!* magazine, saying she was "always a courageous woman, capable of confronting governments but not men." In the interview, which made news in the U.S. and all over the web, Fonda called herself "a chameleon, the woman men wanted me to be."

What's even more interesting is where she places the blame — on her father, Henry Fonda. "I don't want to make a cheap analysis," she was quoted saying, "but when you have, like I did, a father incapable of showing emotion, who spends his life telling you that no one will love you if you aren't perfect, it leaves scars."

The pornification of our culture; our own insecurities; daddy issues; how society feels about women getting older, looking sexy and enjoying being sexual at any age — all of these things have to do with who we choose to listen to and what tape we allow to play in our head.

We control it all.

Talk Dirty to Me

It was September 11, 2001.

I had the early shift that day and had gotten up around 5:30 A.M. and turned on NBC's *Today Show*. I was living in the flats of Beverly Hills, around Doheny Drive and Burton Way.

Matt Lauer had just broken away from an interview, ready to go live, when everything sort of stopped. "We have a breaking story, though..." Once into the 9:00 A.M. hour, 6:00 A.M. in Los Angeles, Katie Couric joined Lauer saying, "Apparently, a plane has just crashed into the World Trade Center here in New York City. It happened just a few moments ago..."

Then, along with everyone else watching NBC's *Today Show*, and no doubt other stations as well, I watched the second plane hit the other World Trade Center Tower.

Couric had eyewitness Jennifer Oberstein on the phone, as the history continued to play out before our eyes, all of this still preserved online for posterity through YouTube.

What I was watching unfold seemed utterly unreal. But I watched it throughout the day, sound on mute once my phone-actress shift started, my head pounding with one of the worst migraines I'd had in recent memory, my mind reeling.

To say I was lousy at phone sex is an understatement, though the second time around I wasn't as freaked as I was the first, which barely lasted a weekend. I'd been doing phone sex this time for about two months or so. The stint as Relationship Consultant had solidified my expertise. The massive interaction I had with men and their views on sex during my thirteen months at the soft-core site had given me knowledge about them few others had.

After watching the events of 9/11 play out that day, I cared absolutely nothing about the book I was intending to write that would compile my sexual education and relationship secrets together. Everything immediately became secondary to what I'd seen on the screen and the revelation of what it meant to our world, which had just come crashing down, quite literally.

I'd been a student of politics because of when I grew up, including living through Vietnam, so I knew all hell was about to break loose. Not many had been around as I had at the start of new media, and 9/11 was a moment I had to cover; the international politics involved in telling the story was something I couldn't miss. I'd have to put writing about relationships, women, men and sex aside, trusting that another time would come. Bailing on phone sex within days of 9/11, I moved to covering politics as I had been doing since I started writing. This time what I'd be writing about was different, the stakes higher, because our country had just been attacked.

But on 9/11, I still had my shift, though it would be a short one, just a few hours, with very few calls.

Some things you don't forget. That day I had three calls, all from men who said they were air traffic controllers. You must take all identification when interacting with strangers, whether it's the extreme example of phone sex, or even something more benign as social media, with a grain of salt. However, I have little doubt that the men, on this day, were who they said they were and did what they say they did. No one talked about sex. None of the men wanted to do anything but just talk about what had happened that morning. How freaked out they were. Only one man stayed on for very long with me. I had no way of knowing what the other girls were experiencing, because I wasn't on the more popular lines that day. Besides, it was very early Tuesday morning, not exactly a banner shift in the best of times.

Looking back on the research and anecdotes I have compiled over the years, whether it was the adult soft-core business, the phone sex industry or my job as a Relationship Consultant, the impetus was about understanding the human animal, our emotional and sexual urges. It's our imperfect selves who long for connection and emotional and physical confirmation of our importance, affirmation that we matter, especially to someone else, if possible.

How did Miss Missouri end up excavating sex on a phone sex line? It's never one thing that starts you on a quest to quench curiosity and answer questions rolling 'round in your mind. That I landed on earth amid the sexual, political and feminist revolutions played a big part in it all. In the mix was making sense of my own life, too, which is the one job we all share in common.

When my long-term relationship ended with porn-obsessed Jeffrey, I was liberated from the excruciating humiliation but left with all sorts of questions. The first was how such a sweetheart and hunk of a man, who was very successful, could make such choices. It wasn't like I was unattractive, inattentive or sexually stiff. At least I knew it wasn't my problem that Jeffrey wasn't interested in satisfying a libidinous feminist who enjoyed sex and wanted to take turns leading the way sometimes.

However, since Jeffrey's porn fetish was all-consuming, not only was I sure I couldn't be the only woman experiencing this, but it set a fire in my erotic brain center to find out why men choose porn even when they have a hot and ready woman in their bed. Very few men reject sex for pornography, especially when it's a daily option. That's just stupid. They enjoy it in addition to what they're getting, which if they're smart is from a woman they adore.

Porn is about variety, the strange and the unknown. It satisfies the frequency some men need, which porn makes easy, especially when their partner isn't available or the guy just wants to get off fast. For a minority of men it's an addiction, as I saw first-hand.

Thankfully, my relationship with Jeffrey, who was a listless screw when he did get it up — with apologies to Erica Jong, because I was incapable of the "zipless fuck" — came amid other interesting men.

One of the most sexually satisfying and deliciously life-affirming triangles a girl could conjure up in her imagination, let alone actually experience, proved to me that not only can a woman have sex without committing to the men she was bedding, but every girl should try it at least once. It also proved to me that you can be crazy about two men at the same time.

I highly endorse being loved and devoured by two virile men at the same moment in time, if not in the same location and bed. You may be curious about threesomes, but they're not my thing. But dating and having sex with two different men you care deeply for can be deliciously satisfying, not to mention great for your ego.

Of course, I was lucky, because the two men I simultaneously bedded were both nuts about me. Nothing was more thrilling, confidence-building and out of character for me than being chased and caught by one man, then the other, then back again and again. It was a roller coaster ride that was one long, sustained, ever-crescendoing and crashing, multiple orgasm. They didn't have any complaints either, at least not sexually.

I distinctly remember giggling while driving from David to Mike's place, after having been sufficiently satisfied before the journey, with the added joy being that both men knew what I was doing. I hadn't lied. That wasn't in me. I wasn't sneaking around, which takes too much energy and, for the life I was living, didn't fit. I simply told them both that I loved them both and couldn't choose, wouldn't choose, didn't want to choose, at least not yet. They would have preferred a decision, but the sexual gladiator inside them, in most men, took on the challenge.

An ode to Venus is required here, because it's tremendously freeing to have such a sexual education delivered through the able mind, hands, tongues, penises and hearts of men who aren't afraid of a woman's uninhibited libido. Trojan condoms made a tidy profit on the three of us. It's the first time I experienced being completely satisfied and quenched, not only physically, but emotionally, too. Ah, but all good things wear out, especially when two men are vying for the same heart.

While it lasted, it turned both men into performance kings, even if hearts were being shattered at the cruelty of sharing someone you wanted all to yourself. I'd warned David off ages before Mike showed up, so it wasn't my fault his ego thought he could win me over. I'd been in a constant state of crazy about men for a long time, but they were never going to be my life's work, so "male suitors beware" was my mantra. I shared it with every single man I dated in one way or another. It was like waving a red flag at a prized bull.

Truman Capote's words from *Breakfast at Tiffany's* also come to mind. Holly's warning is a lesson from her own life. "Never love a wild thing. ... You can't give your heart to a wild thing: The more you do, the stronger they get." I wasn't close to Capote's Holly, but I definitely recognized the dangers of falling in love with "a wild thing." I craved the attention and adoration of these two men and others who came before, especially sexually, all the while knowing I was only passing through, even if the guys were clueless. I was a wild thing, in many ways still am.

It's difficult to explain, but the thing that attracts women to bad boys inhabits the same space. That scoundrel who is starving for love and drinks it up, but isn't able to return it, only makes the woman loving him even more determined. He keeps drinking until he finally is satiated by the thing all humans require, connection and validation, until he's ready to start a new adventure. When he hits bottom again, he'll find solace again. Oddly enough, I didn't have a smidgeon of guilt about bedding Mike and David at the same time, which actually surprised me. It was so unlike me, what I'd been told. I found myself happier than I'd ever been, and I'd never known such expansive liberation.

Don't get me wrong. I never took strangers to bed, because one-night stands weren't for me, though I know many women who delight in them. Well, maybe a couple of times, but I was a serial monogamist, minus a few casual flings. They were all in a stream of mostly fabulous bachelors to me, even when they acted like jerks, because I wasn't looking for a husband. I liked the connection when I was having sex with the same man regularly, knowing him with his guard down. I just wanted to be able to end it and dash, once it got too comfy and we started the expectations game and making plans I couldn't fulfill.

I'd warned every man I'd dated, including Brian, the one I briefly married after college, who knew me my whole life and should have known better, that I wasn't the marrying kind. On the other hand, I had no problem using the marriage card when it benefited me, either dishonestly playing it when it suited the moment and my mood, or using it to scare a guy off and change the dynamic. I'd even ask for marriage at the most inopportune moments, but only because I knew the request would be denied. I never asked a question of a man I didn't already know the answer to.

It's positively predictable how your average bachelor reacts when the woman he's smitten with proclaims she's not interested in marriage. But invariably, at some point he starts expecting things, because he's got time invested. People never took me seriously in the first place, because how could any woman, especially an artist whose finances are unpredictable, say no to a constant breadwinner? Why any man couldn't see me coming is beyond me, because I was a man's mirror image in many ways, especially when it came to guarding my freedom.

The thing about romantic love is that it's a yearning to connect and has absolutely nothing to do with whether a union is smart, will make you happy, or has any hopes of lasting through your first combustible orgasm, if he can even get you off or cares to. It's often romantic yearning that's misinterpreted as love, which leads to all sorts of drama and real life madness, sometimes on the wings of unrequited infatuation that hits men hard.

My passionate triangle ended with me choosing Mike, who happened to be one of the hottest chefs in Beverly Hills at the time, a man whose sexual ego was centered around himself and his glorious anatomy. Any promises he would make about giving me the world were consummated in bed, then quickly forgotten. As long as the sex was frequent, I could enjoy it, squeezing out an orgasm myself, because I was on my own due to his cluelessness about women. He was worthless to anyone but himself, something I never once saw when David was in the picture, too. It made me immediately second-guess the guy I'd picked, because David was everything a girl could want, loyal, loving and generous. Unfortunately, a true partnership with him wasn't possible, because he never really got who I was. That didn't stop him from being there for me at one of the worst times of my life, long after we broke up, something I'll never forget or be able to repay.

Once Mike had me all to himself, he became as emotionally insecure and volatile as I was restless and artistically flailing. The immense manhood he brought to bed with him was his gift to me, or so he thought. He also delighted in exhibiting his penis to whomever he could whenever the moment presented itself, which I'd heard from several people who'd witnessed his exhibitionism. His penis was who he was, and he let it hang in all its meaty glory in at least one locker room. Eventually, even that failed him in our relationship.

One evening Mike came home late from work, then wound down with a cocktail. I walked into the bedroom wearing a black bustier, garter, hose, push-up bra and high heels, telling him to take his clothes off and lie down. He did as he was told, smiling.

So good, so far.

I walked over to the bed, sat and swiveled over to where he was, then straddled him fully, a vision of black silk before him. The foreplay began. It was going well. We were both into it and having a blast. One thing led to another, then he flipped me over, panties flew off, and in he came, but it was all happening way too fast. It was over for him before I could even begin to make sure I was taken care of, too, and when I suggested I was close but hadn't been satisfied, he flew into a rage and stormed out of the room screaming at the top of his lungs.

You see, he thought being inside me was enough. That his large penis would slay my appetite, never knowing or even considering what an orgasm was for me, which I knew must mean he didn't have a clue or didn't care where my clitoris was or how a woman was quenched in the first place. It wasn't the first time I'd experienced this with him, which is why I planned the maximum effort in black silk in the first place.

Why are some of the most well endowed cocksmen so incapable of finding a woman's G-spot, let alone caring that it's the doorway to our euphoria? That's easy. There are still some men out there uninterested or just plain clueless about how to get a woman off. Some men just don't understand how much sex matters to us.

Feminists they are not, because the good men I've enjoyed make sure their women are pleasured first and don't demand missionary every night. Any man who doesn't understand that a woman on top can experience double the pleasure is having sex with too many compliant women.

One fling I will never forget came out of the blue when I was single and ran into an old flame from way back. Jake and I had always had a thing for each other, but never acted on it. It was time. We'd have lustful sex together whenever he'd blow through Los Angeles, and our friendship just kept getting deeper. Phone calls would follow, but we both wanted nothing more from each other. One particular encounter we had happened during what would be the hottest and sexiest car ride either of us had ever experienced. I was driving south on the 405 freeway in broad daylight, our hands playing physical flute with one another's bodies, while I tried to keep my eyes open, controlling myself as best as I could. It was the most delicious sexual encounter I ever had fully clothed. Strike that, because it rocketed above some of the times I'd been naked with a man. Jake and I went our separate ways and later even reminisced once about how hot we'd been together, even if we weren't a relationship match. Pure lust is underrated.

Approximately one-third of the U.S. population — 102 million people eighteen years and older — are unmarried, according to the U.S. Census numbers released in September 2012, which included me for most of my adult life. Of those, 53% are women, which translates to eighty-nine unmarried men for every hundred unmarried women. Seventeen million seniors over age sixty-five make up 16% of unmarried people. People living alone comprise 28% of unmarried individuals, up from 17% in 1970.

Single-person households continue to grow, with cohabitation and other living arrangements supplanting traditional choices, though family, however it's defined, will always be valued. According to Pew Social Trends from November 2012, "In 2011, there were an estimated 36.4 newlyweds per thousand unmarried or newly married adults ages eighteen and older. This compares with an estimated new-marriage rate of 37.4 in 2010 and 41.4 in 2008." According to a 2010 Pew Research Center poll done in conjunction with *Time* magazine, "in 1960, more than two-thirds (68%) of all twenty-somethings were married. In 2008, just 26% were."

This is a good thing, because the surer you are about yourself and your own life, the better chance you have of finding your equal, then making it last.

It used to be that friendship was the number one component in a relationship, with companionship intensely important, too. This was the refrain throughout the twentieth century and before, when husbands had affairs easily and were excused for them often, while women remained faithful, because society didn't give them an option except being ostracized.

I've never disagreed about the importance of friendship or companionship, though I've rejected that they're more important than sexual intimacy. I've always known, because of my own life and the many people with whom I've spoken, that sex is equally important, more than is usually mentioned in the modern partnership, with intimacy being the essential element. It's the oasis that allows two people to navigate life's stressful landscape. Nakedness is the path where intimacy builds. Both people in a relationship have to be willing to change and adapt, even experiment, as time goes by and routine sets in. But friendship alone isn't enough to hold a partnership together today. We're now outliving our relationships, which often happens at or near mid-life, when mortality comes into view and we need to feel younger. A hot sex life can revive a friendship between two people, but a lazy friendship that ignores or loses its lustfulness is hard to rekindle.

It's also much easier for the guy to get in and get off than it is to patiently excite his partner until she's either close before he makes love to her, or completely satisfied when they're both finished. It's another reason why porn is popular, but also why sex in marriage languishes. He finds pleasing her to be work, and she knows it; or he wants it quick, and she can't be satisfied that way so she fakes it. It's not friendship that's missing, it's intimacy — the conversation about how to do each other well. It's making the delicious event of physical pleasure enjoyed, which can't happen in a marriage that's weighted down in sexual separateness. Couples need to frolic, which begins with intimacy, getting naked with each other in every respect, the game shifting as life does, too.

In marriage, compartmentalization can become critical to longevity; you just cordon off what's not working and get down to it. But after sex, emotional fissures can often disappear. The physical communion of satisfying sex can vanquish a lot of demon scenarios playing in your head. Sex is incredibly important, because an orgasm is like a release-valve in your system. The rush of endorphins and contagion of physical reactions make you feel like a new person. Satisfaction doesn't have to be a one-moment event either, with many women multi-orgasmic, even if they don't know it yet.

Teaching a man what makes your body sing is part of it. Does it ever occur to you to guide your guy to wait until you've had an orgasm before he's pleased himself? Real sexual technique takes communication, even discipline, which is always a fun thing to bring into a relationship and also tells you where you stand with him and how he's going to react over time. Tapping the multiple orgasm is a delicious journey for couples. You don't have to experience it every time, but it's lovely to work towards and, oh, what a mood booster for both of you! Toys can really help. Learning to be multi-orgasmic can start in private, if it's not easy for a woman.

The men I dated all looked good on paper. Magazines said it. Television preached it, and so did movies. The church lecture was non-stop and always began with the money he made. Pick a man gainfully employed, good-looking if you can, and healthy, someone who'd make a good father. On and on it went. The case being made had nothing to do with a man understanding what it was like to be with a feminist, let alone an artist looking to change her corner of the world. Not to worry, I'm the one who would adapt.

What most of these relationships had in common was that when I got comfortable with our dynamic and started getting sexually assertive, the men retreated. I won't say their manhood retracted like the head of a tortoise, but most were slow in identifying the woman I was and exactly whom they'd worked so hard to get into their bed.

Isn't that just like some men? They rise to the challenge of the chase, but once they've dragged their hot feminist back to their man-cave, it's over. It's done. They just can't live up to what it takes to make her happy, which goes way beyond money, because she's making her own. The strong, sexy, confident girl all of a sudden becomes too much trouble.

But even when relationships don't work, we're sometimes drawn back in or kept entangled. So what draws women back again and again? Is it the challenge of fixing the unworkable, or something else? Is it the money and lifestyle we can have when we couple and cohabitate? The men I'd been dating afforded me a different lifestyle by living with them. Two incomes, one house can do that. My finances were under control, if paltry by comparison, but I'd never been searching for a man to pay my bills.

It was Mike who drove himself to distraction and into a rage more than once, because he couldn't satisfy me, though he didn't even really try. His uncontrollable temper brought mutual friends to our door one night. He'd gotten so unhinged that I'd become frightened, not a first in my life. But that didn't stop me from returning again and again, much to everyone's horror and disbelief. Was I insane?

Why I chose to seek out and run to a modern form of the traditional relationship, with Jeffrey rescuing me from Mike, seemed as inevitable as it was obvious. It was Brian redux, without the marriage, though that was clearly what Jeffrey wanted and assumed I did, too. It's also why getting him to agree to live with me was such an ordeal.

It was also romantic love to the rescue, at least at the beginning, before I found Jeffrey's porn. I was living in that movie script about a girl who'd been wronged and saved by a man on a white horse. It was also why I married Brian and became a quickie divorce statistic along with so many others in the 1970s. Escaping a tough life for a place that was never in my plans and wouldn't make me happy if it had been. You can't run away from yourself. Well, people do it all the time, but it never works out well or makes them happy.

The combustibility of Mike led me to the calm certainty of Jeffrey, who was ready to show me a good time, with no worries about anything. That is, up until our nights of clubbing and great times would end in sleep and no sex, which was always teased but never seemed to materialize. So, instead of Mike, who was all about himself and his cluelessness about where my clitoris was, now I had a hunky, hot man who was great with foreplay, but refused to have sex with me. It was a monogamous relationship filled with frustration.

This went on and on for three years, with his pornography finally the last straw that set me free, though even after I learned of it, I endured for well over a year. I finally had a hot one-night affair, dragging myself home in the wee hours, lying to him that anything had happened, because at that point it hardly mattered. It was over.

Maybe it was all of these events combined, or maybe it was losing to the porn paper dolls that finally did it. I was dying to ask every question, which led me to my first phone sex actress gig on the cusp of the 1990s, not long after Jeffrey and I broke up. It lasted a single weekend.

The first night I was a complete wreck. I felt so dirty about it, imagining in my mind that these strangers would be in the room with me. I was still the beauty queen from Missouri who didn't do things like this. I was acting as if I was going to actually have to touch the strangers I'd be talking to on the phone. Every light in my apartment was on. I had even rented cheerful videos to keep running while I talked on the phone, muting the sound so that I could just look at happy, bouncing Disney pictures on the screen as I sunk into the seamy world of phone sex.

Because I'm trained vocally and have a sultry speaking voice, the phone sex outfit had assigned me to start on the most popular late-night shift. I'd answered an ad and been interviewed out of some girl's home, getting all the paperwork and instructions, as well as getting the once-over from her.

Looking back through the high-tech lens of today, it's laughable all the notes I had on how to get into the intricate phone system, learning to log on and get into the right group for my shift. I have no idea how it all works today.

I'd be on the phone with Pepper, Lace and Mona, which I remember, because I recounted the event briefly in the self-published story I wrote. It chronicles my initial three-day phone sex venture, as well as my year in soft-core smut, when I was contemplating compiling all of my experiences about writing and working in the sex and relationship industries into a book, which was all blown away on 9/11.

The average call for me lasted fifteen minutes, which was short compared to the others. The call back then cost $3.95/minute. Frankly, I was awful at this, and longer calls were just torture for me. At first I tried to give guys elaborate fantasies, when all they wanted to do was get off. During this foray, I never got the nerve to actually finesse the conversation to ask them questions about sex, which is why I'd done this in the first place. It didn't take me long to know that this wasn't going to happen. That changed the whole experience, because I wasn't doing it for the money. I needed answers to questions about Jeffrey that only men could provide, and I couldn't think of a better platform to work it on, because the web didn't exist, and it wasn't like talking to my guy friends was going to get to the brutal truth. I was handling my own stuff, but I desperately needed to know why Jeffrey was choosing to play with his pretty paper dolls over me.

One guy actually did call up just to talk. He was having trouble with his relationship and didn't know what to do. Now, you never know about these things, either back when phone sex was really big, or today in the social media era. What people are telling you may or may not be the truth, unless there is an in-person component and you know the person. Sometimes you can tell when someone is being straight; it's in their voice and the specifics or in the subject they've brought up.

This guy didn't know what to do because his fiancée kept harping on his small penis. He was devastated to learn what she thought and confused about what he should do about it. What does a man do when the woman he wants to marry says his penis doesn't satisfy her? There are a lot of ways a woman can be satisfied, with many women not able to orgasm through penetration alone. Besides, women will take passion over size any day. He still felt he had a decision to make on whether to marry her or not, which I sure as hell couldn't answer for him.

Size isn't how women pick their mate, but studies have proven the guy had reason to be concerned, especially since the girl he was in love with was vocal about her dissatisfaction. A large penis does affect attractiveness for women. Alert the media!

In April 2013, the National Academy of Sciences released their findings, which NBC News reported: The human male possesses the Italian designer faucet of penises. They're pretty big, the biggest of any primate's, relative to body size. And they're showy, too, right out there, front and center on our upright bodies (i.e., they don't retract), as if they were meant to be seen as part of the décor. Why? A study released recently in the journal *Proceedings of the National Academy of Sciences* offers an explanation: Women are attracted to penises, and the bigger the better. "Penis size does affect attractiveness," lead author Brian Mautz, a University of Ottawa post-doctoral researcher said in an NBCNews.com interview.

Also discussed in the NBC News article is what Emory University neuroscientist Larry Young, co-author with Mautz of the book *The Chemistry Between Us: Love, Sex and the Science of Attraction*, discovered: "Young argues that the big human penis evolved into a tool meant to stimulate both the vagina and cervix as a way [to] trigger the release of oxytocin in a woman's brain, activating bonding circuits. Such bonds provide a survival advantage to offspring."

Once I dated a man who happened to be a lawyer for the most powerful celebrities in Hollywood. Phillip had a very small penis. I'm talking little-finger tiny. The guy was charming as could be, and it never stopped him. He had women coming and going from his apartment while we were supposed to be "in love," before I found out that he just wasn't that into me.

It's amazing how many times he telegraphed that message to me, but I had never heard it before that, and I just wasn't listening. His words didn't make a dent until, reduced to spying on him, sitting in my car one night outside his apartment after he had said he didn't feel like getting together and added, "You deserve a lot better than me." I saw him with a blonde through his window. Boy, was his kiss-off an understatement! He had warned me in innumerable ways, but my ego wouldn't hear it.

Phone sex remains the oddest of the realms I traversed. There's something very traditional and comforting, safe, about phone sex. Anonymous connection allows for expressing yourself in a way you likely wouldn't if the person you're talking to were in front of you. When two people know each other it can open up a safe passageway for exploration. If you have a long-distance relationship, or if you travel for work, phone sex is a perfect way to keep connected. It can be delicious. It can even jump start a relationship that's stalled, as long as the attraction is still alive. It can give you an avenue to divulge secret fantasies.

When I tried phone sex the second time during the weeks before 9/11, I was scheduled for the barely legal lines, which meant I was supposed to act like I was eighteen. The results were humiliating. I'd get more click-offs per minute than was allowed to keep me working on a shift. I heard, "Okay, you're done for tonight, see you tomorrow" a lot. Click-offs, as I called them, were guys dropping in to different chat lines to see who was on and if she was worth spending their money on. Some men came on looking for a specific phone sex actress to see if she was working the current shift. When I tried to get my voice to sound younger, I just sucked at it, so I was only put on that exchange if the lines were jammed on a very busy night. Barely legal lines were huge moneymakers, which I doubt I have to explain.

More than one man would come on the lines to explain a sexual scenario that included a fantasy with a fourteen-year-old or some age near or even under puberty. I couldn't do it, so I simply didn't indulge him, making sure he clicked off and went to another line, because the natural intonation of my voice revealed a woman who was anything but barely legal. "Barely legal" meant just that, and some callers wished we didn't even meet that standard. One guy talked about a scenario where he was in the living room of his house watching a young teenage girl play outside his window, with his fantasy never resulting in anything but his lust being quenched by his own actions.

I'm in no way naive to the ways teenage girls manipulate men of their own free will, ignoring their underage status to flirt, tease and titillate, while completely underestimating the possible ramifications of their actions if they meet an immoral man with no impulse control. Rarely do we make allowances for the willful indulgence teen girls allow men who are older, even if they don't know what they're unleashing.

Back when I delved into phone sex, we had monitors who would pop onto the lines and listen in to make sure we were doing our job. But when you're new, they also make sure you're getting the hang of keeping the caller on the line. A big part of it is getting a sense of the caller as quickly as you can. Some guys call in already hot and ready, so it's quick no matter what you do. They may have gotten just about to blow on another line, clicking over to hear another voice.

It seems like a lifetime ago.

But the goal I had when I was a phone sex actress wasn't focused on keeping the guy on the line to make the phone sex company money or to keep the job, which I knew I would. They always needed people, and I was good enough from the get-go and showed up for my shift, so I knew I'd pull it off and wouldn't get fired. There was one girl who kept tabs on me, and we came close to verbal blows a couple of times, because she didn't like that I'd distract the men by asking them questions about women and sex instead of just talking sex. She threatened to fire me continually, but what did she care that the guys liked talking about sex even if it wasn't the normal call? The money still rang up.

The goal for me was to get guys to talking about what I wanted to know. I knew I'd also have to talk dirty to get them off, but the tricky part was getting information on each caller so I could get a clue about who these men were — were they dating a girl, married or not, and why did they enjoy phone sex if they had a woman at home? What kind of man was calling, and what did he do for a living? What did he think about women?

I talked to business professionals, blue-collar workers, lawyers and lots of truckers, according to what they said. Most of the callers had a wife or steady girlfriend, with none of the men thinking that phone sex remotely harmed their marriages or other monogamous relationships. Having talked to women for years about any number of sexual topics, I knew this was bullshit as far as most women were concerned.

If Jeffrey had preferred phone sex to porn magazines, would it have made a difference? The problem for me wasn't the pornography; it was that he wasn't having sex with *me*.

There were the phone sex pros, the supervisors who ran the shifts at the phone sex call center and were very kind to me when they monitored a particularly rough — meaning long — call, and came on the line to soothe my nerves. When, after my initiation into the phone sex actress scene, I began getting talkers who would stay on the call for an hour, the pros started treating me differently.

After about a week, I was left pretty much alone on my calls. The first three days were as bad as it gets, because I couldn't keep anyone on the line for long. I wondered if I'd just have to bail on the idea in the first place. But phone sex was the only avenue I hadn't fully excavated, my first stint ending way too quickly to really learn anything substantive. I couldn't give up yet.

One of the things the guys loved to talk about, which I always initiated through what became a logical and easy ice-breaker, was why they were calling in the first place. The majority of the men called the lines to get what they couldn't get at home. They wanted a fantasy their girlfriends or wives wouldn't provide. Sometimes the guy admitted he hadn't even asked her to try. He was sure she'd say no. That says a lot, now, doesn't it? The biggest complaint was the lack of variety in their sex lives. This was a common and regular refrain.

Oddly, it actually didn't take much to get the guys to open up and talk about their lives and how lonely they were in their relationships. They slid from sex to their emotional lives in a stroke, feeling safe, for whatever reasons, opening up on a phone sex line to a woman they didn't know. That's the nucleus of anonymous connection, however it happens. The fake intimacy and lack of required reciprocation allowed the formation of a weird attachment, a bond from the caller to the phone sex actress, if only for the short time we were on the call. For both sides on the phone sex line, when the caller hung up or clicked off, it was over. There was no trace of evidence the call had occurred, except, of course, on the guy's phone bill, though there are ways to get around that, too. The bill didn't hint that the call was for phone sex.

One hilarious call came from a man who said he was a trader on the Chicago Exchange. I recalled this conversation and the others in my one-woman show, *Weeping for JFK*, which dealt with President Kennedy and the sexy '60s when he reigned. The guy had called in to encourage, then teach me how to pierce my genitalia. He became a regular for a week or so, as we went through the histrionics of why I should pierce my labia and the benefits sexually if I did.

At one point, when I had convinced him I was ready to do it, he took me through all of the steps, one at a time, after guiding me in previous calls what I'd need to accomplish piercing my genitalia, something that didn't remotely interest me. Once I launched into the effort it was an acting performance that would have had my friends screaming with laughter if they'd been on the line listening:

"I'm scared."

"Don't be, I'm right here with you, baby."

"It's going to hurt, right?"

"It will be worth it, trust me."

Ditsy now had a new definition in my mind, which included this character I conjured up so I could ask the guy with the piercing genitalia fetish about his love life. Like most of my callers, he was married. His wife had no clue he called the lines. He also claimed to be faithful to her. Phone sex wasn't actual sex to him. It also allowed him to feel free to mess around on the phone without hurting anyone, at least in his mind, and it was safe.

One man who became a regular with me alleged he was a computer programmer from South Carolina. The guy, whom I'll call Carl, was a cross-dresser whose wife had known about it since they'd gotten married and had said she was okay with it. Carl liked to wear women's clothing when not at work, and did so almost exclusively in his life outside his job, including when he and his wife went out. However, he'd just learned that his wife was having an affair with another man. He was devastated.

Carl called regularly, three to four times a week for a month to chat. That's all, just chat. A caller would click on and, like clockwork, eventually I heard, "Taylor?" He'd called looking for me, seeing if I was on this shift.

If Carl missed a day or two, when he'd finally call in, he was a basket case and filled with all sorts of news. One call was particularly entertaining, which came short-ly after he called to say he'd gotten over losing his wife. The euphoria he exuded on the phone was the high before the crash, but it was almost enjoyable. The entire con-versation was about the shopping spree he'd done once he'd come to grips that one upside of it all was not having to work so hard to balance a marriage with a lifestyle he wanted to enjoy fully, but couldn't. He also ended up admitting that his wife had shown signs of weariness for his choices much earlier than he wanted to acknowledge.

Isn't that the way it always is. We know in our hearts something is off, but we can't accept it, so we deny it until we're ready to face it.

Now, I'm not an expert on sexual choices in life or in what a person is driven to own because of biology. I'm just talking about the interaction I had with an individ-ual who actually chose phone sex lines to express his feelings, and perhaps seek some sort of solace, regarding his lifestyle choices and how they impacted his marriage.

Eventually Carl crashed.

After the exuberance subsided, Carl called and we talked and talked about why it had gone so wrong. He'd been honest with her and she'd accepted and married him, so why the betrayal? Why had it ended so badly? I listened mostly, but also felt I did have some knowledge that he should consider. The most obvious observation was that she had once loved him very much or she wouldn't have made the compromise to be with him in the first place. They didn't have children, so it wasn't like that was an issue. They'd discussed it, but that's not where either of them was focused at the time. People change, especially when the two of them had such wide differences at the start.

The other issue was that what seemed like a good idea at first had become too much for her in marriage. Theories about how a relationship will work in close quarters are one thing. How you actually navigate it once you're in it are another. Clearly, his wife wanted something else now, maybe because the years had added up and she just wanted out.

Then Carl called one day to say his wife had asked him for a divorce, ending their marriage for good. He barely got the words out when he burst into tears. I had once questioned whether the scenario I was listening to was real, but now, suddenly, there could be no doubt. Of course, the tears didn't prove Carl was a cross-dresser, but they did signal definite trouble in a life where a man was lonely enough to reach out to a phone sex operator, even if he was using some sort of code to talk through his crisis.

That's the thing about phone sex. It's this surreal world where men phone in and have an anonymous, drive-by, sexual collision with a woman, which sometimes becomes a regular thing. I tried to take all sorts of different shifts, because the calls were different in every time zone.

Sam sounded elderly and called very late at night. He used a variety of different names, but because he called so often, I could recognize his voice. I talked to him whenever they scheduled me in the wee hours of the morning. The calls Sam and I had were always long and included a host of characters as wide as I could think up. He'd say things like, "Who's that over there?" and I'd have to come up with a scenario. It was ludicrous at times. He'd throw in all sorts of descriptions that created roles for a menagerie cast of six or more types of sexual partners, everything from buxom twins to a gorgeous transvestite to animals, which quickly caused me to jettison out of the conversation. It may have been his dime, but that was simply a bridge too far for Miss Missouri.

Sam had a wife, but she went to bed early, he said, which enabled him to play on the phone sex lines late into the night. He would invariably reintroduce his favorite farm animals, but I never played along. Bestiality is something I just can't get my head around at all, not even on the phone. I don't even like "furries," those people who dress up in animal costumes and have sex, sometimes with another costumed person, sometimes with a partner who's naked.

As many calls as I did in the six weeks or so I was a phone sex actress, it still amazes me all of the time I spent just talking to the guys. Invariably, the conversation would begin with asking me what I looked like. If I wasn't quick and direct about it, they'd click off. The illusion of the fantasy being real was critical, even if the whole dance was in his head. Big boobs you'd think would be the big thing, but it wasn't. It was making the picture real and being real while making it. The voice was a very big deal, too, and one reason the barely legal lines, which were the busiest, were a bust for me.

Let's face it, when it comes to sex, this is where men live, in their heads. They fill out the girl they think you are before they get to know you. Another regular liked to call the lines after his wife went to bed. He giggled when I first asked if he was married or single, confessing that his wife was upstairs at the moment. He got off on getting off while his wife lay sleeping and completely clueless about his sexual excursions in the dead of night. Naughty boy.

There was a type of caller who would signal quickly that he was simply calling to talk. One of these, a man named Mike, would call to talk about his wife taking his daughter away from him. It was an ugly divorce, where she was going for custody of his little girl, and it was killing him. Mike might have had another issue altogether that helped bring him to tears when he called, but I talked to him several times that week, and he was clearly overwrought.

Talking dirty to men who are strangers on a sex phone line could also turn creepy, and I burned out quickly on being able to handle the harder core stuff. The sheer volume of the calls was mind-blowing. What it meant that all those men were calling over and over again, along with a nonstop supply of newcomers, staggered my perceptions. Coming on top of everything else I had learned, phone sex was the last course in my sexual education, outside my own life.

So when I woke up on September 11, 2001, it wouldn't have taken much for me to walk away and take a long, hot shower from the stuff that was starting to clog my brain.

Our sexual vitality and how we express it is a vital element of a woman's power. How it's received and accepted can vary. Men who are uncomfortable with women having the same freedoms as they do have used terms such as *aggressive*, *emasculating*, *ball-busting* and all sorts of other derogatory descriptions. There is no doubt that the Pill, coupled with the modern feminist revolution, changed the male-dominated status quo. But for those of us who are lucky to have experienced liberated males, we also know there is a great relief and even gratitude coming from our mate at having equal partners, who are recognized as sexual beings. But accepting women as equals, including sexually, hasn't been an easy road. It has come in a combination of lurches and backtracks for American society's traditional structure.

It begins with understanding that when men duck out and disassociate from their hot-blooded sexual partners by choosing outside sources of gratification, the loss is incalculable for both parties, especially when frequency and level of intimacy are sacrificed. A decrease in sexual interaction in marriage may be normal to some people, but to the hundreds of men and women to whom I've spoken over a ten-year period, as confirmed by the sexual education I've had over my lifetime, I'd say we'd all be a lot better off if we started rejecting other people's definition of normal. That measurement has changed significantly in the modern, sexualized era, with more rewrites required, as needed.

The Pfizer Global Better Sex Survey, completed in March 2006, is the largest global survey of its type, utilizing telephone interviews with 12,588 women and men, age twenty-five to seventy-four in twenty-seven countries. The study's stated goal was to measure levels of sexual satisfaction and learn about couples' unmet sexual needs around the world. Pfizer, of course, makes Viagra, so the company has a commercial interest in the subject, but the study, conducted by Harris Interactive, adhered to strict scientific standards in its research. The first thing that was confirmed was that "all aspects of sex are very important to both men and women." This is basically what the Kinsey Reports revealed in 1953, which brought the conservative right, starting with the esteemed Rev. Billy Graham, down on Alfred Kinsey's head. As recently as 2006, researchers were still finding it important to make the point that women and men held sex equally important, no matter their age.

The age issue is critical, because in American society it's seen as gross to hear or have a discussion about older women and men being sexually active. There is almost a cultural lust for media reports and storylines that celebrate hot, young passion. That two people over fifty would be using erotic movies, sex toys and fashion to excite one another has been traditionally seen as unseemly. Sex once was thought to be unimportant for women over fifty, which is likely why so many men over fifty were starting second families. But today, people over fifty are sexually active in all sorts of non-traditional ways that were never made public in my mother's generation, when women became matrons, while men found mistresses. That's over.

Sometimes we forget that things like depression and even our level of irritability, not to be confused with fierce bitch, rise in inverse proportion to the amount of sexual activity we have in our lives. There are innumerable studies from which to pull data proving that having sex releases a whole host of friendly chemicals through our bodies that have the potential to boost our immune systems, not to mention our moods. Some women experience euphoria after orgasm, which can trigger a contagion of positive after-effects.

The daily grind of our lives is reason enough to work harder at making sex an integral part of our reality, just like working out at the gym. When single, there are more hurdles to making it regular, especially if you're busy and not in a relationship. However, that doesn't mean you cannot enjoy at least half of what's offered in a sexual exchange by having toys and other goodies around to make sure you remember what the fuss is all about. I say this as someone who spent most of her life single while sifting through men to find a great sex partner who could deliver his half of the equation by accepting me for who I am.

If you're in a relationship, cohabitating or married, the excuse of being too busy for sex is as lazy as it is potentially destructive. Again, there is a lot of evidence that sexual intimacy is great for our overall health, boosts our level of productivity and makes us happier. It's simply not a good decision to always prioritize two more hours of work over scheduling a date-night with your significant other. Part of that time must be spent on pleasure, the purely physical kind.

The Pfizer study also found that among women and men, "one-third indicated they are having 'less than the right amount of sex,'" while 50% of the respondents — both women and men — say they are "very satisfied" with their sex lives.

One of the interesting findings in the Pfizer study was that among eleven advanced nations, including the United States, women actually topped men in thinking sex was important. Another profound result, however, shows that not all respondents are satisfied with their sex lives. In the United Sates, the survey showed 57% of women and 53% of men were very satisfied. Those numbers are significantly lower than in Brazil, where 58% of women said they were "very satisfied," compared to 71% of men; or Mexico, where it was 78% for men and 71% for women. But U.S. sex partners are more satisfied, according to the survey, than those in Taiwan, where 27% of both women and men expressed satisfaction, or Italy, where sexual satisfaction hovered at just 19% for men and 18% for women.

"Erection hardness" was a common complaint, no matter the country tapped in Pfizer's study. In France, 77% of men were "not fully satisfied with erection hardness," compared with 72% of the women. In Great Britain, more women than men felt this way, 51–41%. In the U.S., it was 56% of women who were not fully satisfied with erection hardness, and 43% of men.

MensHealth.com reported on the Global Better Sex Survey, pointing out that "90% of men say that confidence in sexual ability is critical to having a strong, loving relationship."

A brief blog post on *Discover* magazine's website in April 2013 revealed something that should get everyone's attention. Razib Khan reported on a special issue of the *Journal of Sexual Medicine*, from 2010 research, focusing on "Sexual Behavior in the United States: Results from a National Probability Sample of Men and Women Ages 14–94." The sample was 2,936 men, 2,929 women. One part of the results from the abstract were as follows: "The proportion of adults who reported vaginal sex in the past year was highest among men ages 25–39 and for women ages 20–29, then progressively declined among older age groups." The graph Khan provided from the study peaked for both genders at 25–29, from there looking like a downward ski slope, with women affected the most as we age, according to this study.

I'd like to think that more women are being satisfied outside vaginal sex and that the sexual life of American females is vibrating, so to speak, with expanding opportunities. There's no doubt women masturbate, which is good for everyone. However, having covered women for more than twenty years, from relationships to politics and everything in between, the way women are depicted sexually as we age could use a sex-lift. Men can be sexy and powerful at once. With women still fighting for power equality, being sexy at the same time is confounding to cover for U.S. media, which puts women in an either/or position. That's a loser for us.

The study also concludes that, "Masturbation was common throughout the lifespan and more common than partnered sexual activities during adolescence and older age (70+)." Sexual interest is compulsive when we're young. As we get older, we change. Life can beat us down. We get busy, our jobs more demanding today. I wonder if it's a coincidence that these statistics show up as more people are living happily alone. Of course, vaginal sex certainly doesn't preclude masturbation. We also have to work harder at getting the kind of sex we want as we get older, and that can be the case inside or outside marriage. The effort's worth it. Our health gets in the way of our sex lives, too, but we can do a lot to combat that, and we should.

I'm not a nutritionist, but I started on a health kick long before it was making news, way back in my late teens. It's astounding to me that people don't make a correlation between diet and quality of life, including their sex lives.

There's a reason nutritionists talk about certain foods being aphrodisiacs. When you're feeling lousy or have an illness, it's not by chance that your libido takes a dive. Your energy skyrockets when you start and sustain a healthy diet and workout regimen. Talk to any nutritionist and she will tell you that proper nutrition is critical for hormone production and basic body balance. As you get older, these things become the backstop in maintaining your sexual energy and interests. Weight also has a great deal to do with health.

In the introduction to *7 Keys to Lifelong Sexual Vitality*, written by Drs. Brian and Anna Maria Clement, the authors write something that is taken for granted far too much by your average Jill and Jack American: "Besides diet and exercise, nothing will naturally enhance your health throughout your life more than remaining sexually active. Healthy sex is one of nature's most potent medicines."

There's no doubting that generalizing about sex is a mistake. As Drs. Clement write in their book, borrowing data from *The Sexual Brain*, by University of California, San Diego, biology professor Simon LeVay, "In India, many couples abstain from sexual activity after fifty years of age, particularly after a woman becomes a grandmother."

How healthy this is for the woman is worth questioning, even if it's considered culturally important to India. It may be "normal" there as well, but there's no evidence I've been able to uncover that a woman in India over fifty is any different from any other woman hormonally. That is, her mind and body and life experience would benefit from throwing off the yoke of culture, and even religious traditions where they apply, and remaining sexually active, whether her family approves or not.

This is likely scandalous to even posit, because what business is it of mine what a grandmother in India does in her sexual life? I don't have the power to shake the world's grip on keeping women in their place in certain cultures, but as a chronicler of world politics and women's freedoms, it's of interest to me that we tear down these taboos about women as we age, debunk them thoroughly, especially where staying vibrant sexually is concerned. Men would benefit from it, too.

Another statistic in the Clements' book: "In many South American countries, teenage girls are taught by their mothers how to simultaneously remain 'virgins' and satisfy sexual desires by engaging in heterosexual anal intercourse, rather than vaginal penetration, until they marry." It's preposterous to argue that anal sex can help a teenager sustain her virginity, which I've run across in other research as well. If this doesn't give you a taste of the tortured cultural roles girls and women are forced into accepting, nothing will. Virginity prioritized over the health and safety of the girl is a human rights offense. Ignoring it doesn't change that fact.

America has its own cultural deviances, too — like promoting abstinence without also providing people with the facts on the powers of sexual desire and the condoms to use when overwhelming urges hit. A healthier society would arm people with tools to protect themselves when their own humanity rears its passion in the face of the best intentions. That would mean free condoms for everyone, including those who shouldn't be using them yet.

It's not immoral to be sexually active as a teenager. What's immoral is to think that acting on impulse, which impacts society and is all of our business, doesn't come with personal responsibility. It's moral to accept that sexual education and reproductive health information are not just private, family matters. This responsibility to inform and protect is equally shared between people and their community.

It's not like underage people aren't sexually aware. The modern era is sexually charged, no matter how you're brought up, as *Sexy Baby* taught everyone who saw it and didn't know already. Information is the only offensive weapon, and it should come from people who know the world of relationships and sex and can help others navigate it, so as not to be drowned by it.

There's no escaping the porn-style visuals that inflame men's senses and impact the way women are perceived in our society, all of which filters down to our lives in one way or another. We can talk about it with our girlfriends, but it can also impact the way our lovers see us, unless we reject that as our only role and educate them otherwise.

There's also a healthy challenge to see through it all, so we don't allow ourselves to settle for less. But that's up to each of us to decide, too. What are we going to accept? The answer to that goes all the way down to our very basic sexual satisfaction. Instead of living up to the Victoria's Secret standard, we must define our own version of it. What's your sexy? That's the ultimate question. Because a good man doesn't want a carbon copy of someone else's idea of a healthy, sensual woman. If he's attracted to you, or if you're seeking to attract the right guy, he wants to see your authentic sexuality and how you carry it every day.

How you react to the barrage coming at you is the whole romantic ballgame. Your choices make your life.

My Year in Smut — No Fifty Shades

The website Amsterdaminfo.com offers a good place to start, introducing the city's famous Red Light District this way: "Amsterdam prides itself, and rightly so, on its wholly liberal and tolerant attitude, embracing the fact that people may be into prostitution, soft drugs and pornography — and this is only human." Unlike Hollanders, though, Americans remain very provincial about sex and soft drugs, specifically marijuana, and it's not helping anyone. It's why states and cities are finally going their own way on marijuana. If Americans were a little less uptight, we might have a lot more happy relationships and marriages. Today's Internet and social media smorgasbord has thrown our puritanical propriety for a loop, which is evident everywhere you look.

The first interviews I did with legal prostitutes were in Amsterdam in the early 1990s. Sitting in a legal hash bar after meeting Red Light District prostitutes during their work hours and asking for interviews, I basically just let each girl talk and tell me her tale. Being a legal sex worker in Amsterdam meant health care for a woman, a regular shift, a boss, maybe even a child and a life, while she paid her taxes, too. That didn't mean the banks wanted to lend her money to get a house, however.

Back in the early '90s there was still a pickup zone, or tipple zone, as Amsterdaminfo labels it, which I witnessed from a cab. Cars would drive by, and prostitutes would engage with customers. Some would get in, and they'd drive off. Those days are now gone.

Political correctness often smacks up against sexual liberation and being a feminist, especially when you get into excavating the collision of sex, dating and love through advice, phone sex and soft-core porn, which can get intense, the subject matter and propriety conflicting at all points. It's better not to worry about what everyone might be thinking or saying, and just jump in.

G-spot shot anyone? Growing up I had a journal, and my g-spot wasn't a topic I covered. Nobody knew anything about a g-spot where I lived. For all I knew, it hadn't even been discovered yet.

Now there's G-Spot Amplification or GSA, both of which have been trademarked and are patent pending by gynecologist David Matlock, who is helping women to feel more intense orgasms. His website, thegshot.com, claims, "In a pilot study, 87% of women surveyed after receiving the G-Shot reported enhanced sexual arousal/gratification." The site advises that "results may vary," which is probably the truest statement of all. "Feel the rush" is the goal.

The needle used by one gynecologist for the g-spot shot was shown on TLC's *Plastic Wives*, which reveals the truth about a lot of plastic surgery. Physical enhancements come with varying degrees of discomfort. Whether it's worth it is in the eye of the reconstructed. Beyond just beauty, it's now about pleasure, too, but in the business of porn, it's always about making money.

The first porn-type film I saw was in an independent theater. At least, it's what I considered porn at the time. *Last Tango in Paris* was forbidden fruit in St. Louis, Missouri. I had a crush on a guy ten years older than me who wasn't quite sure about me, probably because he wasn't stupid and knew I didn't sleep with anyone. After the film, we went back to his place where he invited me to lie next to him, then literally begged me to touch him. How clueless are some guys anyway? But considering this was the year of *Deep Throat*, I guess I should be thankful the guy didn't force himself on me, then say I'd asked for it by going to the movie in the first place.

I desperately wanted to be sexually liberated, but I just wasn't. I absorbed the career part of liberation early, by making money performing, starting in my teens, but my body and my mind just didn't talk to each other, and erotic desires were out of the question.

When online dating started to explode, I found myself restless. Still at the *LA Weekly*, I'd been given a taste of what was just beginning online. So, it didn't take long before I was contacted out of the blue about joining a soft-core adult business that had found its way onto the World Wide Web early. It was 1997, and I was gnashing to learn all I could about the Internet, which had already shown me the way I was going to keep writing.

I knew from the cataclysmic changes absorbed by the adult industry when the VHS tape arrived that entrepreneurial lust would inspire them to latch on to the web quickly and exploit every aspect of it to make money. So when I was asked about joining a soft-core company, I simply couldn't resist. The tech world was exploding with possibilities, professionally and financially, which meant I'd be there at the very start, when it all began, a time when my lack of technical expertise wasn't prohibitive, especially with me joining a company that wanted me on the management side, as well as to direct the content.

The film *Boogie Nights* was made the year I dropped into the soft-core side of web smut. The film starred Mark Wahlberg as porn icon Dirk Diggler, whose résumé for his job is his huge penis. Burt Reynolds makes an impression as a porn-king filmmaker facing the moment when smut flicks go from film to video. Julianne Moore plays the porn mama, in an outrageously audacious portrayal that takes on the professional and personal sides of women in hard-core porn.

The company I joined was at the other end of this spectrum — high-tech and web-based only, with offices that represented a legit corporation. The company betrayed none of the seediness most would automatically associate with the adult industry, because it produced only soft-core fare.

The company was called Danni's Hard Drive (DHD). It was launched in 1995 by Danni Ashe, a stripper who had decided to take her fan club onto the web after "a table dance that crossed local decency regulations" got her arrested, as the *Los Angeles Business Journal* reported it in 1997. It was all female when it started, except for one lonely male. Danni Ashe, whose real name was Leah Manzari, was the most popular woman on the Internet at the time, her images having been downloaded an astounding one billion times.

What I never expected was that my boss would be the woman who would become one of the very first to make money on the web, beating all the boys. NBC News' Internet Underground website reported in 2000 that Ashe was the first woman to establish a major adult site on the web. By extension, did that make me the first female editor-in-chief of a soft-core website? Likely, but who cares? I kept my clothes on and managed the content, creative and tech teams behind the scenes. What I inherited and how the team I brought on board supercharged what Ashe had started, allowed DHD to take the next leap forward, which would be one of many that continued long after I'd fled the scene.

My story begins in July 1997 and abruptly ends in September 1998. Danni's Hard Drive was bought in 2004, then sold again in 2006 to Penthouse Media Group, Inc. for $3 million. Whatever happened after I left has absolutely no connection to what I write about here. One reason I decided to take the job in the first place was because the site was strictly soft-core, which meant I could learn the Internet without stepping into the worst of hard-core pornography. Back in 1997, there was a stark distinction between the two.

I self-published *My Year in Smut: The Internet Escapades Inside Danni's Hard Drive* in 2000; it's now long out of print. In its review, the website for *Adult Video News* (avn.com) wrote: "Marsh, a sharp sociopolitical writer, says Ashe insists on soft-core image but never says no to hard-core profits." Adriana Manov, producer/host of KPFK's "Feminist Magazine," wrote, "*My Year in Smut* is an alchemy of the sleazy with the feminist, and the results are pure political gold! This is an emancipation proclamation!" David D. Waskul, a professor of sociology and author of empirical articles covering Internet cybersex, featured excerpts of my story in his book, *net.seXXX: Readings on Sex, Pornography and the Internet,* writing that it was "a rare glimpse into the inner workings of a major Internet pornography corporation."

For me, it was never about reviews or sales. It was meant as a record, which is why I can recount it with accuracy today. What it was like at the beginning, one brief moment of Internet history, when the economics of the Internet were harnessed, which happened through the adult industry. Danni Ashe, a self-starting, determined and difficult woman, led the way, and I was there to see it and mine it.

Ashe wanted to cash in, so she taught herself the tech basics, starting with HTML coding, to launch the site herself. She was one of the very few naturally big-breasted beauties who didn't do sex scenes with men, though soft girlie scenes were a subscriber favorite. She wanted to succeed, she said "by promoting non-exploitative erotica." She wouldn't call it *porn* when I was her editor, only *erotica*, after Hugh Hefner's model. "I just hate the word *pornography*," she'd say. That was Danni Ashe, determinedly trying to separate herself out from the hard-core purveyors. What she was doing back then doesn't exist in the same way anymore in an online industry that has now become a hard-core flesh-fest, due to competition for eyes on the page and the frenzy to draw subscribers to pay up.

A pioneer of the subscriber model that would become a craze, Ashe was no dumb blonde. She knew a lot of strippers, including big-name babes, all of whom had girlie pictures galore. Boasting around eighteen hundred photos on DHD, the subscriber portion of the site, the HotBox, had more than fifteen hundred video channels and counting. Ashe offered models, strippers and XXX-rated actresses a page on her site in exchange for a photo, the girls providing information for a short DHD bio, which included a link to anywhere they wanted, even back to their own sites. DHD instantly became the number one big-breasted, naughty-babe portal on the web.

The model bios were simple, personable and as digestible as a piece of chocolate. Ashe's model was inviting guys to indulge their ultimate fantasies with girls they'd created fantasies about in their minds, but now could do so in the new online world, which offered the ultimate in privacy — their own homes or dorm rooms. Subscribers even got a chance to interact with girls during online shows, including chatting with their favorite big-breasted babe or XXX-rated "actress," using that term very loosely.

In an era of boob-job mania, Danni's naturally buxom figure was a huge draw. What Ashe performed in herself was different from what the HotBox site offered. But she had no trouble providing all sorts of pornography in HotBox, content that DHD didn't produce. It mostly originated through outside web porn channels and external feeds that subscribers could peruse. Danni Ashe was represented by the gauzy cover of a soft-core front, but behind the paywall was everything the adult film industry offered. HotBox was not under my jurisdiction, thank Eros.

Ashe's artistic model for the pictorials featured on the site was complicated. There were no penetration shots during the time I was at DHD, not even with toys or dildos. So, a woman could have a dildo in her hand, but she wasn't allowed to put it inside herself. A man and woman could be seen about to have sex, including the woman holding the man's penis, but the woman wasn't allowed to take the penis into her mouth or her vagina. But remember, all bets were off in HotBox. You could also view Ashe exposing herself fully through all sorts of spread shots, see pictures of her in bondage scenarios and fetish-wear, and enjoy her bisexual gal-pal romps, but men were never involved.

When Ashe found out that someone working for a company providing video feeds of live performances to subscribers had offered one of her DHD models fifty dollars to pee in a cup on camera, she just about came unglued. Golden shower variations on DHD? Not going to happen.

Not all the models could figure out what Ashe was offering. One big-boob stripper confronted her while she was signing autographs at a Las Vegas convention event, screaming at her in front of fans and adult biz purveyors that she was taking advantage of the DHD models by using their images, but not paying them. Ashe kept her cool, didn't say a word, while the model unloaded. Ignorant of what being on a huge site meant for her own tiny stripper site and her booking possibilities, she soon found out when she was scrubbed from DHD.

According to a 2006 study by the Top Ten Reviews website, pornography is a thirteen billion dollar industry in the United States, with worldwide numbers at $97 billion. However, itworld.com reported in February 2012 that the U.S. is around 58% of the world's total $4.9 billion porn bucks. The exact numbers may be up for debate, but it's big bucks.

Back in 1997-98, DHD made around $2.7 million, which sounds like chump change today. But when the Internet first blasted off, DHD was one of the leading moneymakers on the web. After I left, in November 1998, *Entertainment Tonight* reported Ashe was expected to clear four million dollars that year. It got Ashe featured on the front page of the *Wall Street Journal* at the time, making her the only woman ever to be on the front pages of the *Journal* and *JUGGS*. She was whip-smart and insecure all at once, though few ever saw the latter.

I did, because we clashed from the start, which didn't abate until I walked out the door after thirteen months of combustibility and an intense course on diva mania. I was there at the birth of the online erotic emancipation of women. Porn was the beginning.

According to the same itworld.com article referred to previously, as of February 2012, Utah had "the highest online subscription rate per thousand home broadband users (5.47)." This is not shocking to me. Religiosity often leads to sexual outlets other than through a spouse or relationship, because desire is so tied up in judgment and shame that men don't feel free to be mere mortals. This comes with a lot of messy and delicious physical proclivities. The U.S. city "with the most searches per capita of the terms *sex, porn* and *xxx*" is Elmhurst, Illinois.

Nearly twenty-five million sites are pornographic, which is 12% of all websites. But only 20% of men admit to watching porn, which is laughable. Sunday is national porn day in the U.S., though it's not acknowledged. The worst day for the porn industry is Thanksgiving, for obvious reasons.

A search by a teenage boy or a grown man might start with "free naked pictures of girls," which back in 1997-98 might have taken him to DHD. Girls, too, because we like to look at pretty women, we just don't like to pay for it. So the ample, free model shots likely would appeal to curious girls, not to mention lesbians, just as much as men.

The adult industry's history is an all-male power vacuum, with females being the exploited talent with no choice or power. The Internet changed that and gave girls in the adult industry a way to trump the guys.

I didn't even know what an areola was when I walked through the doors the first day. That changed quickly. For those of you equally ignorant, it's the darker part of skin that surrounds the nipple. How a grown woman who'd spent her life in show business didn't know the specific names of her own body parts is hard to imagine, but that's basically how I went through life on the sexual front. It also explains why my life took the trajectory it did: It was guided by the pure curiosity of a tight-assed beauty queen.

The job came with fluffy publicity, because walking into the company's head-quarters you felt you might as well be walking into a small business success story. The message: Girls are just as serious about making money as boys. The site was covered in *U.S. News & World Report*, the *New York Times, Los Angeles Business Journal, Los Angeles Times*, ABC News and CNN. Anywhere Ashe was featured back then, she usually hit the headlines.

A *USA Today* piece, titled "How Small Operators Can Make Big Killings on the Web" told the tale, and getting our picture together in *USA Today* validated our business status in an industry where few were making money yet. I'd fallen into the perfect place to learn about the web, but also to exploit the opportunity to do what Hugh Hefner had done with the magazine *Playboy* — use one of the most highly trafficked websites in existence at the time and see what readers thought about politics. From a liberated feminist's point of view, the faceoff between Susan McDougal and Ken Starr during President Bill Clinton's impeachment became a gold mine. It seemed a natural for our site, and for a brief time I was one of the first political writers on the web who also had a huge audience, made possible through tits and ass.

There was a lot of drama at DHD, including a blockbuster stripper out of control and a company that was in chaos when I arrived, because Ashe had outgrown what she could handle on her own. I was hired, not to handle the sex side, but to try to get her business operations in order. There were no deadlines and no set working hours, with content going up whenever it came in and someone uploaded it. What I did first was fire the one person doing any work, Ashe's good friend and someone she couldn't bring herself to fire. Jill was unmanageable and rarely showed up, so no one knew when things would be posted. Then I hired an entire new creative, design and tech team, as well as a model representative, someone to deal one-on-one with the strippers.

I was in the land of estrogen, an almost all-female enterprise of women making money on their own terms, the way Hugh Hefner had done. I knew that for me to be involved, I had to be empowered to write political commentary that would give meaning and context to the sexually liberated women making the choices they were making. Erotica without a political component didn't interest me, and I wouldn't have taken the job if the agreement didn't include a great deal for me. My advice column, "What Do You Want?," was central to "The Editor's Desk," which was part of our deal from the start. A section titled "I Have a Past," which is on my new-media site (www.taylormarsh.com) today, was first launched back in 1998 and gives the reader a tour of my professional life, because it's been such an unpredictable odyssey.

Men would email me through my advice column asking me all sorts of questions. One that regularly came up was over whether two women with one man might drive a wedge between the primary male-female couple: "Do you think it could hurt our relationship if we try this?" Obviously, there is no one answer to this question, because it depends on the two people involved, the relationship and the candor between the couple. That said, I've heard about more fallout from bisexual experimentation than I have happy endings. Most times couples jump into a threesome adventure on a whim, without talking everything out first. Often people do it liquored up or drugged, which is always a mistake.

One story I chronicled in *My Year in Smut* involved a guy and his girlfriend who started role-playing master and slave scenarios, à la *Fifty Shades of Grey*, only with another woman joining in — something that would never have happened with Christian Grey and Anastasia Steele. According to his emails to me, after two satisfying months of playing together, he woke up to a note from his girlfriend saying she had left him for the other woman, who understood her needs better than he did. The guy was devastated, but not just because he lost his girlfriend. He hadn't been able to recast her with an equally submissive, bisexual female who liked experimenting. Draw your own conclusions about why he was actually upset, which to me sounded more about his sexual needs than an emotional connection that is the relationship glue that keeps people together.

Sex alone won't do it in the end, just like love is often not enough either. There's a bit of magic dust when you meet someone and everything hits, including the elements of friendship, desire and deep understanding. When it does, you don't mess with that chemistry for anything, because you absolutely can find romance again, but a true connection is harder to find.

I'll never forget the bulletin board that took up more than half the wall space in one of the corporate offices. It was filled to overflowing with fan letters and pictures that had been sent in from guys from all over the world. Most of the snapshots were nudes or at least partial nudes of men showing their masculinity in full, erect glory. A few guys also sent in pubic hair and even body fluids, which were quickly discarded. Most of the notes were heartfelt and some were hysterically funny.

One note came from a guy who was pictured fully clothed and smiling broadly. He was handsome and masculine, with a very wholesome, collegiate-type look. The contents of his letter detailed with great pride, abandon and explicitness what he felt was the delicious aroma of his farts. It included written descriptions of the sounds he made as he admitted farting throughout his entire letter writing session. A fart fetish. We were constantly amazed.

Another common email I got through "The Editor's Desk" section on the website came from men asking why many women don't like to experiment and only like sex a certain way. That's a question that has threaded through all of my work in the sex and dating industries. Guys from all corners talked about their shy wives, some who only liked missionary, and asked how to change them. I don't ever try to play sex therapist, so I could only give them advice on what I'd learned.

Two people have to talk to each other about sex, preferably when they're not in the throes of passion. To get naked sexually enough to experiment requires a degree of trust and comfort that often takes women time. People have to also be careful how they react to one another. You've got to stop and take a breath if you hear something from your partner that shocks you. Be gentle and kind, then ask questions and allow him to talk.

If you can't talk openly about sex in a relationship, you're really screwed from the start, especially if you want something lasting. Over time, talking about your sex life together becomes even more important, because you've got to keep mixing things up.

You also have to guard what discussions take place in the bedroom. My advice is to make the bedroom a place of corporeal communion, a primal and physical den of iniquity whenever possible. If children invade the space, it's only temporary, with sensuality easily reestablished if you're determined. Talks about money shouldn't happen here, because it kills the mood.

For the endorphin rush alone, sex is sublime. It offers a complete physical escape.

At least I haven't found anything that feels as great, even when I have a headache.

Why do you think porn is big bucks? It's not just about looking at naked girls. It's about the payoff at the end. That feeling. That's what the guy is after, and when it's a do-it-yourself adventure it's easy. The majority of men also want a deep relationship, connection and love, just as much as a woman. They're a lot more fragile when they're in love, too, which is why when a woman cheats she often pays a bigger price. Once a man is vulnerable he will give you everything, often risking anything to see you happy. Cheat on him and he may never forgive.

Men are also more willing to take risks and venture outside their relationship for sex than women, which almost always has absolutely nothing to do with their partner.

A great example of the compartmentalization some people are capable of is represented through a *Mad Men* episode that aired in April 2013 titled "The Collaborators." Written by Jonathan Igla and Matthew Weiner, it revolves around Don Draper who, as played by Jon Hamm, is one of the best characters ever created that allows women inside the mind of an insatiable philanderer.

Sitting in bed with one another one morning, Sylvia, played by Linda Cardellini, asks Don, "You don't mind sitting across the table from your wife and my husband?"

Don Draper responds, "I don't think about it..."

"I suppose that has nothing to do with this," Sylvia replies.

"*This* didn't happen. Just in here," he says pointing to his head, meaning that for the two of them it can only be real in their minds.

The next night Don and Sylvia get in a heated discussion about their affair at dinner, their spouses unable to attend. She's upset, but he's not sure why. "Is that what's bothering you, that everything worked out perfectly?" Sylvia keeps jabbering. Then, after taking a sip of his cocktail, he levels a deadly gaze at her, saying, "Now I understand. You want to feel shitty right up until the point where I take your dress off, because I'm going to do that. You want to skip dinner? Fine, but don't pretend."

She then confronts him, wondering if their spouses had come to dinner, "Would it be someone else's dress?" Don's confused: "What are you talking about?"

"Weren't you the one who told me you were drifting apart? Isn't that what this was about?"

Don glares at her. "I want *you*. I want you *all* the time. And if you've suddenly decided you want something more than that, well then that's news, isn't it?"

Sylvia sits there, stunned at his brutal candor. She's been called a hypocrite by this hunk of a man, and all she can do is bow her head in response. When she looks up again they lock eyes and you can feel the heat through the screen. It's molten.

Underneath the dialogue, the dramatic Italian aria "Casta Diva" (Norma) plays, while on screen, the scenes are cut in such a way as to alternate between moments of Don and Sylvia first coming through a door, then back again to the table where they're shown arguing, then back again, as they carnally devour one another. Don takes off Sylvia's dress and they fall onto a bed, ravaging each other as if they'd not had sex in weeks.

When Sylvia apologizes for being jealous, Don stops her. "This is just us here tonight," he reminds her. She replies, "We have to be careful. We can't fall in love..."

That's it, the heart of infidelity — physical lust and longing that are separate from love. Having the ability to live in the eye of passion, blocking all else out, not allowing the complications of feelings and emotions to enter the arena of desire. Nothing exists but two human animals fucking and finding their way to explosion.

At the end of the episode, Don Draper returns home, with "Just a Gigolo" playing in the background, the lyrics emphasizing the cyclical futility of his thirst: "Just a gigolo, everywhere I go. People know the part I'm playing.... Selling each romance, every night some heart betraying." Don can't go into his apartment, but instead slumps in the hallway on the floor, ruined.

Carnality can catch you up in its vortex, where you can find yourself doing things you never dreamed of before. Sexual acts of unbounded moral lethality or unlimited imagination can take you over a pleasure cliff you never knew existed, and over which you feel you have no control. The abandon is instantly sublime, and you can't, you won't, deny yourself. When an affair is moored in the physical alone, no earthly responsibilities attached, the escape works like a narcotic; it becomes an obsession. It's equally deadly. It can be confused with love, because of the sustenance sex supplies to parts of ourselves that are wounded.

It inevitably turns to pure torment. Infidelity isn't romance, though the excitement often masquerades for it. Romance is ultimately about safety that allows you both to be vulnerable. Cheating is dangerous, especially if one of you has more to lose than the other. It rarely has a happy ending, because the carnage unleashed when it's discovered can extinguish whatever brought the two people together in the first place. Brad Pitt and Angelina Jolie are an exception, not the rule.

There are also things some men won't ask their partners to do. They can be afraid of judgment or rejection, or they may be just embarrassed or shy. That's when pornography temporarily soothes the beast. A man might want extreme sex-play or "kinky fuckery," but doesn't want to admit it.

The more sexually liberated the woman, the better off a man is.

There's a reason why romance novels and soap operas have ruled for decades, and why *Fifty Shades of Grey* blasted onto the book scene and took off. *Fifty Shades* should finally obliterate the notion that women aren't visual, because the entire three-volume trilogy takes place in each reader's head. The movie that's on its way will expand the visuals, which will likely do a much bigger on-demand and home-video business than in theaters. Erotica is a very private thing, and the notion it's just for men is suggested by the ignorant. Women also like to keep their erotic secrets tucked away where others won't mock or tarnish their fantasies with judgment.

Women have always been titillated by erotica. We just like it different than men do, though even that depends on the woman. However, it helps to have connection between the characters, real ties of emotion, along with the lust, with the woman equally in charge, even when she submits. When love is tangled with lust, it's a blockbuster.

One thing in my job description at DHD was that I had to write erotic stories to go along with a set of pictures of a couple together every week. It was creative torture for me. That I did my damndest to deliver I can only tell you, but the resulting product was always a disaster. When I used the phrase "fluttering action of a feather," the emails I received were brutal, though nothing was as bad as when the girl fell asleep and had a dream fantasy. Epic rejection ensued, with men emailing me that it was the most juvenile porn they'd ever read. E.L. James I am not. When the stories were dropped, the only people more relieved than myself were the men.

One thing about DHD is that you had to quickly distinguish between office talk and a hostile work environment. It takes a certain type of individual to stare at female genitalia day in and day out, which made me glad I was on the management side. Okaying the images was the boss' job. The conversations in the office went like this:

"Look at those tits!"

"Are they natural?"

"Natural? She's a size triple-H, for God's sake."

"How big is triple-H?"

"A lot bigger than you."

"Does she have the biggest tits?"

"They have cat-fights about that all the time."

"How do they run?"

"Run, hell. How do they sleep at night?"

The creative team smoothed out stretch marks on the girlie photos, which were evident when the women had boob jobs. They removed corns from foot-fetish photos, smoothed out tummy wrinkles, and performed amazing feats of magic with butt shots. That included removing very nasty hemorrhoids, making bend-me-over backdoor close-ups look presentable, if there is such a thing.

When it was time to hire a model coordinator, because I sure as hell wasn't going to do it myself, we ran a blind ad in *Variety* and *Hollywood Reporter* for a "talent coordinator," with no one knowing it was the soft-core megasite DHD. The response totaled literally ten pounds of résumés. We actually weighed them. They included résumés from people who'd worked at Disney, as well as with Johnny Carson on *The Tonight Show*. One applicant had managed the talent for Barnum & Bailey Circus. That was all I needed to know. Managing circus talent was the perfect requirement for corralling the crew of misfit models, strippers, and XXX-rated porn actresses that crossed DHD's doorstep.

The stress at DHD when I was there, at a time when Ashe's business was realigning, was intense. Every day we worked to satisfy subscribers, get new images uploaded, and create the e-zines CyberBeauties, NaughtyNewbies, Nippleodeon and NetFetish, all to feed the insatiable voyeurs who paid our salaries and made DHD a multi-million-dollar company out of the gate. This was the original twenty-four-hour, seven-days-a-week web enterprise that made the news industry pale in comparison. We worked like dogs, and I made sure we blew steam off when the cork was about to blow. The trick is not to quiet creative spirit, but to harness and focus it. We had a tight team, with Ashe on the outside as boss, something she had a difficult time accepting.

About as outlandish as it got was when the performance-enhancing substance GHB was overnighted to the corporate headquarters for the private use of a big-breasted star stripper and headliner who was flying in for a highly publicized, upcoming charity event. I hadn't even been there a month when this blew into an epic row. When answers to my questions became a babbling stream of incoherence, because she never imagined anyone would challenge her, "Star Stripper" became the second girl I sacked in the first month. Evidently, there had been lots of partying on a previous Las Vegas trip that made her believe no one would care if she was loaded on stage. That was before I landed in the middle of this diva-drenched scene, knowing very well what the combination of GHB, drinking and a striptease in front of a packed crowd could bring.

This charity event also included limousine rides that could be purchased by the guys, with strippers going along for the ride, insert your fantasy here. At the cost of seventy-five dollars per ride, champagne would flow and plenty of carousing could be crammed in, so more money could be made for the charity, and the strippers. Who knew where that would lead? The answer led to the event being canceled.

Whatever *boob job* means to you, if you've never seen a big-breasted, top stripper, you've not seen anything, though I have no idea what's the norm today. The girls ranged from a normal 34B to an unbelievable 125ZZZ. One gal had a 55EE bust line *after* a reduction. The biggest strippers back then made anywhere up to five thousand dollars a week and more than a hundred grand per year, and earned every penny, though keeping that going was not easy for many. Whatever glamour might be attached, it dulls quickly, when you watch how the sex industry grinds these girls down.

After one event where DHD's model representative had won a kissing contest with a popular stripper, he arrived back at my office with the prize he'd won wrapped in an old Tiffany box, complete with a large satin bow. It contained a latex replica of porn star and model Nikki Tyler's vagina, complete with synthetic blonde pubic hair, and he was giving it to me! My beauty queen mind was regularly blown.

It's this dismemberment part of porn that incites critics and anyone else who can't imagine having sex with a body part of a woman without anything else tied to it. It's not even a blowup doll, the complete "girl." Masturbation is something we all share in common, but the body part thing, well… Many girls love their Rabbit dildos, but that doesn't seem like the same thing. It's different from a plastic vagina replica of your favorite stripper for a man to stick his penis into. The plastic vagina is meant to represent Nikki Tyler, a specific person, which is a lot different than a sex toy.

Body part fetishes are big in the sex industry and it starts with huge boobs. There's a big downside for the girls. It wasn't uncommon during the thirteen months I watched this industry to hear of girls having a breast collapse, due to a faulty implant, though given the extraordinary sizes, we're not talking about your next door neighbor's boob job. When you're a triple-E, a quadruple-F, not to mention a multiple-Z, things can pop, with the ensuing mess nothing to laugh about. More than one girl told me she was saving up to repair her boob collapse, while the oozing material remained in her body. One supersized stripper had to get five thousand dollars together to pay for one of her implants that had started leaking, with the other one in danger of doing the same. It wasn't the doctors; it was the size of the tits, which were as big as shoe boxes on the very largest strippers I saw.

When I got a chance to interview any of the girls, I always attempted to do it without their "managers," often known as their boyfriends, present. But that rarely happened. Male control over some of the girls obviously remained, especially the XXX actresses, even as others broke free of the male dominance of the industry. Stronger women in the adult industry, including strippers, became web pioneers by taking power back from the men who put pornography on the map and did so by cutting out the women who made the industry possible.

One popular stripper had appeared with Howard Stern, Geraldo Rivera and Jerry Springer, and was a featured dancer who reportedly performed in front of more than a hundred thousand men per year. Julie was a seemingly smart young woman, unable to see the signs of what was coming when she'd gotten mixed up with a bad boy, even if everyone else could. When she finally decided it was time to dump him, she got scared of what he might do. She'd discussed how she was going to get away with her friends and family, and everyone who heard about her troubles at DHD pleaded with her to be careful. Julie just kept saying she had it under control, but that she couldn't leave everything she had behind. She kept trying and almost made it out. Almost, but not before he threw her into a wall, badly injuring her kneecap and taking her out of exotic dancing and modeling for quite a while. When she showed up at DHD with a broken leg it was heartbreaking, but not surprising. When a woman is in an abusive relationship, the moment she attempts to leave is the most dangerous. Who can ever forget Nicole Brown Simpson?

More than one stripper had custody troubles, with judges often saying her exotic dancing meant she couldn't be a good mother. Strapped for cash, strippers, also moms, would augment their breasts further to become bigger draws, but it wasn't a great image for the courts. The cycle was dizzying to watch. As Nikita Cash talked about in *Sexy Baby*, it's not easy getting out. At least Cash's dream of having a family panned out. Pictures of her and her husband with their son Rocco on The Daily Beast website and other outlets indicate a better ending than most.

Female porn stars have gruesome adult-film war stories, but that's an industry I know little about, even if their tales are often seen on the web. On The Daily Beast, which was once Tina Brown's baby, I was flipping through stories one day to see what was making headlines, and I came upon, "Blood, Sweat and Sex: My Hard Life in Porn," with the porn actress writing: "My first on-set injury happened with a rapacious male performer who held little regard for my body and slammed into me like a rag doll. It was the first time I'd been torn; the director suggested we use extra lube and keep going."

Feminists, conservatives and most women rail against pornography and legal sex workers, which is understandable, there being many sad stories and bad endings to use against these choices. I've only seen it up close through one soft-core website when it first started, which is nothing compared to what's available today. I'm not immune to the impact of what porn and the sex industry do to objectify women, because that's the nature of pornography. Much of it offers little eroticism, no *Fifty Shades of Grey*, because it's all based on extinguishing hunger quickly. Nothing else matters.

Pornography today amounts to mindless surfing to get hot and get off. It's a way to enjoy other women without cheating, at least as far as the man is concerned. I've interviewed enough women over the years to know many feel differently. Many women judge men looking at pictures of naked women, as well as watching viral video smut or DVDs, as something dirty and wrong, including thinking it's cheating. I honestly don't know what to say to you if you're one of these women. Fantasy isn't cheating. Virtual voyeurism isn't either.

Men like to look at naked women. This isn't news. Some have fetishes, from feet to toes to big and beautiful, to anything you can name. It doesn't mean anything, as far as I can tell, except that it's an outlet, a release valve, a quick and easy way to get off that doesn't require much energy.

Are the women exploited? It's their choice how they make their money, with their ages verified, and children kept out, both of which matter to every legit purveyor in the industry.

Are there porn addicts? Absolutely, just like there are addicts for any number of other vices. I've been there when a man preferred porn over me, and it hurts. It also can destroy a relationship, but that's not the norm, as far as I've been able to learn. A man can watch porn, get turned on, then turn around and make you the receiver of his lust. This is particularly true in long-term relationships, but also when a man hits a low testosterone point in his life.

I'm not sure policing your partner's visual eye candy is a good idea, mainly because it's just not going to work. What do you care if he loves you and you're the one he's sleeping with? Because it's icky to you? We all deserve some privacy, as long as it's recreational, singularly experienced and not obsessive. A woman's ego and pornography can be a combustible mix.

Does the pornification of our culture hurt young men? Absolutely, especially in a vacuum of dialogue, including serious conversations with women about how they feel about it.

It brings us back around to *Sexy Baby* and the "meat curtain." You can't possibly keep up with a man's expectations if he's in a moment of his life where porn has become his visual fetish, as he devours it nightly, masturbating in volume to satiate a hunger that's taken control of him. It usually doesn't last long, especially once he meets a woman that delivers the sex along with the emotional component not found in pornography. There are some who can't be satisfied with a flesh and blood female, but it doesn't mean you have to put up with it. That's an easy choice to make. Walk away.

Sex trafficking and violence against women and children are serious issues, both of which are endemic in the international sex industry, much of which I have covered in my political writing that has evolved well beyond where I started as Relationship Consultant. Child pornography is another scourge of the sex industry, especially beyond the U.S., with real efforts being made, depending on the country, to keep predators away from children. Not only do the child pornographers need to be found, reported and prosecuted, but men traveling to sexual destinations to exploit underage kids trafficked into the sex trade should be identified and prosecuted. The world is a smut sewer for anyone trolling, with untold victims of sex traffickers, pedophiles, young girls and boys being sold, molested and used for horrific crimes. The international laws aren't strong enough to stop this scourge that shows no end across our globe.

What my perch inside the blastoff of the adult industry provided me was access to thousands and thousands of men. Guys who were opinionated and very comfortable giving me their views on all sorts of topics, including sex, relationships and politics. That I was online, writing as a political editor on the biggest soft-core site on the web when the Monica Lewinsky scandal broke was a gift.

What had to be one of the very first online sex surveys, however unscientific, was the one I did asking my readers what the presidential blow job meant: Was oral sex really considered sex, and did the president and his intern have a "sexual relationship"? The verdict on President Bill Clinton, when I asked, came back overwhelmingly in his favor. The guys didn't think a blow job came close to an impeachable offense, even if he lied about it.

I haven't interviewed or met a man who, if confronted, wouldn't first lie about cheating on his wife if he thought he could get away with it and sometimes even if he knows he won't. The shame is just too great to admit it outright. A good example is Representative Anthony Weiner who got caught sexting pictures of his penis. Men want to skirt the consequences and the pain as long as possible, not just for themselves, but from seeing it in the eyes of the women who trust and love them. Few men have an affair wanting to get caught, unless it's payback or a desperation cry. Louisiana's diaper-fetish senator, David Vitter, hardly thought of the ramifications of his actions.

Women responding to my survey on Clinton and Lewinsky agreed with the men over a blow job not being an impeachable offense, even if they were outnumbered a hundred-to-one by male respondents.

I asked which of the following acts constituted the minimum requirement for a sexual relationship to have occurred: penetration, oral sex without penetration, kissing and fondling, heavy petting, cybersex, phone sex, with a final choice of all the above. Forty percent of my "Editor's Desk" readers back in 1998 responded that any of the preceding acts would constitute a sexual relationship; 22% said oral sex without penetration constituted a sexual relationship; 15% said only penetration constituted a sexual relationship.

To this day, it still boggles my mind that right-wingers, led by adulterer Representative Henry Hyde, railroaded President Bill Clinton into impeachment, all because of a consensual affair.

"Men are only as faithful as their opportunities," claims Chris Rock. Well, that very much depends on the man. Chris Rock is hilarious, and the statement certainly made me laugh when I heard it, because I've interviewed plenty of men for whom that's exactly the case. However, there are even more men for whom that statement rings patently false. There are many more good men out there than dogs, including feminist-loving guys who want nothing more than a deeply committed relationship with one woman, including marriage. A punch line isn't rebuttal evidence, though it reveals that you need to make sure of what you've got before you invest in it.

You need to know whether a man thinks a relationship is exclusive or not, and whether he intends on a long-term relationship with you or is just dating you steadily and having a good time. There is nothing wrong with any of these options, but if you want one thing and assume that's where you're headed without confirmation from the guy, big trouble can result. Whether he thinks he's in an exclusive relationship or not is a distinction that makes a huge difference, with actions often getting misinterpreted by the female more often than by the male.

The interview I did for the *New Republic*, with Joe Matthews, titled "The Hugh Hefner of Politics," back in June 2008 explains why I left DHD by quoting my self-published story on my soft-core odyssey:

> ...she tells the story of a "strong and sassy authority-bucking female writer (me) who, while accomplishing a lot for her boss, would ultimately become the sequin-studded g-string that cut just a little too tight up Danni's derriere." Mixing the political with the prurient, she tried to make the website an outlet for those, like her, who believed that porn should be

feminist, or at least socially conscious. But when Marsh couldn't convince Ashe to kill a pictorial of a naked stripper on a school playground ("It was like holding up a welcome sign for pedophile fantasies"), she quit the same day. "There comes a point in time when you have to say: This is wrong," she says. "And you walk out."

That's the long and short of it, with a *What in the hell is wrong with you people?* implied. I just didn't get why Ashe couldn't see how crazy wrong it was to publish the photo shoot showing Tawny Peaks naked on an elementary school playground in broad daylight.

Gloria Steinem went undercover as a *Playboy* bunny trying to get the dirt on Hugh Hefner and how he treated the pretty girls working at his Playboy clubs. She famously wrote about it in a 1963 piece, "I Was a Playboy Bunny," which became the movie *A Bunny's Tale*, starring Kirstie Alley as Steinem. ABC, NBC and other sites, including "Frontline" for PBS, which included an interview with Danni Ashe, have focused on the Internet porn industry many times. People are titillated by an industry they see through body parts, sex acts, women's exposure and men's crudest nature. But there is also a world of erotic equality and sexual desire being mined by other companies trying to expand the nature of what's offered to men, women and couples. Utilized as companion tools for enjoying sex, these shopping marts of wonderful sex toys, creams and tools can make sexual fantasies sing. You can screen out the ugly and find the fun, believe me, and depending on what you want, it can be worth it for you both.

Being at DHD was a grueling stretch for me and has never been easy for me to write about, but the education also became my liberation. I'd discovered the world that I'd been tipped off to as a little girl when I discovered *Candy* in our garage attic. There was a whole world out there I was being protected from, except that I wasn't. Kids are inquisitive and always find a way to root out the truth.

The coverage of who watches pornography has changed a lot, as has the image of the person who enjoys smut. In 2010, a report was released by the U.S. Securities and Exchange Commission Office of Inspector General, and covered by CNN, revealing that during the worst financial crisis since the Great Depression, "Securities and Exchange Commission employees and contractors cruised porn sites and viewed sexually explicit pictures using government computers." The SEC OIG report covered five years, with the employees monitored making between $99,000 and $223,000 per year. One senior attorney at the SEC "downloaded so much pornography to his government computer that he exhausted the available space on the computer hard drive and downloaded pornography to CDs or DVDs that he accumulated in boxes in his office," according to CNN's report.

"Revenge porn" has now popped up, too. It's a porn site where women's pictures are uploaded, without their permission, by former boyfriends or others who want to get revenge. In February 2013, as reported in the *Houston Chronicle*, GoDaddy.com shuttered a site when John S. Morgan, a Beaumont, Texas attorney, filed a class action lawsuit on behalf of two dozen women who had been "cyber-raped" by a website posting explicit photos without the women's permission.

The first state to ban "revenge porn" was New Jersey, with California following in October 2013, making it a misdemeanor. The California legislation was described in the *Guardian* as the act of posting "nude images" of another person "with the intent to cause substantial emotional distress or humiliation." It also requires "personal identifying information" of the other person pictured. New York has now stepped up, the next state to take on "revenge porn." The Cyber Civil Rights Initiative found that 80% of revenge porn victims had taken the photos and videos of themselves, with these images called "selfies." The New York law would include "selfies," making it a crime to distribute these photos or videos as well, with California moving in that direction as well.

When the Steubenville, Ohio rape trial burst onto the national scene in 2013, it did so because of a disgusting Instagram photo and viral video of the "rape crew." Student athletes Trent Mays and Ma'lik Richmond were convicted of brutally raping a sixteen-year-old female, who was drunk and incapacitated, the details horrifying. Was this animal act the result of the pornification of America or the American sports culture that too often protects violent predators? The Penn State child sex abuse scandal also comes to mind, with the men's club protecting Joe Paterno, but also Jerry Sandusky, whose crimes went unreported for years.

The Trojan condoms U.S. Sex Census included one study that was conducted online in March 2011 in ten major cities: New York, Los Angeles, Chicago, Philadelphia, Boston, San Francisco, Dallas/Ft. Worth, Washington, D.C., Atlanta and Houston. It was found that 19% of Americans say they have engaged in sexting, and 19% say they have had "online sex." Ten percent of the people surveyed said they had discussed sex on Facebook or Twitter. The survey also found that 15% of men were likely to discuss their sex lives on Facebook and Twitter, compared with 6% of women.

The same Trojan survey found that 31% of men described themselves as "sexually liberal," while only 16% of women did. A car rated highest as the "most sexually exciting place" to have sex, at 48%, followed by sex in someone else's bed, at 33%. When asked where they'd like to have sex but haven't tried yet, 33% of men wanted to try having sex on a plane. This means standing up and making it quick, which is likely why women didn't choose that response. For women, 26% want to try having sex on the beach or in the sea.

That women like erotica in different ways than men isn't news. What women have always enjoyed is getting off on romantic tales of a hot man swooping in and devouring a woman. This has always been the case, as seen through romance book sales, which have been taken to new heights and exploited in the *Twilight* movie series.

E.L. James' *Fifty Shades of Grey* has proved that women can be ignited in a flame as hot and kinky as anything porn can do for a man. It's not a sophisticated story, and some reviews have taken on the writing itself, which misses the point completely. The scenario that's whipped up between Anastasia and Christian is irresistible to women who have never dined on romance novels, while offering an entry into pleasures unimaginable to many. The simplicity and awkwardness of the storyline mimics our own clumsiness when our heat for a man boils out of control. The sadomasochism and "kinky fuckery" quickly dissolve into love, then marriage, offering legitimacy and a transition into the known for readers. It includes adventure and a dangerous intruder that threatens the lovers' world. Christian and Anastasia even take turns playing hero. The tied-up romantic ending is a bit much, but it gives women a safe landing.

On her site, Ms. James labels her trilogy "provocative romance." Talk about imaginary marketing to hit a mainstream audience. It is a romantic story, but it's also more than provocative, when a man has a "red room of pain," and women willingly walk in and put themselves into his hands, first signing his nondisclosure agreement and contract, which includes all sorts of demands. Yet women of all ages have eaten it up and keep coming back for more, with spinoffs coming in a contagion of e-books as fast as writers can think them up.

Never before has an erotic romance trilogy relied so heavily on condoms in a way that made them sexy, beyond their practical protection imperative. Christian is never found without one. In August 2012, the *Wall Street Journal* blogged about Trojan brand's Vibrations line, which the company Church & Dwight said was doing big business, thanks to *Fifty Shades of Grey*. From the *Journal*: "On second-quarter earnings call, CEO Jim Craigie says he's pleased with distribution and sales of the Trojan brand's Vibrations line of sexual devices, which we believe has been aided by the popularity of the *Fifty Shades of Grey* novel."

The novel is talking about sex and blasting past boundaries in a way that is relatable for a larger number of women. Whether it's "mommy porn," a conversation starter or something for the decency police depends on your frame of mind. Blunt, empowering and feminist conversations about sex are now getting mainstream coverage. At the Sundance Film Festival, sex was selling big in early 2013, starting with *Lovelace*, starring Amanda Seyfried. Joseph Gordon-Levitt's *Don Jon's Addiction* scored the "biggest domestic deal ever for a Sundance title," including P&A (prints and advertising), as reported by *The Hollywood Reporter*. Whether traditional press will be able to digest what's unraveling is a crap shoot, even if online new media is taking advantage of a language and subject matter that older, traditional media cannot.

Amanda Hess of Slate.com put it this way: "It's great that companies like New Sensations, and outlets like CNBC, are helping to legitimize women as viewers of pornography. But female interest in the genre is nothing new, and the collective fantasies of half of the human population can't be served by one narrow niche. 'Porn for women' is not for all women...."

The worst article on the subject landed in late January 2013 from ABC. The blaring headline descended back into the "shame" label: "Romance Porn Lures More Women, With Loss of Shame." It goes like this: "For decades, the female market has eluded pornographers, whose all-male lenses zoomed in on body parts and had little context or dialogue. But today, with cultural and technological shifts that make pornography more acceptable and accessible, Noelle has a fan base that includes women — lots of them."

The popular site Jezebel took ABC's version of events very personally, as did I. Women should care how our sexuality is being talked about when the word *shame* is being hoisted on us in headlines, this time in the second decade of the twenty-first century, no less:

> It's awesome that some women are into Noelle's porn. But blanket statements about what women currently and historically jill off to are getting really old. Calling Noelle's work porn that "lures women without loss of shame" implies that women can only shamelessly enjoy porn that's "romantic" and that all women were too afraid or turned off by other forms of erotica until now. It also insinuates that men are only into more hard-core porn and couldn't possibly enjoy emotional erotica. Filmmakers like Noelle should definitely be profiled, and it's worth noting that there are different types of pornography out there, options that are easier to privately explore, thanks to the Internet, and appeal more to some segments of the population. But why does it always have to be framed as "ladies be watching the porn"?

It's interesting to me that the conversation is being couched as it is today. The adult industry exploited the financial possibilities of the web first, as it did before that with home video. There were pioneers like Candida Royale, to whom I could link when covering the industry, because clicking on her site wouldn't freak my readers out and lead them into a body part extravaganza. Royale calls her product "Erotic Cinema" and highlights female directors in the genre.

This has been around for more than twelve years, likely before E.L. James started thinking about Anastasia Steele or Christian Grey, whom she says were inspired by the *Twilight* movies. Women aren't porn's "new market," as Candida Royale proved years ago, and she was hardly alone.

Slate.com talked with Jacky St. James, a screenwriter, director and publicist for New Sensations, in January 2013. Asked what she felt was the biggest misconception about porn for women, St. James answered: "Women weren't sexualized by *Fifty Shades of Grey*. They've been watching porn and reading erotica for centuries. It's shocking to me that there's suddenly a consciousness that women are sexual. We've always been that way. *Fifty Shades* has allowed us to make it more of a talking point. And that's the only positive thing I can take away from that f—ing book, because I thought it was horrible."

What *Fifty Shades of Grey* has done is put liberated characters and an intensely erotic plot into an era where our major reality is the pornification of modern culture and the reality that labiaplasty is the third most popular cosmetic surgery, because women want to look like porn stars to please men. *Fifty Shades* is the opposite bookend to hard-core pornography.

What remains unknown is whether the millions of women who put the trilogy into the publishing history books, which inspired the Hollywood film version, will come out and see the film. DVD sales and on-demand options should break records. The other aspect is whether the filmmakers will be true to the books. An NC-17-rated *Fifty Shades* is assured if the screen version follows the heart of what E.L. James created.

Will women go for a *9 1/2 Weeks*-type film, the 1986 screen shocker with Kim Basinger and Mickey Rourke, based on Ingeborg Day's memoir, and bring their men out to see it? Possibly, because women put the fantasy of Christian Grey and Anastasia Steele on the cultural map and they remain intensely engaged on every report on the film's development.

The E.L. James dark-and-twisted romance starts with a magic moment, irresistible attraction. It escalates into hot, kinky sex, but what develops in *Fifty Shades* becomes a role reversal, with Anastasia the driver of the relationship and sexual boundaries that include extremely erotic experiences where she's taught the endless bounds of passion and how to say no to what goes too far for her. She also refuses to accept anything less than she deserves, while lapping up the domination, making Christian want to be a better man. It leads to the aggressively dominant male being taught sexual intimacy, something Christian Grey has never experienced and ends up healing his tortured heart. The two find middle erotic ground, add in villains that continually work to derail their happiness for drama and suspense, which is all tied up in a relationship bow that makes for a satisfying end for *Fifty Shades* fans.

However unbelievable, this is what romantic fantasy is all about, turbocharged with kinky extremes. Love, mind-blowing sex, a great marriage and kids, with no money problems, it's the ultimate happily ever after, because Anastasia gets everything she wants, multiple orgasms included.

When Katie Couric had E.L. James on her ABC daytime show *Katie* in early 2013, the former *Today Show* host showed up dressed in a figure-hugging leather dress. The entire show was geared toward the audience that had put *Fifty Shades* on the map. Graphics were handcuffs and erotic intros and exits, with the conversation taking the sex James included in her novel seriously, which is a major milestone, even if it's because she's monetized erotica in a new way.

One of the men invited on *Katie* that day to talk about *Fifty Shades of Grey* was Craig Carton, who'd recently featured the topic on his morning talk-radio sports show on WFAN. Carton had a sense of humor about the James book, but delivered the truth to men who cared to hear it: "It literally proves that the average guy is either not good in bed or not satisfying his woman to the point where she could be satisfied," Carton said to Couric. He's exactly right, too. Women want more from their men in bed, and for the man who delivers, the reward will be worth it.

5

Being Jackie, Being Hillary

How'd we get here? The state of women's angst about dating and relationships seems to be at a high again. We've been hit by a boomerang of back-to-the-past nostalgia, brought on by amnesia, or invigorated sentimentality for something that won't work any better than it did the first time around.

The most revolutionary arrival to the conversation is Facebook COO Sheryl Sandberg's book *Lean In*, which demands that women ask men to handle fifty percent of the domestic duties in addition to their careers, just as most women do, versus women opting out of leadership roles, because expecting a man to do as much at home as a woman is still foreign territory in American culture.

We've been here before — that moment where progress stops and retro becomes fashionable again. We're on the cusp of equality in our relationships but can't quite tip the balance, because corporations, government and our culture in general won't do their part unless women convince men to do theirs. When did the amnesia begin to set in, despite the obvious clues that the backward boomerang is a circular spiral downward?

Betty Friedan's *The Feminine Mystique* was published in 1963, at the time when Jacqueline Kennedy became America's representation of womanhood. It was a cultural and political collision, as Mrs. Kennedy's perfect image blasted across television sets at the moment when the stitches of the traditional American family quilt were fraying. The embodiment of female perfection, Jacqueline Bouvier Kennedy was Madison Avenue's picturesque personification of a woman who couldn't be happier than living her life through her husband and children. Uninterested in the education and talents she had dropped like a hot rock when she married the man who, along with her children, would become the center of her universe. What woman could hope for more?

The Kennedys became American royalty, Jackie Kennedy the queen personifying what it meant to be a woman at the time. Jackie married Jack in 1953, when Alfred Kinsey's *Sexual Behavior in the Human Female* landed like a thud. The timing was epic. It was the height of what became an era where it was "unquestioned gospel that women could identify with *nothing* beyond home," as Friedan wrote, in the Introduction to the tenth anniversary edition of her book, emphasis hers. After World War II, America would present to women a challenge that would be met by women's magazines redefining what roles were good for women now that the boys were back. Jackie Kennedy exemplified this perfectly.

As Michael Beschloss writes in the introduction to *Jacqueline Kennedy: Historic Conversations on Life With John F. Kennedy*, Mrs. Kennedy believed at the time that "the old-fashioned style of marriage is 'the best'" and that "women should stay out of politics because they are too 'emotional.'" In these conversations with Arthur M. Schlesinger, Jr., Jacqueline Kennedy describes her first social secretary Letitia Baldrige as "sort of a feminist" and "so different from me." They were indeed different, but the private Jacqueline Kennedy has been revealed in subsequent books to be quite a different person than what she wanted America to think she was when she was first lady.

According to Sally Bedell Smith in her book *Grace and Power*, Jacqueline Kennedy's beauty regimen included "sprinkling cologne on her hairbrush ('fifty to one hundred strokes... every night')," and that was just for starters. Letitia Baldrige is quoted saying Mrs. Kennedy watched her weight obsessively, "with the rigor of a diamond merchant counting his carats," with the stress and pressure of female perfection always present. Jackie Kennedy was "addicted" to L&M cigarettes but hid her habit from the world, including those in the Kennedy circle. That she ditched first lady responsibilities is rarely covered, but she knew there was always someone else in the Kennedy entourage to sub for her. If not, Lady Bird Johnson could always step in. All the American people saw was the perfect first lady, a woman to be emulated, never the stomach-churning reality of a woman playing a role that seemed superhuman.

While America adored the first couple, and women wanted to be Jacqueline Kennedy, the Kennedy marriage behind the scenes was an emotional blender, a sham even, unless you lived inside the jet set. John F. Kennedy was a legendary womanizer and cocksman, which everyone in their orbit, including the media, knew. It was not only accepted behavior in men of this era, but the wives were expected to look the other way. The media sheltered the truth about John F. Kennedy's philandering, because men will be men, after all, and what's an affair, anyway? "But we didn't know that there were that many!" Robert McNamara exclaimed in an interview, quoted in Bedell Smith's book.

The role of the American man after WWII was all-powerful conqueror of the land he surveyed. The country was shifting, driven by the explosion of the easy suburban lifestyle.

Married women took comfort in their appliance-filled homes, which were intended to make for easier and fuller lives for women, who had only one job. Making her home a perfect haven for the returning warrior, or if your husband had been in the factories, you made way for his shift in professions.

Underneath all of this was what Friedan labeled the "feminine mystique," the foreshadowing of an American society that was about to come unglued, because nobody realized that what was being seen on the surface came with percolating discontent at its roots. Women weren't seen as individuals, but instead were objects, with their only acceptable role being to please their husbands on the way to having babies. By *being* female a woman was, through her biology, destined not to *do* anything, a boiled down version of what Friedan saw.

There were some professional women, with Friedan herself a perfect example. She worked in the *Mad Men* world depicted in the popular AMC series, but also came to blame herself for her part in creating the happily ensconced, picture-perfect female, completely content with a domestic bliss storyline.

In 2012, the book *Mad Women* was published. The author is former advertising executive Jane Maas, who was billed as a "real-life Peggy Olson," as Salon's Emma Mustich wrote in her February 2012 interview. Ms. Maas talked about her existence as a professional woman in advertising in the mid-'60s: "There were very few working mothers at Ogilvy, because, as I wrote in the book, it just simply was not done in the '60s to work full-time if you had children under the age of twelve or so. Other women looked down on you and said, 'What do you do if they're sick?' That was the first question you were asked. And men thought you must be married to a bum, otherwise why were you there working?"

Maas received the Most Obnoxious Commercial of the Year Depicting Women award twice from the National Organization for Women. Salon's Mustich asked her if she was conflicted about creating the ads that won? Maas' response was blunt: "No, I wasn't conflicted. Not a whit. One of the products was Dove-for-Dishes — Dove dishwashing liquid. The whole premise of Dove-for-Dishes is that it kept a woman's hands soft and smooth, even if she had to do a lot of dishes. The whole object there, the whole strategy behind the product, was that it was 'made for a woman's hands.' And the National Organization for Women berated me that I didn't have men doing the dishes. Well, that never crossed my mind...."

All these years later, too often it still doesn't cross the minds of women *or* men, which partly explains why reactions to Sheryl Sandberg's book have been electric on all sides.

Maas goes on to talk about the 7 A.M. to 9 P.M. working juggernaut that was Madison Avenue advertising in the mid-'60s, with husbands spending little time with their wives and ending up getting "lonely." From Maas: "I think part of it was just pure sex, and part of it was that they were kind of lonely. Here were all these young women — many of them single — working as secretaries but wanting very much to get professional jobs, and they'd be happy to sit down and talk about the brands that these guys were working on, and the future of the agency, and what was going on in the office. And they were also sexually available...."

Fast forward to the second decade in the twenty-first century, and the equivalent you have is wives with their own careers and professional lives that are often demanding. Add to that the need for two incomes in today's competitive economy, and you've got a lot more stress on relationships. As we learned through the reckoning of the feminine mystique, modern women enjoy having a vibrant home life but also being engaged in the world. It makes modern relationships more challenging, and we haven't even gotten to the longevity aspect, with people living longer. Mates people take in their twenties or thirties, by the time fifty-something rolls around, have already seen a full marriage by twentieth-century standards.

The Kennedy marriage was described through interviews in Bedell Smith's book as nomadic and separate. John F. Kennedy's sexual promiscuity wasn't really about sex, which these things rarely are, but more about "having his own secret life." Bedell

Smith writes that JFK's "profound disloyalty defined their marriage."

What also defined their marriage were the times in which they lived. Jacqueline Kennedy was forced to carry a heavy weight, living her "own secret life" behind the scenes at a time when American culture was telling women they had to live a certain way.

Given what was expected of her, but also the outsize role she played in American life as the wife of the fabulously handsome and glamorous president, who himself was seen as the new light of the western world, is it any wonder Mrs. Kennedy was addicted to cigarettes or that she obsessed about her weight and ducked out of first lady duties whenever she could? It drove Letitia Baldridge nuts enough to want to quit. There was much, much more to Mrs. Kennedy, which was seen through her historic hand in the restoration of the White House, as well as making Washington, D.C. the cultural and entertainment center of the universe, where everyone from Los Angeles to New York to London and beyond, wanted to be seen. However, these talents were also feminine in nature. Quite different was her journalism training, which she would embrace later in her life, long after the JFK era, once her children were grown and she became a successful editor in her own right.

But being an editor when she was young wasn't an option, because of who she was, where she came from, and her era. These constrictions grew even tighter when she met and married Jack Kennedy, then became first lady. Not only did she play the role to perfection, but as a PR machine, nobody was better. After JFK was assassinated, her last interview on record was mind-blowing. "Jack so obviously demanded from a woman — a relationship between a man and a woman where a man would be the leader and a woman would be his wife and look up to him as a man," Mrs. Kennedy said to Arthur Schlesinger. The historian had said to Bedell Smith that Jacqueline Kennedy had "an almost European view" about her husband's disloyalty. Jackie Kennedy called her marriage "rather terribly Victorian or Asiatic." Mrs. Kennedy also said, "I think women should never be in politics. We're just not suited to it." All the while, she wove the image of her slain husband so tightly around the myth of Camelot that it has managed not to unravel throughout the ravages of history.

She also talked about when "violently liberal women in politics" preferred Adlai Stevenson over her husband, it was because they "were afraid of sex." Eleanor Roosevelt was a dedicated Adlai Stevenson supporter and uninterested in Kennedy's 1960 campaign until he reportedly pushed his case to her personally. So even though Mrs. Kennedy's words came after Mrs. Roosevelt's passing, they carry a hint of innuendo. When talking about Madame Nhu, the South Vietnamese first lady, and former congresswoman Clare Boothe Luce, Jacqueline Kennedy whispered to Schlesinger, "I wouldn't be surprised if they were lesbians." The other implication of Mrs. Kennedy's statements was that women interested in power obviously couldn't also be interested in men. That was in 1964, with Jacqueline Kennedy still playing her role, validating that power is masculine.

In late October 2013, *The Letters of Arthur Schlesinger* was published, revealing new insights from the famed historian through his private letters, never before seen. In a letter to Tina Brown, dated 8 July 1999, Schlesinger recalls having lunch with Jacqueline Kennedy in 1993. The topic of Hillary Clinton came up, whom Schlesinger had not met, though he knew her husband. He said to Mrs. Kennedy, "I gather that she is a very intelligent young woman, but I imagine that she is awfully earnest and humorless, a real blue stocking." Jacqueline Kennedy replied, "I saw something of Hillary during the campaign last year, and she is a delight, filled with fun and irony. You will have a jolly time."

When you contrast Mrs. Kennedy to Eleanor Roosevelt, it reveals the twentieth-century trap women fell into after World War II. Mrs. Roosevelt was as contro-versial as Jacqueline Bouvier Kennedy was traditionally conventional, at least in her public persona.

In 1933, when Franklin Delano Roosevelt was inaugurated, Eleanor revolutionized what it meant to be first lady. She had a newspaper column titled "My Day," which sixty years later would inspire Hillary Clinton to do the same. Mrs. Roosevelt held press conferences and was very involved in political issues of her own. Eleanor Roosevelt would be the first to address a convention. According to "legend," reported by Elizabeth Deane of WGBH Boston, Mrs. Roosevelt squeezed Democratic presidential nominee John F. Kennedy into creating what would become the President's Commission on the Status of Women in exchange for dropping her resistance to campaigning for him in 1960. She is considered the very first person, a public official in her own right as first lady, to use what we know as mass media to publicize the issues she was championing. She and her husband also had six children, even though Eleanor Roosevelt admitted, "I do not think that I am a natural-born mother," which came out in Hazel Rowley's book, *Franklin and Eleanor: An Extraordinary Marriage*. Rowley describes their partnership as "one of the most interesting and radical marriages in history."

It was radical, indeed, because Franklin and Eleanor Roosevelt "gave each other space" to have relationships outside their marriage. Rowley's book takes us inside the relationship, which NPR covered when it was published. It was an open marriage, once Franklin had his affair with Lucy Mercer, who had been Eleanor's secretary. He worked to persuade Eleanor to stay, promising to end the entanglement, but also that they would sleep in separate beds, because Eleanor had her pride and had no intention of being made a fool. However, Franklin couldn't stay away from his mistress, and the relationship reportedly lasted all of his life.

Eleanor's romantic life thrived and included men, as well as Lorena Hickok, a lesbian, beginning around the time of FDR's first inaugural. It was obviously the stuff of great gossip, to which Eleanor Roosevelt wrote to "Hick," from Rowley's book: "And so you think they gossip about us... I am always so much more optimistic than you are. I suppose because I care so little about what 'they' say."

It's positively unfathomable today to think of having a first lady being in love with other men and having her own sexual life that would evolve into a lesbian romantic life — no matter what her husband was allowed to do. People in the throes of living their lives at the pinnacle of power are now forced to navigate personal complications and human proclivities in a different manner. Back in the Roosevelts' day, independence was possible. In our mass media environment it is not, especially since our puritanical society remains in a permanent pubescent state.

There were suspicions about President Eisenhower and his driver Kay Summersby. Historian Gil Troy, writing in the *Washington Post* in 1998 about the rumors, brought up something I find far more revealing than any affair gossip: "The willing-ness to turn the uncertainties about Eisenhower and Summersby into fact says more about us than about him, and suggests that when presidents fail to act according to a higher standard, they can indeed damage the nation's moral fabric." That our nation's moral fabric is still seen to revolve around the politics of sex instead of the morality of American policy is revealing.

Politicians are often complicit in their fantasy portrayals that the media foist on us. John F. Kennedy himself worked hard to create the 1950s image of marriage by hiring Richard Avedon to capture them in his photo book, *The Kennedys: Portrait of a Family*. The photo session happened on January 3, 1961 and was written about in *Vanity Fair* in 2007. The story "As Camelot Began..." was written by Kennedy historian Robert Dallek, whose book on John F. Kennedy, *An Unfinished Life*, is arguably the most revealing in history, especially on the seriousness of JFK's medical condition and the medicine cabinet filled with drugs he took to keep himself alive and highly functioning. A total of seventeen Avedon photographs appeared in the February 1962 issues of *Harper's Bazaar* and *Look*, though many more were taken. Richard Avedon told *Newsweek* after the photos were published, "When I took

Caroline's picture with her father, he was dictating memos to his secretary. When I'd ask him to look around, he'd stop dictating. But the moment I finished, he'd start in where he left off."

Ronald Wilson Reagan's image was pure Hollywood myth, a casting director's dream, along with his marriage to Nancy Reagan, which was a great love affair. He had none of the grit revealed through Kennedy's World War II heroism, which led to JFK's great skepticism about war and the upper echelon military brass. The steel exhibited through Reagan's physical persona was manufactured marketing to make him the man he was to the public. The perfect actor was cast as president, which worked. Few people today discuss the generation of men lost to AIDS through Reagan's indifference, his multiple, even historic, tax hikes, or his crimes during Iran-Contra, which are part of history. Reagan built his pitch and his fan base by traveling the country as a front man for General Electric, honing his political patter one slick stump speech at a time, that is, until his bosses got wind and fired him. It's impossible to imagine John F. Kennedy as a G.E. spokesman, but then, imagining J.F.K. as the faithful husband, as Ronnie was to Nancy, is an equally ridiculous exercise.

JFK's legacy includes the established craft of a politician working the media and concocting a public persona based on what he wanted the American people to believe, which hid many secrets. It's what encourages voters to have a cult-like fascination with our presidents, which makes their celebrity more important than anything else. Considering John F. Kennedy was first a prince-in-waiting, it's very likely that looking at Jacqueline Lee Bouvier in the early 1950s, what he saw was a woman with the breeding and image of the Perfect America Wife.

Of course, she was also cultured, beautiful and fascinating. Ruthless, too, especially when it came to JFK's image after his death. The widowed Mrs. Kennedy was not only shrewdly focused on her husband's legacy, but brutal when comparing him to his older brother Joe Kennedy Jr., who was being groomed before JFK to run for president but was killed in WWII. In the 1964 interviews with Mrs. Kennedy, Arthur M. Schlesinger Jr. asked whether the stories were true that Joseph P. Kennedy, the family patriarch, "expected Joe to be the great political figure of the family." Mrs. Kennedy's answer is revealing: "I've got a feeling, from what I think of Joe and everything, that he would have been so unimaginative, compared to Jack. He would never have — I think he probably would have gotten to be senator, and not much higher. I don't know if that's prejudiced, but I don't think he had any of the sort of imagination that Jack did."

This wasn't just a widow talking, though one can only imagine the crushing loss she felt. Mrs. Kennedy knew that in these interviews, which would become the last she'd speak of him or their life together, she was establishing John F. Kennedy's legacy. Her assessment of Jack's older brother was biting, while elevating her slain president husband. This all came from an educated journalist who knew what she was doing. She also had to learn from watching Jack.

This was a woman who had written since high school and in 1951 had entered a *Vogue* Prix de Paris contest, which required, according to a FirstLadies.org biography, "an original theme for an entire issue, illustrations, articles, layout and design, an advertising campaign that could be tied into the issue's content." Out of 1280 entries, she'd won, but her mother wouldn't let her leave the country or accept the other part of the prize, which was becoming a junior editor for *Vogue*. Subsequently, before marrying JFK, she also worked for the *Washington Times-Herald* as its Inquiring Camera Girl, earning $42.50 per week, interviewing local citizens. Her first subject was Pat Nixon, with Richard M. Nixon eventually also becoming a subject, as did her future husband, John F. Kennedy. The former first lady knew how to craft a story and likely also knew her audience would be fully trusting of the mythology she was crafting, which purposefully elevated Jack above all others.

Jack and Jackie became who they were because their glamour played so well in the television era. The style and radiant hope they emitted through the television screen further attached people to the couple. Meanwhile, the media world had been invested in the image of the perfect wife and husband, so once Jack and Jackie were crowned America's answer to royalty, to say it was an inconvenience that Betty Friedan was blowing a whistle on all that Jacqueline Kennedy embodied is an understatement.

The Kennedy bubble allowed First Lady Jacqueline Kennedy the privilege of crafting her image through activities that kept her well away from politics, which was odd considering it was the early 1960s, when American culture was shifting underneath them. Mrs. Kennedy became the first lady of the White House to have a press secretary. It was an era when politicians were still granted privacy, which allowed her also to escape the humiliation and scandal that would have embroiled the Kennedy legacy and made the creation of the Camelot myth impossible. It's likely one reason she never spoke on the record again after her taped conversations with historian Arthur Schlesinger, Jr., Mrs. Kennedy Onassis had no intention of answering questions that would open and allow a rewrite on the Camelot book she'd closed.

Jacqueline Kennedy was not oblivious to her reality, which is why she fled the White House whenever she could. She knew about all of her husband's extramarital escapades and at times made sure people knew she wasn't stupid. When talking with a reporter from *Paris Match* during a tour of the White House, Mrs. Kennedy shifted into French and said, "This is the girl who supposedly is sleeping with my husband." She was referring to one of the infamous Fiddle and Faddle girls, who played sex games with the president on the White House grounds on innumerable occasions.

Jacqueline lived with her husband's womanizing and compartmentalized it to make his presidency what it remains today. Mrs. Kennedy's active role constructs the most impossibly tortured picture of a marriage you can get, at the start of the sexual revolution. That it manifested in an era when American culture, the U.S. media and JFK himself were complicit in the fantasy, is part of the spellbinding story of these two complicated creatures who draw us in to their epic historical drama every time the era is revisited.

What Arthur Schlesinger described as "reciprocal forbearance" read much more like the misogyny that typified the age of the feminine mystique. Jacqueline Kennedy played out the role for women across America so they could see what they were supposed to be doing. But just like Mrs. Kennedy, with her injections that were the equivalent of speed, many women who came of marrying age in the era of the 1950s and 1960s were masquerading as happy on the outside, while doing what was ex-pected and taking pills to get through the day, because American society had written a script that didn't come with choices.

The Kennedys miniseries, which was picked up by Reelz because Kennedy loyal-ists — Democrats and others — pitched a fit and got the History Channel to dump it, went into detail about Jackie's indulgence of amphetamine-laced shots from John F. Kennedy's physician, Dr. Max Jacobson. Jace Lacob, who covered the miniseries for The Daily Beast, wrote that even the whitewashing of *The Kennedys* went through its own scrubbing. One of the lines Lacob reports was cut from the miniseries is John F. Kennedy saying, "I love lobster, but not every night. If I don't have some strange ass every couple of days, I get migraines." It doesn't comport with the public image of JFK's eloquence, but why should we care if we learn something about the man? It doesn't make his leadership during the Cuban Missile Crisis any less impressive. A line given to Jackie in the original screenplay, according to Lacob, painted a picture of the much-admired first lady that nobody wants known, beginning with the fact that she wanted to divorce Jack due to his philandering. Joseph P. Kennedy, Sr., offers to pay her a million dollars, which makes it into the miniseries *The Kennedys*, but what was scrubbed was Mrs. Kennedy's worry about getting an STD, to which Joe Sr. replies that if it happens, she can "name her price."

Can't have the wife of a legendary president revealing herself as someone who knew what was going on and had no intention of risking her quality of life for a man whose obsession with mortality could take her with him. People like to bubble-wrap their heroes.

Just like other American women of the time, Jacqueline Kennedy wasn't satisfied sexually either. "He just goes too fast and falls asleep," she's quoted by Bedell Smith as saying. If only we could ask Judith Exner, who was bedding both mobster Sam Giancana and Kennedy, even if the latter couldn't remember the names of many of the women he slept with.

When Exner died, not even the venerable *New York Times* could bear to tell it like it actually was and what Exner asserted with enough details to prove she was telling the truth. It resulted in the *Times* having to print an Editors' Note apology, because they'd doubted Exner's story and omitted what had been proven by the FBI:

> September 30, 1999, Thursday — An obituary on Monday reported the death of Judith Campbell Exner. It quoted assertions she had made over the years that she had had an affair with John F. Kennedy before and after he was elected President. The article reported that aides of President Kennedy's, including Dave Powers, denied the affair. But it should also have reflected what is now the view of a number of respected historians and authors that the affair did in fact take place. The evidence cited by various authorities in recent years has included White House phone logs and memos from J. Edgar Hoover.

Thirty-five years after John F. Kennedy's death, what once was the paper of record in America still has trouble reporting the facts in a woman's obituary, because she's talking about an affair she had with President Kennedy. There were scores of such women, but few held a position with Kennedy equal to that of Exner, who got the last word, backed by J. Edgar Hoover no less, something that had to make the tortured FBI megalomaniac gleeful from beyond.

The year before *The Feminine Mystique* was published, Mimi Alford was a nineteen-year-old virgin intern when she claims to have had an affair with President John F. Kennedy. She recounts the details in *Once Upon a Secret: My Affair With President John F. Kennedy and Its Aftermath*. She even serviced JFK's friends. Writing about the book for *The Atlantic*, Caitlin Flanagan describes Mimi's relationship with Kennedy this way: "The president schooled Mimi in all the skills a mistress must know, from performing fellatio to making scrambled eggs."

It wasn't until 1975, after Jacqueline Kennedy Onassis had raised her children and her second husband had died, that she returned to New York City and began her career as a consulting editor. As *Vanity Fair* reported in an excerpt from Greg Lawrence's book, *Jackie as Editor: The Literary Life of Jacqueline Kennedy Onassis*, she'd admitted to one of her friends, "I have always lived through men. Now I realize I can't do that anymore." Of course she could; after all, she was Jacqueline Kennedy Onassis, who could do anything she wanted. However, she chose something else. As the story goes, Letitia Baldridge suggested she talk to her publisher at Viking, Tommy Guinzburg, whom she'd know for twenty years.

The job at Viking turned into drama, when a book with a plot line about an assassination of the America president was published and Jackie got caught between the Kennedy family and Guinzburg. Assuming she'd been involved in the publishing of the book, a *New York Times* review called the book "trash," and said, "anybody associated with its publication should be ashamed of herself." Jackie resigned through her social secretary, which was a statement in itself about the rarified world of Mrs. Kennedy Onassis. Not long afterward, she landed at Doubleday, where she would shepherd Michael Jackson's memoir *Moonwalk* to print, which would take four agonizing and drama-filled years.

"If you produce one book, you will have done something wonderful in your life," Jacqueline Kennedy Onassis once said, and if that applies to anyone, it does to her. She also stated that it "helped me to be taken seriously as an editor, for my own abilities."

Jacqueline Lee Bouvier Kennedy was an educated woman at a time when "to-getherness" was being sold to the American female, with pictures of the perfect marriage and blissful homemaking life filling the media; when women weren't seen fit to have any thought but marriage and home life, which wasn't making them happy. The myth of feminine mystique was that this was all women required. Nothing outside the home could possibly make her a real woman. If she dared show interest in the world, the next thing that would happen is she'd lose her man to a woman who was content with her femininity. Again, the secret was to just *be*.

I've studied and researched John F. Kennedy, written and produced a one-woman show about him that includes Jacqueline Kennedy, too, so I know the personal flaws of the man made public. Regardless of his human weaknesses, Kennedy earned his enduring image and public importance through his words and intentions, much of which Lyndon Johnson made manifest. The JFK mythology is sewn into our history, which Jacqueline Kennedy played the instrumental role in creating, even knowing that the truth never matched the myth. It was JFK's vision of America and what we can help make the world — not his personal, sexual compulsions — which crystallized what our country is supposed to stand for in the modern era.

The gorgeous, sophisticated and educated Jacqueline Bouvier Kennedy and the raised-for-greatness war hero John F. Kennedy had to happen in the era of the feminine mystique. It's not a coincidence. They epitomized the model male and female of the moment, when WWII was shifting our culture and re-crafting the American woman into a happy homemaker with all of the appliances she needs to be the perfect wife and mother. While magazines screamed what women should be, Jackie's American hero husband seduced the world. The politics of sex embraced Jack and Jackie, who exuded desire, romance, sex and power, and became the embodied dream of the perfect American marriage.

According to Betty Friedan's research, by the end of the 1950s "the average marriage age of women in America dropped to twenty, and was still dropping, into the teens."

In the early 1960s the Kennedys were dreamily ensconced in the White House at the same time Friedan was interviewing women who were so disconsolate that they were seeking out doctors for "the problem that has no name." That was Friedan's label; doctors were naming it "the housewife's syndrome," aka "occupation: housewife." It plagued women who supposedly had everything, but had "blocks," as Friedan reported it, to "fulfillment as a wife and mother."

In June 1960, a *New York Times* story reported, "The road from Freud to Frigidaire, from Sophocles to Spock, has turned out to be a bumpy one." That same year, a *Time* cover blared the opposite in, "The Suburban Wife, an American Phenomenon." Inside, the story characterized these women as, "Having too good a time… to believe that they should be unhappy." *Newsweek*, in March 1960, was more nuanced: "She is dissatisfied with a lot that women of other lands can only dream of." On the article went, quoting Freud's famous dictum, "Anatomy is destiny," while critiquing a woman's discontent just years before Betty Friedan would document it, and going beyond what Kinsey would say, that women are sexual, to proving that women are also individuals with brains and thoughts and cares about life outside the home and motherhood.

Redbook weighed in, which Friedan cited, too: "Few women would want to thumb their noses at husbands, children and community and go off on their own. Those who do may be talented individuals, but they rarely are successful women." *Look* reported that the "more than twenty-one million American women who are single, widowed, or divorced do not cease even after fifty their frenzied, desperate search for a man."

It was rarely digested that the people assigning and editing these articles were men. Today, according to a study by the women's literary organization VIDA that looks at the publication trends by gender, the amount of men who get bylines, have their books reviewed, or are assigned essays, towers over the number of women getting the same opportunities. Whether you're talking about the *Atlantic*, the *New York Times Book Review*, the *New Yorker*, the *Times Literary Supplement*, or other publications, with the notable exception of the *Paris Review*, men have more literary light shone on their work than women. Slate.com covering the VIDA study in February 2011, wrote, "VIDA's study raises questions about how seriously women writers are taken and how viable it is for them to make a living at writing." By March 2013, VIDA revealed it wasn't much better.

Into this mix, throw in the most famous actress in the world, Marilyn Monroe, whose love affair with John F. Kennedy made the myth of the man even stronger. Hers was the ultimate tale of the sexual woman about to turn into parable.

Written about in innumerable books, the affair between Kennedy and Monroe played out at the Hollywood home of Patricia and Peter Lawford, who were JFK's sister and brother-in-law. JFK was Mr. America, Marilyn Monroe the goddess he'd earned. Their union came at the beginning of the decade that would represent a sexual explosion, as our country began convulsing.

Legendary investigative journalist Seymour Hersh, in his book *The Dark Side of Camelot*, reveals a fascinating detail that has gotten lost over the years. After Monroe's death, the head of the medical legal section of the Los Angeles district attorney's office, John Miner, was given special confidential access to a psychiatric "stream-of-consciousness tape recording" of Monroe, which Hersh reports in the book was recommended by her psychoanalyst, Dr. Ralph Greenson. Miner's transcript of Monroe's tape was made available to Hersh for publication in his book, after Greenson's family gave their permission.

Marilyn Monroe's words reveal the swoon of a woman who could have any man she wanted, but besides being the president, the power John F. Kennedy seemed to exude intoxicated the legendary movie star and actress, wholly taking her into his spell. Monroe was bewitched well beyond JFK's sexual hold on her. From Hersh's book, the transcript of what she said to Dr. Greenson:

> Marilyn Monroe is a soldier. Her commander-in-chief is the greatest and most powerful man in the world. The first duty of a soldier is to obey her commander-in-chief. He says do this, you do it. This man is going to change our country. No child will go hungry, no person will sleep in the

street and get his meals from garbage cans. People who can't afford it will get good medical care. Industrial products will be the best in the world. No, I'm not talking utopia — that's an illusion. But he will transform America today like Franklin Delano Roosevelt did in the thirties. I tell you, Doctor, when he has finished his achievements he will take his place with Washington, Jefferson, Lincoln, Franklin Roosevelt as one of our greatest presidents....

Included in the footnotes of Hersh's book is a quote from Hugh Sidey, who was part of the White House press pool the night of the now-infamous "Happy Birthday, Mr. President" performance by Marilyn Monroe at Madison Square Garden. Twentieth Century Fox had forbade Monroe to go to New York, because she'd already caused so much trouble during the filming of *Something's Got to Give*. Robert F. Kennedy reportedly called the studio and berated a board member for refusing to give permission, even calling him names, but the studio wouldn't budge. Being JFK's "soldier," Marilyn went anyway, and the birthday boy was evidently as overwhelmed as everyone else, according to eyewitness Hugh Sidey. "It was quite a sight to behold, and if I ever saw an appreciation of feminine beauty in the eyes of a man, it was in John F. Kennedy's eyes at that moment," Sidey told Seymour Hersh.

Baseball great Joe DiMaggio, once married to Monroe, was intoxicated by her his entire life. When she died, DiMaggio commissioned Parisian Florist in Los Angeles to deliver flowers to Ms. Monroe's crypt at Westwood Village Memorial Park Cemetery three times per week, which continued for decades. Buying flowers myself from Parisian Florist back in the 1990s, I met the owners and had them verify the stories that have now become legend.

Marilyn Monroe's *being* proved the power women can have over men, and the lengths we will go to use it, even in the midst of our own struggles to be recognized for our individuality beyond our sex. To separate the two is not only futile but stupid. The problem arises when we're not allowed to *do* that which goes beyond being a woman, to get taken seriously for our talents. Any feminist ideal that obliterates one for the other is doomed. We cannot do it and survive whole, because we are most vital in that collision.

Romantic tales of overwhelming lust and taboo sexual collision between a powerful man and a beautifully seductive woman have been captivating us for centuries. The casting of a dashing bad-boy with overwhelming stature or power over the world in which he lives is the "ultimate aphrodisiac," to quote Henry Kissinger. It's indeed about power. Charm and the ability to make a woman feel like she's the most wanted woman in the world at any given moment is part of the potion. The life-altering and sometimes life-shattering repercussions of entangling yourself with a man of this description can be irresistible. The narrative is too seductive, the adrenaline-pumping highs rationalized as worth it, regardless of the bone-crushing lows.

Mere mortals are not immune either, though we have much less lofty or name-worthy romances, even if the emotional roller coaster performs the same type of adrenaline jolt.

Barron was decades older than I, married, wealthy and bored. It was a high-wire act in one respect. He was a well known Wall Street mogul who was recognized wherever we went, the restaurants from Los Angeles to Las Vegas to New York, including the floor of the New York Stock Exchange, which he took me on one day before we had lunch in SoHo. He introduced me to outrageous players, including the infamous Bob Guccione, whose home we attended one night for a lavish party and an exhibition of his legendary art collection. Guccione greeted us with his dogs, his ever-faithful companions. Barron and his wife no longer had a sexual relationship in a very long marriage that was comfortable and cold. We were very discreet. The fun lasted for years.

This was exactly what I wanted at the time and the first and last such relationship I ever had. I admit to having flirtations with many a married man, though I never acted on any other, even if I could have many times. His children were grown and long gone, something that mattered to me. I may have been scandalously adventurous, but I had no intention of ruining anyone else's life in the process of having fun, which is the only thing I wanted. I didn't want his money, and I certainly didn't want to take him away from his wife, whom we mutually agreed to never discuss. When we were together, it was just us. I always kept my eyes open for other interesting men. I was single.

Nothing did my Relationship Consultant image more good than getting three-foot tall, massively exotic floral arrangements delivered to my *LA Weekly* office. Not to ruin your picture of the whole thing, but my "office" was actually a stolen area on the Classified Advertising floor that I partitioned off from everyone else so I could have intimately private conversations with women placing personal ads, which always involved salacious banter.

Between floral arrangements there were also the limousine pickups late on Thursday, when I'd be whisked off to LAX for weekend trips to Las Vegas. There we'd spend weekends eating lobster and quail eggs, drinking champagne, seeing shows, playing craps and having sex. If you're picturing Sharon Stone in *Casino*, standing next to a toad of a man who's rolling dice at the craps table, that couldn't be further from the truth. We simply were having the best time and enjoying each other's company to the maximum extent, with absolutely no strings attached. The sex wasn't bad either, nor were the dinners with his old Vegas pals, which included some of the original Strip landowners made wealthy when casinos moved in. They told the most outlandish tales.

Most relationships with married men end, which was what I'd always expected. For us it began the night he and I met for dinner and he started on this soliloquy about what it would be like being his wife and what he'd expect of me. I was sure my heart stopped for just a split second; my brain definitely froze, paralyzed, in absolute shock. This was not what I wanted, and there was no way it was going to happen. I just stared at him as he laid it all out, not really looking at me at all. He was obviously going through his own thing, admitting to himself out loud that this is what he was now contemplating. At some point, I got up to pee and try to breathe again, and when I returned we finished the bottle of wine and dinner, then left. Things quickly unraveled after that, even if it didn't really end for months and months. I just got busier and busier. We quit traveling, then it all just dwindled... out.

I guess everyone's got to try things like this or maybe fantasize about them, but the truth is, the complications are really uncontrollably inconvenient. I know this may sound terribly tedious, but anyone getting involved with a married person with children at home deserves to have his or her head examined. There are all sorts of open marriages that exist today, even if they're not declared. Once was more than enough for me. I got lucky, though, because we had a blast and didn't hurt anyone but ourselves, because you can't have a long-term fun- and fuck-buddy without mourning the am- putation of the attachment, even if you're the one who whacks it off.

Living in Los Angeles, there were many rich men to enjoy. It's a miracle I even lived through the 1980s. On one of the most bizarre nights, among many spent partying, a millionaire spied me in an upscale bar with my girlfriends, and started sending me champagne. It ended with me in his Jaguar that night, though nothing happened, because I was his twenty-four-hour project. When he dropped me at home, much to my chagrin, the instructions for the next day were that I was to wear a see-through blouse with no bra. It was a test, but I complied. The next day we spent together, along with his blond Labrador retriever, in the hills of the beautiful Pep- perdine University campus, as this gorgeous but very lonely man spun a yarn about who I really was and what I deserved, including that I should never be in a bar, and that he was the man to take me 'round the world. It was a fantasy day that I seemed to watch from outside my body as he performed for me, giving me life advice to take into my next chapter, which he felt would be wiser after his counsel. We never took our clothes off and didn't see each other again.

Watching men be men is what I spent thirty years devouring.

The "trapped American housewife" story finally broke into the open in 1962, after the Pill freed women, and the sexual revolution of the 1960s was in full swing in the White House, though the media wasn't talking. At the time, *McCall's* was reportedly the fastest growing women's magazine. The world was in upheaval, but in *McCall's*, there was "no mention of the world beyond the home," again according to Betty Friedan's exhaustive research. Their readers were judged to be "housewives, full time."

When Friedan's *The Feminine Mystique* blew the lid off of the American myth of the happy housewife who needed nothing beyond home, it foreshadowed the launch of the modern feminist revolution that would open a path to feminism breaking out in 1972, which introduced Gloria Steinem, the cultural daredevil of our time.

Feminists took back what the pre-WWII heroine had begun, before the post-war era stuck women back in their traditional role. Feminists of the 1970s, led by Steinem, again reclaimed power that included intelligence and education, as well as encouraging the abilities a woman had to create exactly what she wanted by *doing* something to earn it.

Back in 1939, according to Friedan's research and films of the times, the "New Women" heroines "were almost never housewives." In January of that year, *Redbook* published "A Dream to Share," where the husband and wife were partners in life. The story of women in 1939, according to the magazine, was that "if she kept her commitment to herself, she did not lose the man, if he was the right man."

In 1939 we had Scarlett O'Hara, who scandalized the South in every way possible, including by being a good businesswoman, but even after everything falls apart, she comes back repeatedly, living her life her way. There was also *The Women*, starring Norma Shearer, Joan Crawford, Rosalind Russell, Paulette Goddard, Joan Fontaine, Hedda Hopper and other talented, accomplished actresses. There were wives but also women who had jobs, lives and individual strengths. It's the story of a wife, played by Shearer, who is losing her husband to a hot single girl, played by Joan Crawford, who has sex with him and is trying to get him to leave his wife. Shearer throws him out when she finds out, because she has no intention of allowing it or turning her head the other way. She also won't make allowances for some sexual appetite that she's supposed to suffer through as her husband beds another woman, even if she's dependent financially.

Fast forward to 1959 and Tennessee Williams' *Suddenly Last Summer*, with Katharine Hepburn, Montgomery Clift, Elizabeth Taylor and Mercedes McCambridge. Here's the IMDB description, though I've added the names of the cast: "The only son of wealthy widow Violet Venable (Hepburn) dies while on vacation with his cousin Catherine (Taylor). What the girl saw was so horrible that she went insane; now Mrs. Venable wants Catherine lobotomized (Montgomery Clift plays the doctor) to cover up the truth."

In 1956, *Inherit the Wind* featured Lauren Bacall as a shadow of her 1944 *To Have and Have Not* self. If Kinsey had seen Bacall make her screen debut in that earlier film, her classic line to Bogart, "You know how to whistle, don't you, Steve? You just put your lips together and... blow," might have set him to work a lot earlier than 1953. This time around, in 1956, she plays a woman who falls in love with rich bad-boy Robert Stack, while Rock Hudson pines for her, with Dorothy Malone playing what Hollywood now called the "nymphomaniac." The role, with all sorts of warning signals about what happens to an unmarried girl who likes sex, landed Malone an Academy Award for Best Supporting Actress. Bacall gets slugged around and has a miscarriage, but at least she ends up with another man to take care of her.

Butterfield 8, 1960, has Elizabeth Taylor playing a good-time girl who falls for married man Laurence Harvey, while Eddie Fisher pines for her. Taylor ends up dead. Sex with a married man kills. Funny how that's never the case for men in these films.

In *His Girl Friday*, released in 1940, Rosalind Russell is an ace reporter, with her boss Cary Grant also her ex-husband who just can't let her go. Russell had what was considered only a man's job by the time the 1950s rolled around, and was single with no children in sight. She was also the heroine.

This all illustrates, at least to me, what happened to women's roles, which had taken off with vigor in the 1920s, when we got the vote, and stayed strong on screen throughout the pre-censorship era until WWII ended. The history of women in film tells an important story about the world in which our greatest screen icons grew up and which shaped their lives and their choices. Digesting this at a time when some are decrying feminism, talking about a post-feminist era when we still don't have equal pay or equal power in media, corporations or politics, we should make sure we remember the lessons from women's history already there for us to see.

Sheryl Sandberg's book, *Lean In: Women, Work, and the Will to Lead*, is a message in an era when women are bailing out, even when they can afford not to do so. Progress can be overturned, as it surely was in the mid-twentieth century, when the feminine mystique took hold after WWII and a half-century of women working and producing next to men.

By the mid-1950s, career housewives were told they needn't be concerned with the world, because only children and home were important. In a March 2013 article in *New York* magazine titled "The Retro Wife," meant to rebut the urgent need for women to keep pressing for progress, the main female subject of the piece says, "I want my daughter to be able to do anything she wants… But I also want to say, 'Have a career that you can walk away from at the drop of a hat.'" The privilege of being a woman who only wants to do what she wants when she wants is the very definition of bailing on what women have already built. It's a position that rejects leadership at a time when we need female leaders more than ever, which also means women must inspire men to step up to help this manifest. Who a woman partners with either makes leadership possible or not, with America's role in the world hanging in the balance.

Hillary Rodham Clinton graduated from Wellesley in 1969. She was thirteen years old when Jacqueline Kennedy entered the White House, never imagining that she would one day refer to swimming with "my friend Jackie," as she did in her memoir, *Living History*. Clinton's heroine was Eleanor Roosevelt, someone who is left out of the conversation at this point in feminist history, but is foundational to it. When Hillary Clinton decided to change her life and move to Arkansas to be with the love of her life, Bill Clinton, it was Eleanor she heard in her head. Hillary writing in *Living History*: "I knew it was time for me — to paraphrase Eleanor Roosevelt — to do what I was most afraid to do."

You're not going to find two women who were more different in the White House than Jackie and Eleanor. Of course, the marriages of all three of these women are something else, but the women themselves are far more interesting to contemplate in a country that still pays women less than men for the same job, while being seen around the world as a beacon of female freedoms.

Hillary Clinton learned from both women. It was Eleanor Roosevelt's famous line that a woman in political life must "develop skin as tough as rhinoceros hide," which became a "mantra" for Mrs. Clinton as she "faced one crisis after another," again quoting from *Living History*.

One prophetic warning from Jacqueline Kennedy reverberates, which Mrs. Clinton chose to include in *Living History*. Hillary said Jacqueline Kennedy "spoke frankly about the peculiar and dangerous attractions evoked by charismatic politicians." She warned Hillary that, like Jack, Bill Clinton had "personal magnetism that inspired strong feelings in people." It was obvious to Mrs. Clinton that "she meant that he might also be a target." Mrs. Kennedy warned, "He has to be very careful. Very careful."

I can't help but wonder what Jackie and Hillary thought in terms of the role both Jack and Bill played in setting themselves up as willing targets for "peculiar and dangerous attractions." This was inherently dangerous, especially for a president, but that's obviously part of the thrill. As for "peculiar," I think I've proven to you by now that this isn't all that odd for a wide spectrum of men, regardless of class or stature. There is no such thing as "very careful" in today's modern era, which hangs on the risk of who has more to lose.

Upon leaving the State Department, Hillary Clinton was more popular than any man in politics, looking very much like the only woman in history on the ramp to becoming the first viable female presidential candidate of the United States. She got close in 2008, which I chronicle in my book *The Hillary Effect*. Her years at the State Department have only sealed her prowess as the most powerful woman on the scene today. She was the first person at State to make women a priority in our diplomatic mission, something that she started as first lady when she went to China to speak to women there and declared "human rights are women's rights."

Growing up watching Jacqueline Bouvier Kennedy must have been something for a girl moored in midwestern religious traditionalism and clearly affected by politics early on, no doubt because of the opportunities growing for women. An accomplished woman, Clinton's own career as a lawyer included a 1974 stint on the impeachment inquiry staff, advising the House Judiciary Committee during the Watergate hearings. Hillary Rodham gave up her own ambitions to move to Arkansas and marry William Jefferson Clinton, whom she simply knew was headed for the presidency.

Caught between the ages of the feminine mystique and feminism, but also falling madly in love with the force that is Bill Clinton, there are few female leaders who have confounded younger women more than Hillary. This is borne out by emails and comments I received, and conversations I had, on the front lines of the 2008 election season. Women continually contacted me confused and resentful over how such a powerhouse female would choose to stay married to a serial philanderer. The story is generational, one that modern women can't relate to without context of history, which includes the roles that have been expected of females before the age of Gloria Steinem. The human collision of feminism and marriage to a man who humiliates you is difficult to dissect and accept.

You can certainly see the parallels in Eleanor Roosevelt, Hillary Rodham Clinton and even Jacqueline Kennedy Onassis, who was caught between them, in an era we can't seem to escape. Eleanor had her own policy world, a world that John F. Kennedy ironically needed when he was trying to wrestle the nomination, pleading with Mrs. Roosevelt for her endorsement. Mrs. Kennedy built the Kennedy mystique to last, and it continues to reverberate. Hillary is a woman who saved her husband's presidency at a time he was being hunted politically.

All three women had the duty of making the success of their husbands' presidencies possible through independent actions, which established their own legacies along with their husbands'. The media looked approvingly at the architectural work Mrs. Kennedy oversaw when she refurbished the White House, over the design and artistic elements, the social affairs and whirlwind glamour. These were all part of a woman's duties in the days of the feminine mystique. However, Eleanor Roosevelt and Hillary Rodham Clinton were seen as lightning rods in the presidencies of their husbands for daring to have voices, platforms and places in policy creation. Coming before the World War II dividing line, Eleanor had no chains; Jackie grew up in the throes of the war, whose ending created the feminine mystique that caught her up; Hillary was a product of both, her persona burnished by history and Eleanor Roosevelt's power, at a time when the feminist revolution backlash was producing a puritanical second wave of "occupation: housewife."

Michelle Obama's political position has the gift and burden of race, but not the other trappings of Eleanor, Jackie or Hillary. The first African-American first lady in U.S. history, Mrs. Obama is clearly shaping policy from behind the scenes as a strong adviser to her president husband in a way that has benefited women and families, with a special focus on the military. In addition, she has impacted the way children eat through her Let's Move! initiative. She's still making her legacy, so it's unfair to weigh her impact, which already has been very real and potentially lasting, especially if you look at her role in emphasizing childhood obesity and the importance of real food in our diets. By planting the first ever White House garden, complete with beekeeping, she has made a historic statement on health and lifestyle.

Going beyond Eleanor, whose assertiveness as first lady was revolutionary, Hillary took on health care policy for President Clinton, heading the President's Task Force on National Health Reform. The knives came out and filleted her for her efforts, which went well beyond just evaluating the mistakes that were made. The true partnership of Bill and Hillary in the White House was seen as an overstep, even if it was a perfect picture of how the modern marriage can work. Hillary's fierce commitment to make policy work for people resurrected the stereotypical feminine mystique picture of power being masculine, which meant the femininity that described the traditional nature of the first lady was challenged. The male-dominated media couldn't wait to pick it up.

When FDR was sick, Eleanor became his legs. Jack was sick his entire life and presidency, but Jackie was never his political stand-in. Hillary was a political partner, feminist representative on policy, traditionalist's target, and savior.

When Hillary was slapped down for her health care efforts that failed, a new role was immediately created for her. She was *Jacquelineized*, or at least, that was the goal of the White House image-makers. This happened even after she was said to have "taken Capitol Hill by storm" in the first months of the health care debate. A noted Clinton critic and MSNBC host, Lawrence O'Donnell, was the Senate Finance Committee's chief of staff at the time of "Hillarycare," as it was derisively called. In a May 1994 *New Yorker* article, "Hillary the Pol," O'Donnell described the difficulties she faced with health care at the time, saying, "She held her position in the face of questioning by these senators around the table, many of whom know a great deal about the subject. And she was more impressive than any Cabinet member who has sat in that chair."

She'd failed on health care, so it was back to feminizing Hillary, but quick. To put it in one sentence from someone other than myself, Michael Tomasky in The Daily Beast wrote in February 2013 of Hillary's post-health-care debacle period back in the '90s:

> She had to endure this little woodshed period of acting like she was passionate about historical preservation, trotting off to places like Edith Wharton's house and handing out plaques (her historical interests, she once told me in an interview, really extend back to ancient civilizations, marveling over questions like "How many generations it took to figure out what you boiled and put in the sun to cure a dread disease").

But her inner-Eleanor wouldn't be denied long. In 1995, she gave the speech heard round the world, saying, "human rights are women's rights and women's rights are human rights," that would herald the greatest cause of her life, the empowerment of women and girls across the globe.

A woman who, like Jackie and Eleanor, had helped make her husband's presidency possible is now on the cusp, at the very least, of having the option to take another shot at winning the presidency. When African nations have had female presidents but we haven't, it's a scandal. Still, people — *women* — shrug and wonder why it's important.

Some people still wonder what kind of woman would permit her husband's philandering and not leave. Jacqueline and Eleanor were captivated by bigger things, as was Hillary. It wasn't just a marriage that was at stake; it was America itself, as well as what each man stood for, and the opposing forces that would have benefited if their presidencies had been destroyed. How many divorces hinge on such a world-shaking pendulum?

In 1998, if Hillary Rodham Clinton hadn't fought for Bill Clinton's presidency, it all would have ended. All of it, because Democrats were so upset at the lying and deceit of it, the dangerous risks taken when it was clear the Republicans had hunted Bill Clinton from the start, plotting for the moment to take him out. Hillary's the one who stood in front of congressional Democrats and told them they had to stand fast. The American people were behind William Jefferson Clinton, having decided it was just sex and they couldn't care less.

We cannot possibly understand what it must have been like growing up in the generation of Jackie and the feminine mystique, caught between the expected "occupation: housewife" and the sexual revolution, as Hillary was caught between that and Gloria Steinem feminism. Eleanor likely would have understood both, because she had the freedom of being beyond both. These women were and are the last of their kind, women who helped, then capitalized on their husbands' statures to make bigger and broader lives for themselves, even as they were responsible for keeping their men and their myths alive in deadly times. They were archetypes that don't exist today.

Being Jackie and being Hillary were both a lot different from being Eleanor. Today, women can choose anything we want with nothing out of bounds. We have to beware to not go backward again, as happened between Eleanor Roosevelt's time and Jacqueline Kennedy's. The ground of equality in relationships, between marriage and work, is not solidified. Expectations of women's roles are being argued again today at a moment when we have a chance to shatter not only corporate glass ceilings forever, but also break open doors to equality in our homes.

At the end of 2012, Suzanne Venker, the daughter of Phyllis Schlafly, the crusader against women's equality and the ERA, wrote an article titled "The War on Men," in which she proclaimed that "women aren't women anymore." Then Venker sets off in the direction of 1950:

> The so-called rise of women has not threatened men. It has pissed them off. It has also undermined their ability to become self-sufficient in the hopes of someday supporting a family. Men want to love women, not compete with them. They want to provide for and protect their families — it's in their DNA. But modern women won't let them.

Never fear, there's an answer. All women have to do is "surrender to their nature — their femininity — and let men surrender to theirs." What's our nature? It's to nurture, Venker says, to stay at home, to let men be men, which means women can't be in the workforce, because competing with them is bad for marriage, which men supposedly don't want anymore.

Why wouldn't any man want a woman bringing home a paycheck, one that might equal or exceed his own? What family doesn't benefit from the matriarch's financial contribution? Maria Shriver found out in her 2009 study on working women for Center for American Progress that many women are not only breadwinners but are also their families' chief financial officers, which Citigroup VP Lisa Caputo first put on the map. There is no going back.

Venker's prescription comes straight out of the post-WWII advertising age, and we all know where that led us.

Being Jackie won't work anymore, economically, romantically or sexually. Philandering as a sport is out, unless it swings both ways, and most men aren't built for that, never mind that it won't make anyone happy.

Marriage requires what Jackie, Hillary and Eleanor all had, to varying degrees. We've benefited from feminism, which has taken the dog out of the male beast as we appeal to their better nature, because women now have the financial option to leave. What's optimal in a modern marriage is a creative partnership that includes children but also allows both partners to think wider, to invest in each other's lives and careers, while sharing an equal role at home and in the family.

What we all need to guard against is being sold an advertising campaign that was bought once before and caused generations of women to suffer. We can't blame anyone else, because this time we have history to remind us. Women have changed; we are closer to equality than ever before. Men have changed, too, and are getting used to what we bring to the table. Now, women have to encourage men to step up and take their share of what used to be called "women's work," because if we don't, we'll lose ground again. Women are allowing the modern era to engulf and overwhelm them, because many can't admit they need a fifty-fifty partner.

We mustn't let anyone romanticize a bygone era that wasn't that good for women. It's not just women who will pay the price this time. Men will, too, and the next generations will suffer through yet another era of boomerang regression, already immortalized by the feminine mystique, and marketed by people with an agenda that has nothing to do with a woman's happiness.

6

How to Catch a Man

Some things never change.

There is no doubt that what you look like matters. It's a lie to think otherwise. But it's not about perfection as much as it is about confidence and knowing how to make the most of what you've got. That includes being comfortable with your own sensuality, whether you're a beauty queen type or a big and beautiful, plus-size girl. At the root of it all, in case you haven't caught on yet, is not just what you look like, but who you are as an individual. The key is not pretending or projecting some magazine's view, but being the person you actually are in your own skin. You cannot do this without knowing what it is that excites you, which goes well beyond externals.

We've got better things to do now than worry about how to catch a man, right? Women are no longer focused on being perfect, because we're more invested in being the individuals that we know we can be. Right? We want it all, and why not? Especially since we are no longer tied down to rules and expectations of behavior that someone else drew up. If men have been masters of their fate forever, at least now women hold the reins to their own destiny, an option my mother didn't have.

Whether women can have it all depends on your personal definition of what that means, which includes the financial means you have at your disposal to manifest it. There's also a lot to be said for making specific choices that cut off other avenues that you have decided aren't for you. It's not feminism's fault if things aren't happening as you'd like. Sometimes, it's just being patient, waiting for life to unfold in its own time, which is the hardest lesson to learn. At other times, we aren't kind to ourselves, harshly judging what really is the best we can do at the time. There are still other times when we have no one to blame but ourselves — when it's all our fault that we've ended up in the mess we're in, often knowing it was coming long before it landed.

As Taylor Swift admits, "I realize the blame is on me. 'Cause I knew you were trouble when you walked in, so shame on me."

That's when it's all the woman's fault. It's a topic I've mined for more than a decade. Obviously, it's not about blaming yourself every time you turn around. It's about those times when you knew he was bad news, but you just couldn't resist. Or maybe it's not that he was the wrong guy, but you just knew it was never going to work, and you plunged ahead anyway. Maybe it was a guy who has been hovering for a long time, who catches you at a weak moment and you succumb, just to have someone to take up the slack in a life that's become too much to handle on your own.

Been there, done that. When I married Brian, a guy who had known me most of my life, I knew it was a mistake. However, I'd spent my childhood, adolescence, teenage years and college life, all working so hard, going through so much; I was just tired and wanted an escape. As if you can escape inside a marriage. There are innumerable other details that inevitably come with thinking you can escape your life into marriage, but they hardly matter to anyone but me, because the specifics come in any number of shades and colors, named by women of every generation in time. I was just another one of them to make the same mistake. I'd graduated early from college, then headed into marriage. It was over before we said, "I do."

What became so incredibly unbearable to me, however, was this man who had known me all my life and hounded me for years to be his, all of a sudden forgot why he'd liked, then loved me in the first place. The greatest passion and purpose in my life was performing, which is one thing that drew him to me from the start, because we shared a love of musical theater. But suddenly, after we were married, out of the blue, there Brian stood after coming home from work one day, declaring to me that I must be relieved that I could now give up all that silliness and not worry about anymore auditions. That I actually thought Brian would understand that I was still on my way to New York even after we got married was my biggest blunder.

He was the guy I'd seduced during Christmas vacation, the day before my family paid for my very first trip to New York City in the middle of my junior year of college, because I was so antsy to get to Broadway that I was ready to drop out of college. And now he didn't get me at all.

What made Brian's sudden pronouncement doubly difficult to hear was that I had my eyes on a dinner-theater-bound road show that would travel across the Midwest, with the plan to end up on the East Coast. When I informed Brian that I had no intention of giving up performing or staying home, he erupted in an explosion of fury I'd never witnessed from him. It scared the crap out of me and was a harbinger of physical intimidation and emotional collisions to come, which eventually led me to flee from the comfy condo and take refuge back home. This delighted my mom and family, because the whole thing had been one colossal mistake from the start and everyone knew it. My un-marriage, as I call it because it was over before it began, cured me forever of tying the knot, or so I thought. I wanted an annulment, however implausible, because that was what I felt about the union, but I was in such a hurry to go on the road, getting out became enough. It's why most people who know me think I've only been married once. It's an uncounted un-marriage, as far as I'm concerned, which says it all.

I can honestly say it wasn't entirely my fault, because I was the same person the day after we got married as I was the day before. That this guy who'd known me since we were kids thought I'd change just because we got married was not my fault. What was my fault is talking myself into marrying Brian in the first place. The clue of what was to come was when his dad, who was an amazing man, took us to a jewelry store so Brian could get me an engagement ring. His dad laughed out loud at him when he freaked out about the cost, because it wasn't like it was a huge ring or that he had money problems. Brian's mother was always a challenge, a woman who didn't drive a car and demanded to be driven everywhere. It was the mid-1970s! I used to tweak her by picking fights about the Equal Rights Amendment, which she viciously opposed. She also complained about the minister I chose, so we had two. Then she started a fight with my family in the middle of our living room as guests mingled at our reception. I've learned a lot since then.

It's really not all that hard to seduce and snare the man you want, but what once was a game of catching the man, today is much more complicated when you get to the fine print. The repercussions when you do set your sights on someone are far more important to consider. What needs to happen from there is a course in managing expectations and being honest with yourself, while making sure you both want the same things and that the relationship is really one built on equality. What you want must be compatible with his desires, because that's how you get there.

Catching a man begins in the oddest place today. You'll never guess where you will need to start. How do your teeth look? Well, that's the number-one issue on the minds of men *and* women, according to a February 2013 online national survey.

The other thing is, the same survey finds that "65% would not date someone with credit card debt greater than $5,000; 54% would not date someone with substantial student loan debt."

USA Today reported on the survey by Market Tools Inc. for the Dallas-based dating website Match.com. The sampling was 5,481 unattached adults age twenty-one and older. The survey found that "38% would cancel a date because of some-thing they found while doing Internet research on their date." Men are also very picky about the pictures they see on a woman's Facebook wall, with 55% saying they broke up with someone because of what they saw. Forty-eight percent of women say they have done the same. Only 38% of men, compared with 48% of women at Match.com, do Facebook research before a date.

This same survey found that 36% said they'd sent a "sexy photo or explicit text." The definition of *sexy* and *explicit* would be significant, but they were not narrowed down for this survey.

There's another finding from the survey I found interesting. As reported by Sharon Jayson in *USA Today*, "47% of singles reported a 'friends with benefits' relationship. And those surveyed last year were more than twice as likely to say it turned into a long-term relationship (44%) compared to 20% the previous year."

The Match.com survey also validates something I've learned, which is what's really important to a man. The "must-have" issues for men begin with "someone I can trust and confide in." Shorter translation: loyalty is number one for men, which explains why when a woman cheats, men are less likely to forgive. Number two on the must-have list is "trusts and respects me," with number three being, "physically attracted to me," which 40% of the men surveyed called a must-have in a relationship. "Sense of humor/makes me laugh," comes in at number four, with "is comfortable with her sexuality" at number five, with 36%.

When women were surveyed about looking for a man, neither physical attraction nor being comfortable with their sexuality showed up anywhere on their top five must-have list. For women, the top quality they must have in a man is "treats me with respect" (84%); at number two is "someone I can trust and confide in" (77%); "has a sense of humor/makes me laugh" comes in at number three; in the fourth position on women's must-have list is "shares the same values as I do"; while, "is comfortable communicating his wants, needs and desires" rounds out the top five. You could surmise that number five is about physical attraction and ease with sexuality, but it's really about *talking* about these issues, driving home women's need for verbal communication as a big part of intimacy.

Feminism liberated women to seek great educations that could lead to fulfilling careers and cash. But as women finally freed themselves of having to depend on men for basic needs and shelter, society's economic dynamics changed, morphing into the "mancession" of the 2000s.

Is the economic competition between men and women the "end of courtship," as the *New York Times* proclaimed in early January 2013? Is it a "war on men," as Suzanne Venker declared, because women want their own money, pitting them against men, in competition for the same jobs? The answer has evolved into what Sheryl Sandberg's book *Lean In* focuses on. Couples must discuss the woman's career in terms of having a family *before* marriage, so we don't continue perpetuating the Super Woman syndrome that is making women feel guilty, stressed out, under-appreciated and inadequate. The movie *I Don't Know How She Does It* with Sarah Jessica Parker didn't work, but the premise made a point. The obvious answer is that she doesn't, because she can't do it alone.

A woman who wants to be a mom and still maintain a career has a responsibility to herself to ask and expect her future husband to understand that since she's committed to both career and family, this means he'll be doing the laundry and fixing dinner for the kids when she has to work late, as well as carting the kids to lessons and doctor appointments when she can't. Oh, and she'll be glad to do it for him, too. If you're a feminist, this is imperative, because what you do at home has direct repercussions for the workplace, with ramifications rippling beyond your own life.

Just a month after Sandberg's book was published, Ben Smith, the editor-in-chief of the popular website Buzzfeed, had the evidence that the book was resonating:

> It's been less than a month since Sheryl Sandberg published *Lean In: Women, Work, and the Will to Lead*, and I've already had two women bring up her name in salary negotiations. I'm not alone: Other editors whom I asked this week told me that women who worked for them had brought up the book — its broadly empowering message, and its specific advice on pushing for a raise. It's a concrete, if anecdotal, suggestion that Sandberg's high-profile effort to start a movement is having real consequences on a dynamic that's well known to managers and backed by volumes of research. Women often ask for less money than they could get, and negotiate less aggressively than men.

What Sandberg's book also proved is that women take on work and the majority of household duties, including parenting, while men never expand their responsibilities to make marriage a truly equal partnership. This might be the one reason why women don't cheat. They don't have time.

In the '90s, everyone freaked out about the end of dating as we had known it, with one big question at the dawn of Internet-dating being whether equality demanded that a woman pay her fair share on a date. The initial meeting for coffee is fine, but once the attraction is clearly sparked, it shifts. Of course, it depends on the woman, obviously, and there are exceptions, with the great news being we can craft what we want. My advice remains that a woman should not pay on the first date, even if she can. Of course, if you're an older woman looking for a boy-toy, well, that's a different story, at least at first. But even then there's a need for the woman to understand the ego of a man, even one who makes less money than you do.

This gets into romantic territory. Just because a woman can pay and the man knows it, doesn't mean both wouldn't benefit from the romance created when a man has an opportunity to buy her dinner. This allows the woman to reveal she can give up control, even if she doesn't have to, while the man shows he can take care of a woman, something that will be in his DNA no matter how advanced society becomes. The balance shifts in this moment: The woman is on the receiving end, an instant that is very much like sex itself, which can only happen if she gives permission. It's the basic dynamic of a relationship. Everything depends on the woman.

Women are claiming that dating has devolved into a series of text messages that end in women "hanging out" with men, without a date ever happening, which is being blamed on the "hookup culture." Citing "asynchronous communication," otherwise known as Facebook, texting and Twitter, as the reason for the demise of courtship and dating, culture-watchers and experts are once again proclaiming that another generation is being screwed out of the pleasure of intimacy. It's leaving them bereft and without hope of what once was a wonderful experience. Man meets woman; man dates woman; man and woman fall in love; write your happy ending here.

Dating hasn't gone anywhere for women who know they deserve it.

And, oh, how quickly we forget how badly we wanted out of what the 1950s offered women, which was no control over our lives whatsoever. A time people are now looking back on with... *amnesia.*

It was a time when women were seen as a "man's wife, sex object, mother, housewife — and never as persons defining themselves by their own actions in society," as Betty Friedan describes it. The images flying through the culture in the 1950s were assaulting American women, "coming at us from the women's magazines, the movies, the television commercials, all mass media and textbooks of psychology, and sociology," writes Friedan. It was the image of the perfect woman, to which we all were to aspire. The "problem with no name" was having all the things a woman was supposed to have, but still wanting more. Becoming overwhelmed with guilt because she "didn't have an orgasm waxing the family-room floor." Unhappy and unfulfilled, but she couldn't name why, because it had nothing to do with the traditional things that women had been consumed with accumulating.

It wasn't long ago that what women wanted didn't matter, because back in the pre-feminism, pre-sexual-liberation years, we were still told what we should want by the media, in church, and through what society would accept as our proper role. This was back when there were no "women's issues." Women weren't taken seriously and didn't much think there was anything wrong with that. Catching the man was the only agenda item, but how to go about it didn't matter as much, because *he* chose *you*.

Today, a match of mutually beneficial goals wrapped in an agreement is less likely to last forever than at any time in human history. On top of this, women are being led to believe there's no good news if you're looking for love. We've come a long way and have a multitude of choices, and now women are suddenly grappling with the notion that dating's dead. It's gone from the "Should I pay my share?" 1990s question to "Courtship is dead," as proclaimed by the Style section of the *New York Times*.

Women are allowing themselves to be whipsawed back and forth from one hookup to another, because a woman's not sure if that last text message that came in — "dropping a line in the water, hoping for a nibble," as the *Times* couched the challenge to women today — is a query a woman should grab for "FOMO" (fear of missing out), or maybe ignore because it doesn't mean anything.

Savvy Hanna Rosin, in an article about the millennial-oriented Gaggle website in the *Times*, published in October 2012, says, "Now feminist progress is largely dependent on hookup culture." She goes on to say that women today are looking for "fulfilling relationships that exist outside the path of marriage."

This is what I've done my entire life, and I'm in a completely different generation than the twenty- and thirty-somethings. I never focused on Mr. Right and loved the company of men for decades, preferring serial monogamy to marriage. It's just that more women are choosing it today and *that* is news. It's not news, however, that the wider your social circle is, the more men you'll meet, but if having a gaggle of men of differing types works, I'm all for it. I just know a so-called post-dating era couldn't happen unless women were buying into it, which isn't a good thing on any level, and I don't have to be a millennial to figure that out.

The Gaggle was founded by Jessica Massa and Rebecca Wiegand as an offshoot of Massa's book by the same name, and considers itself, according to an article in the *Times*, part of the post-dating landscape. On the site, Massa and Wiegand champion the so-called non-date, group non-date and networking non-date.

The mission statement of the-gaggle.com contains a "vow never, ever to publish a piece called 'The 10 Best Ways to Satisfy Your Man in Bed.' Thank the sex gods. Instead, they publish pieces like "Give A F*#!ing Fantastic Blowjob!" written by "a sex educator with five years' experience," the title in all caps, exclamation point! Their advice includes, "If you are fulfilling your man's porn star fantasies, then fuck yeah, swallow."

That triggered my gag reflex, involuntarily. It's déjà vu all over again, with advice that could have come from *Penthouse*.

This latest advice for women, according to this article, is telling a twenty-first century female that in order to fulfill "your man's porn fantasies," you must swallow. Do you want to swallow? That's not a question to be asked, evidently. Some women love it, some don't. But it's not like this is revolutionary stuff or even all that new to ponder.

And I'm still trying to figure out the difference between "Give A F*#!ing Fantastic Blowjob!" and "The 10 Best Ways to Satisfy Your Man in Bed," except that the former is a lot stingier. There's another problem. Advice on giving a f*#!ing fantastic blowjob that includes "fuck yeah, swallow" as its climactic pointer is a bait-and-switch proposition when the post begins with a smart "play it safe" caveat, stipulating that a "mint flavored condom keeps you and your partner safe, but it will get you so minty fresh you'll feel like the porno version of the Orbit girl." I don't know any man, whatever his age, who considers getting a blowjob with a condom to be f*#!ing fantastic.

If you want sex, have it, though I'd suggest you know the guy, because in the modern era, sexually transmitted diseases are still lethal, which I hope at stardate 2014 I don't have to tell anyone. Like to swallow? By all means do. Having sex because you enjoy it won't preclude finding a relationship that matters, which my life proves. If you meet someone and it hits, it hits. That's a way to live life that is vitally exciting. Men were never the center of my universe; they simply added to the joy and excitement of the life I was leading. I had no intention of going without men. They were a spectacular dessert during my bliss-quest.

Much of my dating life was always done on the fly. Dinner reservations? What're those? Some men certainly do plan, plan, plan, but there are a whole lot of people who don't, myself included.

But is this evidence of a post-dating world?

Only if that's what you want to orchestrate and that's the way you want to live your life. Just because guys are into group dates or non-date events doesn't mean women have to start once again playing by their set of criteria. Log this under another event in the cultural boomerang to the bad old days.

The *Guardian*'s Jill Filipovic, who writes spectacularly modern advice on "gender and other agendas," took the *New York Times*' "end of courtship" article down very easily by giving credit where it's due to "feminist victories" that make women's lives today better. She tells her generation, "If your goal is to live a varied life, to learn about yourself through a variety of relationships, romantic and not, and to develop reasonably fully as a human being before you settle down, then there has never been a better time to be alive (especially as a woman)."

Where many girls, including myself, had to take a boatload of grief for not wanting what we were supposed to want in the era of Gloria, today's generations are free and clear of the traditionalist guilt, unless they're dumb enough to listen to it. What Filipovic described is exactly the life I have led.

The means of communication since the Pill all of a sudden turned the language of formal courtship into having sex at will, and screw marriage. Today, it's called simply the hookup. This latest definition of having sex without consequences hasn't shattered all form. It's just been given a new name.

Women have always done that, just without the fancy technology that makes relationships between the sexes even quicker and more disposable. At least now we have all the cards men have, though, unfortunately, the latest generation of non-daters is so intent on equating the era of post-feminism with one of post-dating, that women are negating the power they've got to craft whatever it is they want, whether the men like it or not. Because the one thing that hasn't changed is that women still control what kind of relationship they want and receive.

When a man sets his sights on a woman, he won't get sidetracked. It's at this moment, at the beginning, that the woman has to communicate what she expects from him. The man will also have expectations that he believes the woman must meet. Her response tells him whether he has it right or not, but also sends him a message of her own value. It's the standard she sets now that will impact his respect for her. A good man wants to be worthy of you, because you're the woman he might marry, and maybe have children with. This all comes through a negotiated agreement known as dating. It's the mother of all mating dances that sets up the standards of your relationship, which will never be higher than at the time of courting. This is very serious stuff for a woman, because what she's taking on includes not only the possibility of who will be responsible for her children, but also the life they will share and build together even if children aren't part of the package. When children aren't present, the woman must still convey what type of creative life they will manifest through their relationship, because that will be the foundation of their partnership.

Does anyone actually buy into the notion that men have changed as much as women have? At least Suzanne Venker gets that much right: "Much of the coverage has been in response to the fact that for the first time in history, women have become the majority of the U.S. workforce. They're also getting most of the college degrees. The problem? This new phenomenon has changed the dance between men and women."

It's a continuation of the argument against feminism that hit decades ago.

Venker continues: "But after decades of browbeating the American male, men are tired. Tired of being told there's something fundamentally wrong with them. Tired of being told that if women aren't happy, it's men's fault."

Methinks Ms. Venker doth protest too much on behalf of men.

Men have never had it so good: sex without marriage; women who can help pay the bills; and fewer demands, because the woman is supposed to be responsible for her own life and happiness. After all, she finally is in charge and can make any choice she wants. And if you marry her, she'll not only work as hard as you at her career, but do all the domestic chores, too. What a deal for men.

Once again, women are being lectured to from the same book that birthed the 1950s and convinced women that household appliances were their oasis, and that when relationships and marriage don't work today, it's all the woman's fault. When we pick the wrong man, it is, but when we transparently communicate and act on what it is we do want, making sure men get our signals, it sets men free to either follow or get out of the way for a man who wants an equal partnership, which means more for everyone, including happiness.

When you put this all together, and add in Sheryl Sandberg's *Lean In*, what you've got is the next stage in a feminist, sexual and economic revolution that has a real chance of shaking the dust off of American society and finally manifesting marriages that make the people in them happier.

It all depends on men's reaction to this cultural shift, which is actually an immense opportunity to gain something valuable lost by the sacrifices they have been making without much acknowledgment. If men take women's call for equality at home and in their careers as a threat, seeing women taking their power while the men are asked to take an expanded role at home that's foreign to them, we'll have a collision on our hands. The politics of sex could rear up and this chance could morph into competition. The potential for men to break the pattern of isolation and separation from family life that their heavy workload causes will be lost because they didn't take the leap, which will require a bit of faith.

An article in the *Harvard Business Review* by James Allworth made an incredibly important point on this subject. In "It's Not Women Who Should Lean In; It's Men Who Should Step Back," published in April 2013, Allworth includes a poignant anecdote from Bonnie Ware, a woman who worked in palliative care, with people who are dying. One of the major regrets these dying men had was working too hard, which, Ware said, "came from every male patient" she nursed. "All of the men I nursed deeply regretted spending so much of their lives on the treadmill of a work existence." Women felt the same way, but they were also older-generation females, who weren't the primary breadwinners, according to Ware.

No one is saying this will be easy. It will be a foreign adventure at first. What we all have to gain, if the bravest and most adventurous among us give it a try, might be more balanced lives and a more equitable existence for everyone, with children understanding the value of a true partnership, not to mention seeing a path to happiness. Where no one gets cheated out of the most delicious elements of relationship — love, career and purpose, the myriad of family experiences, all of which makes up life's abundance itself.

Women have never been in charge before, which is only going to expand in the years to come. We've never had everything at our fingertips that a man has had. Now that we do, it's understandable there's some confusion. But it's certainly no reason to throw the social engine in reverse like what happened in the post-WWII era and into the 1950s. That's what led to the concoction of the feminine mystique, which sold America the notion that all a woman needed was children and a husband, or a kitchen full of appliances, because she didn't have a brain in her head that was meant for anything but other people's needs.

Social media and the pleasures of instant intimacy — today's equivalent of cheap thrills, which always cost more than anyone is told — are just the latest distractions for men and women. At least they do hold the hope and possibility of connecting in a way that generations before never had, expanding the playing field. There was once a time when after one bad relationship in a town where everyone knew each other, there was little hope of finding love again. There are ups and downs to online dating, fitting the best of roller coaster analogies, but life's possibilities never offered so much extended value.

Amid all of the technological changes stand women and men and the human craving to connect, touch someone, love someone and share dreams. The first thing that needs to be settled is what it is you want. All these years after the Pill, if there's one thing that modern women have learned, it's that our choices have expanded, but biology is a reality that men don't have to face. But today, for women of means, there are lots of options.

It's easier to be single and have a child if you're a woman; all you need is money and a good nanny. It's easier to be older and have a child if you're a woman; fertility treatments make miracles possible. But the decision to have children is still the one thing women grapple with that can require different dating patterns than those chosen by men, who don't face a biological reality. At least women are not restricted today by choices on how to have children or the time-frame in which they choose to have them. Fertility miracles and options abound, so this puzzle is easier to fit together when you're ready, which was never the case in prior generations.

There's another side to this single-mother story, however, which is that poor women have a totally different reality. According to UCLA psychologist Benjamin Karney, "Girls who think they have somewhere to go in life don't get pregnant; girls who think they have nowhere to go are less careful about contraception." This was just one of the things covered by Karney and other UCLA psychologists in a study on marriage, relationships and values, which was reported in the July 2012 issue of *Journal of Marriage and Family.* According to Karney, these women don't trust the men they're with to be responsible, and so believe any relationship or marriage would ultimately end, a belief that impacts their decisions. Statistics support their pessimism.

Single mothers, especially the poor, value marriage as much as anyone, despite what criticisms have been leveled at them in the media. The difference, according to the UCLA psychologists, is that low-income women have no role model for what a good marriage looks like. Also from the study, posted on the UCLA.edu website:

> Karney said that an affluent eighteen-year-old girl does not want to get pregnant because that would interfere with her plans for college, her career and a future husband. A poor eighteen-year-old looks at what awaits her; she doesn't see herself becoming a lawyer or even a college graduate. "But if she becomes a mother, she gets respect, purpose and someone to love her — and she doesn't need to be married to do that," he said. "She knows she can be a mom; she doesn't know if she can be married forever."

There is an often forgotten world out there of poor, single mothers with limited opportunities for finding good, dependable men. Certainly, Sheryl Sandberg's *Lean In* is not speaking to low-income women either, yet we shouldn't forget that any woman succeeding at the top has a chance to make it better for all women. That's the unspoken pledge in the universal feminist charter.

The post-dating advice contingent and the traditionalists who tell women to relinquish their "war on men" aren't talking to low-income women either. "How to catch a man" for low-income women is more about making sure a girl doesn't marry someone who would put her in deeper jeopardy because he can't live up to what she's providing for herself and her child. A marriage to a man like this is sure to make her life more miserable. Statistics have proven that divorce puts lower-income women and their children in even more perilous conditions, which the UCLA study backs up.

More from the UCLA.edu article:

> "There is a lot you can do with a billion dollars to promote marriage, including helping people with child care and transportation; that is not where the money has been spent," Karney said. "Almost all of that money has been spent on educational curricula, which is a narrow approach, based on false assumptions. Communication and emotional connection are the same among low-income people as in more affluent group. Their unique needs are not about relationship education. None of the data support the current policy of teaching relationship values and skills. Low-income people have concrete, practical problems making ends meet."

Single motherhood is an option, but a Women's Legal Defense and Education Fund report from December 2012 should disabuse anyone of the nonsense that it's a great idea. The study, titled "Worst Off — Single-Parent Families in the United States, a Cross-National Comparison of Single Parenthood in the U.S. and Sixteen Other High Income Countries," and authored by Timothy Casey and Laurie Maldonado, includes this in its introduction:

> This report compares U.S. single-parent families with single-parent families in sixteen other high-income countries. We find that U.S. single-parent families are the worst off. They have the highest poverty rate. They have the highest rate of no health care coverage. They face the stingiest income support system. They lack the paid-time-off-from-work entitlements that in comparison countries make it easier for single parents to balance caregiving and jobholding. They must wait longer than single

parents in comparison countries for early childhood education to begin. They have a low rate of child support receipt.

Nobody is going to tell you that today's dating, sex and relationship scene is easy. It is absolutely terrifying on many levels. At least women are in full control, though that's what is terrifying to some, and helps explain why some women are giving in to men's demands, or society's whims, which will always be whatever is easiest *for men*. I write this as a great lover of men. But, seriously, if men can have it easy in a relationship, they're going to take it easy. If you don't know this, study up. If a man isn't expected to do something, he won't, and with fewer societal expectations and expanded equality between the sexes, why should he? If women want to engage in the same game with men, that's fine. But who says you have to? What if you don't want to?

Women hold power in their lives in a larger way than ever before in human history. This is not hyperbole. It's why we're often met with resistance when giving the revolutionary advice that women need to step up and claim the power we have. This begins with our own lives, of course, with the immediate extension of this power to include our relationships. But not just how we catch a man, because it's never mattered more what kind of man a woman catches.

It's absolutely true that social media makes the need to find out about one another on a first and second date almost obsolete. That's only because the social media blast excited us all, so we jumped on board and engaged in a voluntary personal data dump. Women and men got stoked that we could hook up virtually, verbally and sexually, without boundaries or rules, with a whole new era offering permission to let it all hang out.

Grouper, a social media networking service that brings sets of friends together, is a lot of fun, I'm sure. Do it, don't do it. But it's not going to change the basic desires of men and women or prove anything, except that it's fun to hang out with people and have cocktails. The 1960s and the 1980s pretty much proved that already. Today there are just more innovative and technologically advanced ways to introduce people to each other who could never have met before the new-media era.

What is particularly seductive and misleading about the networking and post-dating rituals is the transient rush of emotions that are connected with a fleeting night of casual flirtation that women can often mis-translate. The rush of adrenaline when you connect actually means nothing. The request for a phone number, when given, often leads to a flurry of texting in a twenty-four-hour period, then stone-cold silence when Monday comes. We re-enter the orbit of real life, and that cocktail-induced meeting is reduced to another fabulous weekend, but that's all.

Romance is created through slowly unfolding intimacy. Longing grows, which can only manifest through curiosity and unlocking mysteries, as well as the hope that builds from knowing something about a person that can't be learned on Facebook in a click. Giving out your phone number in hope of getting a text message is setting the bar very low. That's okay if you're very young and in it for short-term thrills, but it's going to wear your heart out.

Considering the scenarios that continue to suck people in on *The Bachelor*, which has now logged more than seventeen bachelors over twenty-five combined seasons, the number of girls and women willing to give it up in a text message is unsurprising. Desperation is hard to kick.

Hey, I love my trash TV, too. But it makes me wonder what are viewers really after? Is it the long-held notion that a man can sweep you off your feet and fulfill your fantasies of romantic love and happiness? Feminism doesn't change this notion, nor does having a fabulous career. But it rarely plays out as you think it will, especially if you're going to hand everything over to the man to orchestrate. It didn't work the first time out in the 1950s and it sure as hell won't work as the twenty-first century progresses. Or are viewers really into the show for the tabloid gossip and the drama when it all turns into a train wreck? An April 2013 *People* magazine article said the show's longstanding popularity is all about "the drama, cat fights, and hot tub hijinks."

In Season Seventeen, bachelor Sean Lowe and all the dirt that circulated about him after he got a jolt of celebrity made for a lot of tabloid dish, with his appearance on *Dancing With the Stars* adding an additional ego boost. Contestant Catherine Giudici was in the classic no-win situation. She had no one to blame but herself after allowing Lowe to make a fool of her, though if the media stories are even half true, the publicity-hound couple just might deserve each other. What's waiting for them after their glitzy televised wedding on ABC? It's all been great fun, but what happens in the days and months after the party is what makes a marriage.

The money and attention doesn't change the fact that the dynamic is all wrong in this relationship. The minute Lowe started treating Catherine like a bit player in her own life, she should have gathered the courage to walk out, shaking up his world by revealing him to be the boy he's behaving like. Catherine Giudici is using Lowe as her sun, hoping the glow reflects onto her. A smart woman creates her own heat.

A matchmaker on NBC's quickly canceled *Ready for Love*, Matthew Hussey, put it perfectly when he advised one woman, "Men value what they earn." That's absolutely true, and it's something the girls in *The Bachelor* never seem to learn.

But as a soap opera, *The Bachelor* is a reality show bonanza. When the news broke that ABC was going to mine seventeen seasons of the show and eight seasons of *The Bachelorette* to produce a blooper show, I can only imagine how ecstatic *Bachelor* fans were.

You've got to be clear about what you want and not be afraid to ask for it, as well as walk away from adrenaline love affairs that you know aren't going to deliver anything close to what you had in mind, let alone what you deserve.

Contrary to what you might have been told, men love strong women who know what they want, ask for it and don't settle for less. They respect women who have boundaries and aren't going to sell themselves short. They won't think it odd if, at a hookup event, you prefer to keep some mystery to yourself. If you set a date for coffee instead of going for texting it won't scare him off if he's really interested. Of course, if you've let it all hang out on your Facebook page, he'll find that out before you leave the event through the convenience of his smartphone, and you'll just come off a phony.

It doesn't do much good to have that first night connection if everything has already been uploaded for the world to see, or is going to be unloaded when you initially meet. It's tempting, because you think if you don't play the instant intimacy game you'll end up losing to some girl who will, but there's nothing that can keep a guy away if he's ready and you connect with him.

Of course, if he doesn't have a job or has money troubles, it's over before it starts. Hooking up with a guy who is a mess is a dead end road, just like it is if a guy meets a woman who doesn't know who she is. No matter how much you're attracted, it's not meant to be, if he can't deliver at the moment when you're ready for something real. That's not saying a guy who's dealing with financial troubles isn't worth your time, but it's a serious issue you have to consider and discuss.

If we're talking love and marriage, we also have to talk about children. Our lives are no longer defined by our relationships, and that includes marriage and motherhood. A February 2013 interview with Dame Helen Mirren in *Vogue* magazine reveals as much about modern women as anyone has before. "'[Motherhood] was not my destiny,' she says. 'I kept thinking it would be, waiting for it to happen, but it never did, and I didn't care what people thought.'" Of course, it's never that easy. It wasn't women who gave her grief, Mirren adds, "It was only boring old men. And whenever they went 'What? No children? Well, you'd better get on with it, old girl,' I'd say, 'No! F--- off!'"

Like Mirren, I'm child-free by choice. It was a deliberate life decision for me that boggled the mind of my mother and also more than one of the men I dated, which invariably made me more attractive to them and inevitably made them more annoying to me. My mind couldn't be changed or altered by people who said they knew I would change my mind once I found "the right man." It was not about finding "the right man." In fact, the "right man" had shown up several times in my life, and I'd enjoyed his company immensely and never once had the longing for children or marriage.

Modern women are carving new ways to live. A 2010 Pew Research report based mainly on Census Bureau data found that almost 20% of American women do not have children, compared to one-in-ten in the 1970s: "Among all women ages 40–44, the proportion that has never given birth, 18% in 2008, has grown by 80% since 1976, when it was 10%. There were 1.9 million childless women ages 40–44 in 2008, compared with nearly 580,000 in 1976."

There is less of a social stigma for child-free women than ever before in America. Most women today do not have to struggle with the incoming barrage of guilt trips women fought off all of the time in the twentieth century, especially since there are so many role models of happy, contented and fulfilled women who have willingly chosen to be child-free. One's family, however, can be something else, though that was never an issue for me.

The same Pew poll revealed differences according to race: "One-in-five (20%) white women ages 40–44 was childless in 2008, the highest rate among racial and ethnic groups. By comparison, 17% of black and Hispanic women were childless in 2008, and 16% of Asian women were childless. Rates of childlessness rose more for nonwhites than whites from 1994 to 2008."

Childless is an ancient label with obvious meaning, though why it's still accepted should be questioned. A woman isn't "less" if she is child-free.

A study reported on the LiveScience.com website in October 2012 revealed that even though motherhood is "highly connected with adult femininity in the United States," women also show "low or no distress about not being mothers, even if their friends and family want them to have children."

That doesn't keep head-exploding headlines like "Childlessness 'May Increase Likelihood of Early Death'" on websites as important as the BBC's, even if the sub-heading is actually the story. Reading on, you learn it's "involuntary childlessness" that may increase that likelihood. The information comes from a Danish study that focused solely on couples seeking in vitro fertilization (IVF) treatment, with the women who were unsuccessful at conceiving "four times more likely to die prematurely than women who had been mothers." Involuntary childlessness has to be heartbreaking. However, the numbers give the bottom line, with 316 people dying out of twenty-one thousand couples over the eleven-year study.

Knowing our own uniqueness has always been the primary key to happiness, but also is the only way to catch the right man. As you live your life and slog through difficulties and grand experiences, finding who you are becomes the central adventure, along with being the key to what makes you happy along the way. Happiness is greatly underrated, as life quests go, but I've found nothing to replace it as a guide to not only following the bliss that manifests a life lived authentically, but also in leading you to attracting the right man.

There's something inside each of us that drives us, that sends our pulse racing, similar to the high when you meet a great guy. It is that something that draws you like a magnet to discover and eventually experience your own individuality. It manifests through the curiosity that naturally rises when you find something you want to *do* with your life.

You can't ignore the impulses being sent from your heart when you come upon your life's work. Establishing a foundation for supporting yourself is a girl's major priority today, no matter her age. Our extended life span — the real possibility for realizing great longevity — means additional stressors on married life. Where a twenty-five-year marriage might once have lasted "a lifetime," it's now a point at which some modern couples, especially those who spend extended periods of time apart and living separate lives, find nothing left.

When former Vice President Al Gore and his wife Tipper announced their separation, there was a sort of shock wave that rippled through the political world. Washington, D.C. social diva Sally Quinn, who writes for the *Washington Post*, where her husband Ben Bradlee once ruled, wrote: "Watching the Gores is sort of looking at the possibilities of what a good marriage could be, and when it doesn't work for them, you sort of think, 'Oh my God, maybe it's not possible.'" The Gores announced their separation to friends via email, calling it, "a mutual and mutually supportive decision that we have made together following a process of long and careful consideration."

Tipper Gore is an accomplished photographer and has been part of the political universe with Al Gore for forty years, with the former vice president now an international environmental force. Both individuals have their own professional universe beyond their marriage. But in what universe is forty years not a complete marriage? That's a question we've never asked and answered, because it's never been an issue.

However, the twenty-first century brings with it so many advances that allow us fuller lives for longer periods, that the normal course of relationships cannot help but also be altered.

It offers another reason to postpone marriage, to live a little of your own life before committing to someone else.

There's also the image you create of your spouse that over decades can make him or her into a caricature. That's where stirring up the sex can be very helpful. Pedestals and personas can inhibit treating one another like sexual beings with appetites that include imaginative roles. When a woman becomes a mother, that doesn't mean she doesn't still have an inner sex kitten that needs tending. A judgmental male mate, who's always pontificating on his moral soapbox, could use being handcuffed to the bed and shown where his inner animal still resides. Changing the game and the dynamics between you in the relationship every once in a while may be difficult, even risky after so much comfort, but it could save a marriage.

According to a 2011 Pew Research poll on social trends, the median age for a woman to be married her first time is 26.5 years old; with men it's 28.7. In 1960 the numbers were twenty and twenty-two, respectively. Delaying marriage has caused the divorce rate to drop as well.

In 2007, *USA Today* reported that divorce had dropped to its lowest level since 1970. Some say it's because cohabitation has "increased tenfold since 1960." Others say there is a divide, with divorce rates falling for college-educated couples, "but not among less affluent, less educated couples." This same article reported that people are waiting five years longer to marry than in 1970. Bill Chausee from the Child and Family Services of New Hampshire is cited, saying, "People don't see marriage problems as some sort of stigma anymore. They're really interested in learning how to stay married; a lot of them are realizing they need more skill." *USA Today* also reports that experts believe the breakup rate of marriages is between 40-45%, not 50%.

In May 2011, CNN reported that the U.S. Census Bureau found that "divorce rates for most age groups have been dropping since 1996 by an average of about five percentage points."

Studies from Pew Research to Knot Yet all reveal that people, including men, are happier in marriage, so even as rough as it is to make marriage work, there's a reason we keep trying.

A March 2013 Pew poll on modern parenthood also revealed that a significant majority of marriages are now two-income households: "Roughly 60% of two-parent households with children under age eighteen have two working parents," the report states. "In those households, on average, fathers spend more time than mothers in paid work, while mothers spend more time on child care and household chores."

When children are included in the picture, this same poll reveals the real divide, but also a window on what change could make everyone happier:

> Overall, 33% of parents with children under age eighteen say they are not spending enough time with their children. Fathers are much more likely than mothers to feel this way. Some 46% of fathers say they are not spending enough time with their children, compared with 23% of mothers. Analysis of time-use data shows that fathers devote significantly less time than mothers to child care (an average of seven hours per week for fathers, compared with fourteen hours per week for mothers). Among mothers, 68% say they spend the right amount of time with their children. Only half of fathers say the same.... And when it comes to what they value most in a job, working fathers place more importance on having a high-paying job, while working mothers are more concerned with having a flexible schedule.

What if both men and women had equal responsibilities at home, giving the man more time with his children? It seems to me that what a man values as important might be directly related to the opportunity he has to spend time with his kids, just as a woman's valuing of a flexible schedule could revolve around the reality that she's the one with the primary domestic duties, even with a full-time job.

Unsurprisingly, American society still judges the woman as the best partner to be at home with children, but all that's needed to change this is to see a great father in action. First, he has to be given more time to become one. This has as much to do with traditional standards as it does with who is a better parent. A man cannot breast-feed an infant, but he can bottle-feed and rock the baby as well as a woman. We're just at the beginning of having a wider conversation about men being fifty percent of the domestic puzzle, and it's a topic that should have been explored a long time ago, because it's directly related to women still not having full equality.

Each woman's individual path now almost demands she find something beyond a relationship and children, and this can be excavated before finding a partner. This path is something that, when fully explored, can become a constant part of a growing consciousness that leads a woman toward fulfilling her dreams. Living longer demands this.

What can be gained through following the bliss of her personal interests is hard to explain to a woman who has never considered any path beyond finding a man to marry and building a beautiful marriage that blossoms into family. This can be the center of your universe in thought, which today encompasses everything from active dating and planning to visualizing the life you want, all depending on the way you think and create your life. It can also be part of a larger experience that first includes finding something else to accompany the joy of finding love. This makes you someone a man will be attracted to, because of the fascination your interests bring to you as a person, as an individual. It can also be a shelter in life's hurricanes.

When exploring the things you love to do, it's not a coincidence that you may also be led either to someone who has similar interests or who finds the type of things you're interested in fascinating because he or she can't do them. The opposites-attract quotient is powerful in this regard, as is the possibility of you being good at one part of your mutual interest, while a potential mate may have another gift to bring to the table.

Relationships require at their heart something the two of you will create together, beyond the relationship itself, even beyond children. This is the primal key to connecting at the deepest, most powerful level of all. Nothing rivals it or can compete with its grandeur.

Of course, centering a relationship on creating doesn't guarantee longevity either, but a relationship that isn't creative at its core cannot survive, whether it's ten years or forty, the latter certainly a long marriage by all accounts, especially when you consider "till death do us part" used to mean age fifty-something. According to the U.S. Social Security website, "Life expectancy at birth in 1930 was indeed only 58 for men and 62 for women." By Jane Fonda's sexual enjoyment standards, these statistics mean she'd never have reached her peak satisfaction. Tipper and Al Gore would never have lived to separate.

What is often not understood or fully appreciated is that creation in a partnership doesn't require children to make the relationship soar and have the potential to lock in the primal code to give it a real chance and hope of longevity. Older couples and those in second marriages have found this out.

Shared interests can lead to creating something together. Two people can have investments in their own lives, with one person aiding the other in a venture that could benefit them both. For example, women once worked to send their men through law school or to become doctors, and there are just as many men who have shepherded women into business.

But attracting and catching a man in the first place?

The place to start is through your own life. Find something that is yours that you enjoy doing, something that fills your heart with happiness and deep satisfaction. It can enlarge your world and make you excited about your own life. What this does for you as a woman, individual and unique person will change how you look, what you transmit to others, and how a man sees you. You cannot help but be more interesting, even happier, and there's nothing that acts more like an aphrodisiac on a man than a happy woman who is in love with her own life.

You also might be surprised who you can meet along the way to living your own life and exploring who it is you are as an individual. There's no down side to paying attention to yourself and what you want out of life. It starts with making yourself happy in your own skin, about what you're doing with your life and the trajectory you've set for yourself.

No man can make you happy.

All alone, living your daily life, happiness must be the core of what your choices deliver. If you're not happy in the life you've constructed, the first order of business is fixing that now, immediately. It might begin with something as simple as making a list of likes and dislikes about what's going on in your life. Often, it's about things that can be changed, but also can require work, which you've put off.

If you're in debt and that's dragging you down, the answer is simple and has nothing to do with finding a man. You first have to extricate yourself from the financial hole you've dug for yourself. It doesn't take fixing it before you look for a relationship, but your woes need to be manageable, and you must be taking responsibility for them, or any potential boyfriend could back off as soon as he starts connecting. The economic times require that both people in the relationship deal with their own realities before trying to create something together.

The old twentieth-century notion of women catching a man was coined when that was exactly the attitude, not only of society in general but also of women.

The modern era requires a woman to trust that she can attract a man worthy of her. It happens through the life she's leading that will eventually bring someone across her path, whether it's through online dating, friends and social networking, or through her career. It can even happen by chance. But today, women are leading their lives first, because having a man in our lives is a plus, not the means by which we have a life in the first place.

There's no guarantee, even if you're doing everything right that it will all end as you imagine. Life doesn't work that way. We're all dealt terrible blows. The only real weapon to combat life's surprises is the knowledge that you and no one else has chosen the path you're on. To have no regrets because you're living the life you want, even after disappointments force changes, is all anyone can expect of herself.

For a woman, dreaming of a man rescuing you has morphed into being the heroine of your own life. Writing sentences like that makes me wince, but the simple fact is that without this fundamental belief in yourself and having the knowledge that you can live a good life alone, it's very unlikely a relationship will be what you want it to be, even if you create it.

Your choices make your life, and they begin when you're alone.

A man wants to believe in the woman he envisions being with, whether it's a monogamous relationship or marriage, but he can't believe in you if you don't believe in yourself. There is also nothing on earth that can deter a man from pursuing a woman when lightning strikes, except the woman's own insecurity.

Stop listening to the tape playing in your head. You know the drill. It can either play continually or only in those moments of special vulnerability, when you begin to break out and take a risk. You think the words you're hearing cannot be controlled, but they can. You have the remote, so just turn them off. Delete them from your brain-pan DVD. Every time a phantom of them pops up, hit delete. You don't need them, because they likely came from someone else at another time when you didn't have your own voice.

It doesn't matter what's happened in your life. Absorb it, thrash the hell out of it, then move on. A great therapist I once had said the horrors of life may never go away, but they can be muted to black and white. She said it better, but that's the gist. Black and white from color may be overly optimistic, but at the heart is that you survived. Anyone can build on that.

This means we each must acknowledge that we are responsible for our own happiness, not some man, your mother or father, your friend or anyone else. No one owes you anything, but you owe yourself all you can grab and hold on to. Once you get it all together, then you can give back.

Oprah Winfrey has done several interviews with Steve Harvey, who offers the man's point of view on dating, with women asking questions that are quite provocative and worthwhile on her website, Oprah.com. It doesn't mean you need to follow everything or take what he's saying as gospel, because remember, this is your life and you're the navigator, not Steve Harvey. However, he does give excellent insight that validates what I've been told about how men think.

Harvey talks about anxiousness coming off as desperation, especially since men consider themselves hunters. "Keepers" and "throw-backs" is how he describes men's targets as they choose women. But the interesting thing is that Harvey strongly adds that the woman decides which one she is. Don't be impatient, which is built into modern life. You've got time to let things unfold, attracting him into your life.

Harvey is correct. Confident women are made this way through our own efforts. This includes having a life to live whether the man reacts to you the way you'd like or rejects you. Your worth doesn't depend on him. How this plays out when you're dating is visceral when he meets you.

One thing I've learned is that one of the worst things any woman can do is cast the man to type, according to height, financial portfolio and other factors, including in an online ad. You never know who can walk through an open door when you're looking at a whole person instead of stats on a tally sheet. But if you must go that route, then you need to match what you're looking for in a man.

Harvey says he wrote his book, *Act Like a Lady, Think Like a Man,* to empower women, which it does, up to a point. One of the things that resonated so powerfully with me is his assessment that men need three things: support, loyalty and sex. Few have put it more succinctly.

Your attention to the man's main focus, which is usually his career, has to go beyond casual interest. Men must now learn to reciprocate.

As for loyalty, Harvey couldn't be more right. A man's whole world in a relationship revolves around this. Loyalty is so deeply hooked into a man's being that if you cheat on him he's likely never to forgive you and will never trust you again. There are exceptions, but they are rare. It may not be fair, but it's a fact. A man in a relationship considers you his, not anyone else's, and he's territorial about it. If you make the choice to cheat, he gets that it was your decision, and that says all he needs to hear. It may not be fair, but forgiveness comes hard for most men.

As for the sex, it's like breathing for men. It's why when I was Relationship Consultant I was so adamant that women lead with their sensuality. It illustrates confidence, but also is the only way the best men are going to respond. They have to get a sense of your sensual nature before they engage. I'd take it much further to say this applies for women, too, which too many men just don't understand.

However, men easily can have sex after a hard day's work and sometimes actually want it to blow off steam. Women often have so many more duties at home that sex isn't on their minds. The other issue is that it's not all *Fifty Shades* of romance. Sometimes sex is just sex, which is certainly true on a Tuesday night when you just want a release.

There's nothing like a little service sex, as I call it. The depths of your sexual appetite and imagination depending, even when things at work are nuts, it can be the tonic to set you both back in sync. Service sex always goes both ways. It's a moment in time when you decide that you want sex and you know he'll love it, but you're going to forego all the candles, music, wine and delicious fluff and just get down to business. (Toys can help.) It's satisfying yourself and him in a way that doesn't require a lot of time and energy, but gets you to a climax that is thrilling just the same. It's the ultimate stress-reliever.

"Set your standards high," Harvey suggests, and I couldn't agree more.

After I met Mark, my husband of eleven years (and counting), when he called to ask me out I was pretty blunt. I have always known what I wanted and what I didn't, and I also didn't have an investment in whether I married or not, because I was a confirmed bachelorette and happy staying so. What I told Mark on the phone is that I enjoy drinking wine, and wouldn't be wearing a skirt on our date. We'd met at a moment when my whole world revolved around launching a radio show, so although I was flirtatious, I didn't have time for bullshit.

When I eventually found out Mark's reaction to that simple statement, we both laughed about it. He said he panicked immediately, because he was a beer drinker and hadn't a clue about wine, but was intent on pleasing me, so he set out to find a restaurant that served it. When we arrived and I was thrilled, he was in heaven. As for the skirt, when Mark saw me in my ass-hugging pants, high heels and fitted blouse, he couldn't have cared less.

It's not that wine is the ultimate bar for me, but I wanted to see if he could deliver something so simple that would make me happy, but also make him the hero. Win-win at the start, which also gave me a chance to thank him for his thoughtfulness and reward him with a big smile.

In one simple assignment there is communication without a lot of words, the outcome being a conversation that matters.

Who are you and what are you worth? Do you want your door opened? Then stand by the car and wait for it. If he doesn't make a move to open it, you're better off asking him to open it or walking back inside your apartment. Does he ask you to split the tab? If he can't pay the check, he certainly won't take the risks and pay the price required to build a relationship. If he can't call ahead of time to set up a date and expects you to meet in a group, the guy's a child and you need to find someone who actually wants a relationship.

Marriage still requires love, trust and deep abiding friendship that's glued together with the stickiness of sexual friction that only your chemistry mixed with his can produce. This requires time alone together, having fun over many days and weeks and months to nurture into something real that might have the possibility of lasting through moments of marriage hell.

It all begins with a date, the ever-indispensible, dynamically combustible, originating catalyst to connection, long before love ignites. Anyone thinking that it all doesn't begin here is concocting an alternative, false universe.

The post-dating idea fits perfectly into what Steve Harvey frames as "terms that [men] created so you can require less of us."

It's just so obvious, and women are doing it to themselves, which is the only way these things can happen.

As Harvey says, "Chivalry's not dead — it's just not required anymore."

7

God's Outdoors

Organized religion and the men who run it have screwed things up for everyone else. If women had a fifty-fifty stake in the leadership ranks of all religious organizations, perhaps "religiously unaffiliated" wouldn't be so popular. Religion has also not kept up with the times. Most of us still believe in something greater than ourselves — a belief in God, however it's defined — but more and more people are rejecting traditional religion, which is a very good sign for women, as well as for our relationships.

Considering the gender segregation in the overwhelming majority of organized religions, it's a miracle that women still seek out the church to have our wedding ceremonies. It really makes no sense at all, except that there's something about the ritual, the singing, the ties to our roots, as well as the architecture of a great church, that draws us back. Traditionally, many have been comforted by the guarantee of God's blessing to our unions, though modern people have realized that's absolutely no guarantee at all. Church architecture always seduces me, because I cherish privately meditating inside a beautiful chapel. Even as far away as I have moved from traditional religious worship, that's one thing that remains a joy.

Given the institutionalized misogyny in most religions, why a woman would willingly embrace this hierarchal outlet for herself, as a guide to her relationship, defies the basic foundation of our liberation. Churches that continue to encourage, institutionalize and guarantee that only male leadership dictates what faith, empowerment and connection mean have outlived their usefulness, yet too many still support this ancient ritual that denies women an equal role. It's long past time this validation ended, which can only happen if women reject it.

The newfound freedom to mine our spirituality outside the church has the potential of inspiring profound changes in how we live and what we experience in our relationships. Traditional role-playing in a relationship robs women, but also the liberated men who love us, of new ways to make a life together, which begin with shaking up gender roles to embrace full equality. We can define our marriages together, uniquely, rejecting the tired traditionalist rules from past generations that no longer serve the modern family.

Choosing a traditional relationship in today's economic reality is becoming less and less attractive, especially for modern women and men who simply do not benefit from rigidly defined gender roles. Since more women enjoy a career today than ever before, the faster we redefine marriage outside old traditional stereotypes the better it will be for women, their partners and generations to come.

From the 2012 study "Marriage Structure and Resistance to the Gender Revolution in the Workplace," by Sreedhari D. Desai of the University of North Carolina at Chapel Hill, Dolly Chugh from NYU, and the University of Utah's Arthur Brief:

> We found that employed husbands in traditional marriages, compared to those in modern marriages, tend to (a) view the presence of women in the workplace unfavorably, (b) perceive that organizations with higher numbers of female employees are operating less smoothly, (c) find organizations with female leaders as relatively unattractive, and (d) deny, more frequently, qualified female employees opportunities for promotion. It's becoming stark for the average middle class household.

A 2012 article in *Forbes* includes research that shows that women are founding businesses at one-and-a-half times the national average, and that venture backed companies operated by women have 12% higher revenues. The *Forbes* article goes on to say, "Companies with more equalized gender distribution in the upper echelons garnered 30% better results from [Initial Public Offerings]; only 3–5% of all women-owned businesses receive venture capital funding; only 16.5% of U.S. companies have women on their boards; only 25% of the tech industry is women."

The WorldBank.org website on gender points out, "Countries that invest in promoting the social and economic status of women tend to have lower poverty rates." A 2012 World Bank report on "Gender Equality and Development" explains the landscape modern women find ourselves in today: "Women's lives have improved greatly over the past decades. Enjoying ever-higher education, women have greater control over their life choices. They use those choices to participate more in the labor force; have fewer children; diversify their time beyond housework and child care; and shape their communities, economies, and societies. And the pace of change for many women in the developing world has accelerated."

Clearly, women lead differently from men, and in very good ways. In March 2013, a study of 624 board directors in Canada, conducted by the International Journal of Business Governance and Ethics, revealed that women were more likely to use "cooperation, collaboration and consensus building," while male directors more often made decisions by using "rules, regulations and traditional ways of doing business." Women were also more likely to "rock the boat" and be "more open to new ideas" than men. Chris Bart, the study's co-author, said, "Men are pack animals and they are very much quick to recognize the hierarchy of the alpha males in the group. They would be very unhappy with people coming in with different values or views to the board."

During the shutdown and debt ceiling crisis in October 2013, which brought our country to the fiscal brink, Jay Newton-Small of *Time* magazine chronicled how women senators showed the boys' club how it's done. In an article for the magazine's Swampland section titled "Women Are the Only Adults Left in Washington," Newton-Small reported what happened when Republican Senator Susan Collins stood up on October 8, as the United States was on the brink of economic default, saying, "I ask my Democratic and Republican colleagues to come together. We can do it. We can legislate responsibly and in good faith." Democratic Senate Appropriations Committee chair Barbara Mikulski, from Maryland, stood up, saying, "Let's get to it. Let's get the job done." Alaska Republican Lisa Murkowski joined in, too.

Jay Newton-Small also reported something rarely heard of today: "Most of the Senate's 20 women had gathered the previous night for pizza, salad and wine in the offices of New Hampshire Senator Jeanne Shaheen, a Democrat. All the buzz that night was about Collins' plan to reopen the government with some basic compromises. Senator Amy Klobuchar, a Minnesota Democrat, proposed adding the repeal of the unpopular medical-device tax. Senate Agriculture Committee chair Debbie Stabenow suggested pulling revenue from her stalled farm bill. In policy terms, it was a potluck dinner."

Women now either sit or are ranking members in ten of the twenty Senate committees, according to Newton-Small, which gives them a say on the most powerful issues coming before the Senate, from economic issues to military sexual assault. Democratic New York Senator Kirsten Gillibrand has led this fight and confronted Senate male seniority, as well as the highest military brass, to press the fight for the Military Justice Improvement Act. While she differs slightly on a key administrative detail, Democratic Missouri Senator Claire McCaskill is working with Gillibrand to change the horrendous reality that the military men's club continues to ignore. To do something about the 26,000 sexual assaults in the military reported in the Pentagon's own 2012 study, attacks that often come when higher ranked officers abuse their authority through sex crimes, with the victims having no way to get justice without ruining their careers.

California Democratic Senator Diane Feinstein, who turned 80 in 2013, chairs the Select Committee on Intelligence and holds dinners for women in the national security universe, where men still rule. She also keeps her door open for any new female Senator wanting advice on how to make her office effective as she learns to work the Senate.

Senator Heidi Heitkamp, a North Dakota Democrat, is quoted by Newton-Small as saying, "One of the things we do a bit better is listen."

Partisanship isn't allowed between these female senators, focusing only on what they have in common instead. They also don't publicly criticize one another. When Senator Claire McCaskill was facing a tough reelection, New Hampshire Republican Senator Kelly Ayotte refused to work for her challenger, Republican Todd Akin. Not only did Ayotte not campaign for him, but she called him out for his ludicrous claim that biology keeps women from getting pregnant during a "legitimate" rape. As if rape requires a designation of whether it's "legitimate."

Most women today want to work but also need to work, and so, for the first time in history, are fully one-half of America's workforce. In 1967, women were only one-third of all workers, according to the 2009 Shriver Report, done through Center for American Progress, a progressive group that sponsored the study.

A recent, sobering reality is that men lost three out of four jobs in the first two years of the great recession that started in 2007.

The traditional world of our ancestors, a world that depends on organized religion's male-dominated foundation to survive, is gone. With modernity threatening the old ways, organized religion has become obsessed with political wrangling and enforcing rules that no longer resonate, with churches weighed down by scandals of all types.

God's as relevant as ever, but how we convene with this force has forever changed, mostly out of necessity, because the old ways don't ring true anymore, especially for women.

Organized religion is not currently prepared to support the world of today's liberated reality. The entire structure that has defined gender roles from the home to seats of power, from boardroom to the Senate, House and White House, is supported by traditionally male leadership roles. It wasn't until October 2013 that Janet Yellen was nominated by President Barack Obama to be the first-ever female Federal Reserve Chairman in United States history.

The only way to change what organized religion has set up in our society is to replace ancient traditions that no longer apply with what empowers everyone, including places of worship that could become revitalized if they modernized.

Spiritual is now the word heard more often than *religious.*

The openness implied by spirituality also honors modernity and the way more people are living their lives. It respects the original craving for connection once experienced only through religion and the church. Spirituality has become the new modality; prayer in its modern version is represented more and more through meditation. Whatever draws so many of us to organized religion at the start remains important, but the specific rules and regulations of organized religion are no longer of primary importance.

All religions initially act as simple gateways to what lies beyond, which can only be excavated privately. Meditation offers a similar gateway in abundance. The benefits of excavating the mind and body connection through meditation go deeper than religiosity's reach.

The possibility of discovering a broader philosophy that helps answer life's imponderables is irresistible to most. Though it can be accessed through a deity or holy book, we are finding wider reaches independently and beyond. Spiritual freedom changes forever our outlook on what once was the original glue of relationships and marriage, which came with designated roles that promised predetermined lives.

Many now dare to imagine that God is outdoors.

That a connection exists beyond any church or organized religion is a revelation to some. Even as most respect that the holy books were divinely inspired, we seek modern solutions and a more private path to asking timeless questions. We still crave a way to discover the mysteries of life, of God, but we want a more independent experience, one that doesn't include the oppressive male-centric hierarchy, which includes misogyny and bigotry, as well as politics, that we just can't reconcile with any empowering spiritual message that resonates.

What does this mean for our relationships? What if we choose for our marriage or union to be sanctified in God's outdoors or elsewhere and not in a church? We are each free to decide, with the stigma of building your relationship's universe without organized religion at its center long gone.

In the 1950s, religion sanctified relationships and made them valid. Religion made people feel safe and protected in rough times, which remains a reason many still embrace it. My mother couldn't have survived without her faith and the First Christian Church, with her religiosity something she handed down to me, though I bucked the tradition from the start.

Many people, including myself, have gravitated toward modern alternatives.

New-age gurus and spiritual advisers have blasted onto the scene. These include people, teachings and books that offer a more direct route, a personal path to mining spirituality without the dogma, pleas for cash, and the guilt that bears down from most podiums in churches across the spectrum. People like Deepak Chopra, Dr. Wayne Dyer, Marianne Williamson and many others offer alternatives to religion, which were featured regularly on Oprah Winfrey's talk show and now through her website, giving alternative spiritual routes credibility. The web has opened up avenues for questions to be asked and answered personally, freeing people from having to rely on our parents' pulpit.

Meditation has exploded among the spiritually curious and mystically adventurous, offering a private and very personal way to connect the mind and body with no outside interference or interaction. The process revolves around a simple technique that begins with quieting the mind and shutting off that tape playing in your head, as Dr. Wayne Dyer has referred to it for years. With people learning to calm their emotions through meditation, the practice has caught fire, replacing prayer, and bringing creativity and unlimited possibilities with it.

The behavior of organized religion's hierarchy makes me truly sad for all those people who attend church every Sunday, especially the women. The gender power segregation isn't the fault of regular church-goers, which I have been most of my life. But any spiritual person looking for answers to the great mysteries of existence should at least question the relevance of religious organizations that practice the maxim that women aren't allowed to lead and stand with the men who have always run the church.

As defined by twentieth-century norms that have been blown to smithereens, religion is a female's worst enemy, because the entire structure is laid out against us.

It's not an accident that the church's traditional gender roles and power structure have been mimicked throughout our capitalistic, political and economic history.

In most religions, women who crave connection to God actually need men as conduits, because we are seen as unworthy and unequal to men in the church's mind, doctrine and tradition. It's this same structure that gives men power over women, which, in under-developed nations around the world, men are using to control, abuse, torture and kill women and girls.

Organized religion's expectations are a losing proposition for any independent-minded, self-actualized, spiritual female, but also for the men who love, honor and protect us. Unless, of course, you belong to one of the liberal religious factions or choose meditation and contemplation, which are now becoming a primary source of spiritual solace and inspiration for more and more people.

For the record, I'm a rebel Episcopalian, coming from the Disciples of Christ world. I've heard speak and met the presiding bishop of the Episcopal Church of the United States, Dr. Katharine Jefferts Schori. She is the first female elected to this position in the church's history. I remain an Episcopalian in my heart, because the Episcopal Church under her leadership has led the way on supporting marriage equality, and because there are modern Episcopal churches. Schori stated in 2012 that the church "has taken a very nuanced approach on abortion. We say it is a moral tragedy but that it should not be the government's role to deny its availability." This is a modern statement by a true religious leader, a female, who understands the challenges of modernity and that, in some matters, we each have to grapple with ourselves and our God. She has also said that contraception is a "normative part of health care," because "it's appropriate for couples to plan their families."

I've written about my very personal come-to-Jesus moment many times before, including in my book, *The Hillary Effect*, in the chapter titled "Is Freedom Just for Men?" To make a long story shorter here, contraceptives failed, leaving me pregnant in the middle of a road show tour. I had to hide that we were going to get an abortion, a legal procedure at the time, also having to cross several state lines and drive for hours to have the procedure performed. There wasn't a moment I didn't know what I had to do when I found out I was pregnant. An abortion was the only option for me for emotional and very personal reasons, as I explained in my first book in great detail. It's unfortunate that I had to skulk around to get one, because it led to me hemorrhaging one day as I walked around a mall. Thankfully, it wasn't life-threatening, and I kept the real reason I'd originally missed rehearsals quiet, averting judgment and stigma I didn't need on top of everything else. The abortion did make me face myself in every way.

I'd done everything I could not to get pregnant, except not have sex. For most modern women this is not a real choice and shouldn't be expected. It was a tragic situation, but I take responsibility for the way I live my life, with my independence and decisions no one else's business. The abortion had no impact on my spiritual grounding, but did further convince me that "God's will" has nothing to do with anything in life, but is really a *man*-made construct to explain choices we each actually make ourselves, but are afraid to claim.

I also know from personal experience that churches can make a great deal of difference in their communities, for which they should be commended. The outreach by churches to the poor and homeless through meals alone after the 2008 economic downturn became the only source of sustenance some people had. The last church I belonged to was when I lived in Beverly Hills, California. All Saints' Episcopal Church was a lifeline at one of the most harrowing times in my life, which I'll never forget.

It doesn't erase the harm organized religions do through politics and gender apartheid.

When I was growing up, my mother wouldn't let me skip a Sunday service. If I dared to play hooky by pretending to be asleep or act like I was not feeling well, I could sometimes skate, but once she came home, the cold shoulder I got destroyed the whole day. It turned me into a religious person for a very long time, though not someone who automatically followed along with the sermon and saluted. I had a lot of questions that started very early, because I didn't quite appreciate that women were out of the power loop where God was concerned, which was obviously a setup. What made men worthy to run things but not women? When I figured out it revolved around having a penis, it led to quite an epiphany.

Religion was seen as the glue to American society until the late twentieth century. But nothing has caused the world more grief than people fighting over their religion's dominance throughout history. What religion has done in the name of God is equally immoral. The Catholic Church's role in protecting priests instead of children might have turned out differently if nuns had serious leadership roles inside the Vatican. Would the Penn State pedophilia scandal have happened if women were among those who knew about it? Our institutions cry out for women in leadership.

Amid this testosterone-driven environment, women are supposed to find solace and support in the most important union of their life, marriage. Is it any wonder more and more females are choosing God's outdoors as their church?

I blew through organized religion's usefulness a long time ago, preferring daily meditation and contemplation, where I convene as I choose in a manner that has proven to me that I need no conduit to connect. Women don't need a male member of any church to prove the force is within, though I have met holy men whose conversation I have deeply enjoyed. Not coincidentally, I have also had their respect for being a powerful spiritual force of my own. There are men who know women deserve this respect inside the church as well, but they are still a minority, especially in the public voice of organized religion. Still, we need them because we won't change the balance without them. I'm blessed to have also learned much from spiritual men.

One of the main disagreements I have with Steve Harvey's mostly insightful advice on relationships is his emphasis on traditional religion. In many sections of his book *Act Like a Lady, Think Like a Man*, Harvey invokes God, which is understandable given his traditional audience. However, in one section constructed for women, he gives examples of questions to ask potential mates, including "whether he knows the Lord."

Obviously, Harvey and I are from vastly different cultural backgrounds. It's not just about me being a Scots-Irish feminist, and Harvey being an African-American, traditional male, though this is a huge part of it. It also goes way beyond Harvey, because there is a whole contingent of people, including women, who still believe that the structure of relationships and families proselytized by organized religion still applies today and will for the children born to millennials and the next generations.

Throughout my life, I had one dating rule: If a man showed up in front of me and professed his Christianity or his knowledge of the Lord, I'd politely excuse myself, then run from the building. Because what's tied to most men who claim to know the Lord today is the traditional mind-set that is now archaic and meant to make women unequal, but is disguised through words like *respect* and *protect*, which can also mean *rescue* and *control*.

In a hilarious tale revolving around Steve Harvey's definition of "protection," he talks about one time when he was out scuba diving with his wife, a certified scuba diver. Not a diver himself, Harvey was left back in the boat while his wife went exploring. When she was out of sight and in the water, he pretty near panicked: "By the time she was actually under the water, I'd told my security guy, who can't scuba dive, to put on his snorkel and get in and keep an eye on her. I'd also told everyone onboard — from my manager to the captain — that if my wife is not back up here in thirty-five minutes, everybody's putting on some suits and we're going to go get her."

Needless to say, the tour guide for the dive got a bit alarmed, and the rest played out in a scene you couldn't script better if you tried. "'I'm telling you,' I said, getting a little more jumpy with each word, 'either everybody goes down there to save her, or I'm killing everybody on the boat. This boat goes nowhere without her, and if it pulls off and she's not on it, that's it for everybody.'"

Harvey calls this a "primal need" he has "to make sure nothing happens to her." His wife doesn't "trip out" about this; she simply says, "Thanks for caring, honey."

Good for the Harveys. They're obviously well suited, and we should all be so lucky as to have such a long, successful marriage.

Modern women like myself hear Sting playing in our ears, every breath, every move, every step, "I'll be watching you." Great song, horrible way to live.

Harvey also talks about a moment when his father stayed home, because his mother felt intimidated by an "insurance man looking for some money." As he tells the story and describes the man, it sounds like any woman at home might feel intimidated by someone like this. His dad finds out about it and decides to confront the insurance man, making sure he's at home when the guy comes back. The confrontation is intense. Harvey recalls his dad saying: "'If you ever say anything disrespectful to my wife again, I will *kill you*.' Now, that may seem a little extreme, but this is what real men do to protect the ones they love."

If this weren't literal, maybe we all could appreciate the romantic paternalism of this story, if not the actions, which are more than "a little extreme" and go a lot further than what any modern woman expects from her man. Assaulting, let alone murdering, someone and landing in jail would be extremely counterproductive to protecting the ones you love.

Steve Harvey repeats in his book that it's "God first, then family." I've no doubt many people relate to this prioritization, but it certainly doesn't translate to anything that benefits modern women or men in today's world. The search for meaning in life, as well as God, can be a constant in a person's life. But your primary relationship is finding and knowing who *you* are and what that thing is that makes you happy, which no force outside yourself can tell you.

The answers lie within. We are all part of God, not separate from God. If we'd accept that, maybe our actions would change, and so would the world.

What organized religion has done to the natural course of human sexuality experienced between partners is nothing good. The shame, bigotry and exclusionary religiosity that comes from organized religion has resulted in sex becoming dirty, scary and outside the normal course of life's experiences we long to enjoy. Celibacy is not a natural condition of the human animal. It's an aberration, an abnormal condition that is unhealthy and counterproductive, and is only appropriate for the very few who live in seclusion but have no business teaching life-lessons to mere mortals, who benefit from the healthy quenching of natural human desires. If sexuality isn't honored and respected in your life, it will destroy you through its sheer power to be recognized as part of what makes you human.

Modern religion has done much for the poor, reaching out across the world through ministries to help the underprivileged and marginalized. But it has a lot to answer for when it refuses to honor what's real and institutes religious dogma for solutions, which is what happens regularly with condom distribution and reproductive health advice for women in underdeveloped nations, but also through institutional bigotry and misogyny. Counseling that helps women in developing nations plan their lives is a human rights issue, as well as a women's rights issue, borrowing from what Hillary Clinton has said throughout her public life.

Modern women and the partners who love us need to craft a separate path, away from organized religion's hold on society, especially where relationships, marriage and family are concerned. Does this mean there is no value in the Christian or Hebrew Bible, the Quran or in Buddha's teachings? Of course not. Reading any such text is at the very least a challenge for us to mine the meaning for our own lives through the words that come from men divinely inspired. But any holy text is just a beginning. Where extremist fundamentalism resides, however, no matter the religion, there is no room for women to breathe or live independently, which is the point.

People are questioning and finding out answers for themselves, with there not enough vibrant conversation going on outside the church in God's outdoors, where life's combustion lives. That is to say, beyond the boundaries and confines, outside the rules and strictures of religious philosophies that are rigidly discussed. Gender-driven confines have no place in the modern era, with more and more people coming to this conclusion slowly and steadily.

In 2012, the Pew Forum on Religion & Public Life found that one-fifth of the American public and about 33% of adults under age thirty are "religiously unaffiliated" today, which is the highest percentage ever in Pew Research Center polling.

Believe it or not, that's very good news for relationships, as well as for our nation's spiritual health. But for women, it's celebration time. We will never experience full equality as long as there are men in the turrets of some religious building spreading lies that we aren't their equals when it comes to leading religious institutions and those seeking spiritual guidance.

A twenty-first century reformation will happen when hell freezes, right? Or when the money dries up. Or when people with larger imaginations set religion free. Surprisingly, Pope Francis I has shown remarkable courage in the way he has chosen to live, but also through his rhetoric. When he said the Catholic Church shouldn't be "obsessed" with abortion, gay marriage and contraception, but also showed willingness to engage atheists, he made worldwide headlines. Conservative, traditionalist Catholics openly questioned him, ignoring that he'd given hope to millions of people who are spiritually hungry for change.

The inequality, segregation and outright bigotry of organized religion is no doubt why 88% of those unaffiliated also aren't looking for a religion. The religiously unaffiliated believe that "religious organizations are too concerned with money and power, too focused on rules and too involved in politics," the Pew Research Center found.

Not enough people are brave enough to ask why churches getting involved in politics aren't automatically stripped of their tax-exempt status. The answer is simple: It's because politicians are scared to do what's right, which would be to force religion to its higher place, outside of politics, where it does not belong. In a survey done by NBC News and *Esquire* magazine, released in the November 2013 issue, they describe a shift in American politics that includes "a large group of American voters — even a majority — who make up a New American Center," with 59% of these people believing that "churches and religious organizations should have no role in politics."

The number of Americans who say "they never doubt the existence of God" has dropped from 88% in 1987 to 80% in 2012, according to the Pew study.

The wonderful thing that rises to the top, however, is that a survey in 2012 by the same Pew forum, conducted jointly with the PBS television program *Religion & Ethics NewsWeekly*, found that 46 million unaffiliated adults consider themselves religious or spiritual in some way. More than two-thirds, 68%, say they believe in God. More than one-third, 37%, say they are "spiritual" but not "religious," and 21% say they pray every day.

That's a relatively paltry number who say they pray every day. But just imagine if meditation was seen as prayer, and people knew the physical and emotional benefits of it. One of the things meditation does is quiet your ego and emotions for a while, stop that tape in your head that keeps propping up beliefs you've clung to, but which are actually stumbling blocks preventing you from living your most authentic life on your own terms. Meditation is also great for stress, but also for your health, just like sex is.

In a conversation with Deepak Chopra on his website, Rudolph Tanzi, a re-nowned genetic researcher who was dubbed one of the "Rock Stars of Science" by *GQ* magazine, calls this tape playing constantly in our heads the "default mode." It's our normal. Tanzi and Chopra co-authored *Super Brain*, which, they write, "shows you how to use your brain as a gateway for achieving health, happiness and spiritual growth." When your intellect is keeping your emotions in check through gibberish, it is actually also keeping you sane, as Tanzi puts it. But at the same time, it prevents you from living your life in the moment.

You may have had a fight with your boyfriend. Maybe you've had an encounter, and you're scripting your next conversation. Or perhaps you're reciting what you're going to say when you meet that guy for your first date. All of this is your ego squeez-ing your emotional energy into words in your head to keep you from just enjoying your walk to the restaurant or bar, or waiting quietly for a call while you read a book and think about what you're learning instead.

Meditation calms the noise. It allows the brain to relax and open, for lack of a better description, and even leads to intuition and higher thinking that isn't available when all the chatter is rumbling. In a state of meditation, your awareness is more acute. I'm again relying on Tanzi's interpretation, because it also rings true with my own experiences with meditation, which I've been practicing daily for well over fifteen years.

"The brain is like a piano," Tanzi told the *Boston Globe* in November 2012. "You can learn to play it," he added.

The distance meditation offers from the madness is part mystical, part mira-cle. It's all predicated on the practitioner mining her own brain and funneling her energy into complete and total quiet. When you first try it, you'll be lucky to last five minutes, but the effectiveness grows as you practice. The beauty and power of meditation is also that sometimes your mind works out problems. In the silence and peace, an answer rises, presenting itself easily. You often know the answer anyway but can ignore it in the frenzy of your nonstop, ego-emotion conversation.

There are no rules to meditation. Sitting in a pose isn't required. Anywhere you feel comfortable will do, as long as you're alone. For busy parents, this could mean the shower. You can even find a path to meditation through music, using it as a prelude and preparation for learning to sit in silence. A piece of music you love can act as a faithful companion as you attempt to quiet your busy brain.

Meditation does not require religion, a priest or pastor as conduit, or a book of holy prayers to chant. You can be indoors or in God's outdoors, sitting in your car watching the sun set. Church is not required. Tuesday is just as good as Sunday. Meditation is the ultimate liberator. It can also eventually be a step forward on the path to health, including in your relationship.

"Meditation is valuable for all of humanity," the Dalai Lama told Oprah Winfrey in a 2001 interview posted on her website, "because it involves looking inward. People don't have to be religious to look inside themselves more carefully. It is constructive and worthwhile to analyze our emotions, including compassion and our sense of caring, so that we can become more calm and happy."

Turning to meditation, there is a sense of rising peace that is empowering. The religious door you might have once walked through to find faith in the first place has now opened into God's outdoors, and you experience the force that is the creator of life and abundance in a world outside a building, and outside an organization run mostly by men. This is the limitless world of nature, containing the possibility of tapping the mystical formula that is the contagion of life.

All of a sudden, with eyes closed, through the process of clearing the chatter from your head and stopping the tape filled with voices of people who push rules on you that no longer apply, you find your own code.

Or just maybe you don't. Maybe you decide that the buck stops with you, and that's enough. You can live with making your own choices and mistakes, taking the consequences. That guilt imposed from the outside isn't for you. Meditation can still calm the ego and offer massive physical benefits you can actually feel, through a calmer center of self and less angst. You find a place for problems by prioritizing what matters.

The Golden Rule is pretty simple and doesn't require religious scripture, church or whatever hocus-pocus makes atheists go berserk when you cite faith as a foundation of your life. Many utilize Jesus' words in the Sermon on the Mount, which Wayne Dyer quotes in his book *The Power of Intention*: "Whatsoever ye would that men do unto you, do you even so unto them." Treating people as you want to be treated is simply enough spirituality for some.

According to Gallup, the first year they conducted polling on religiosity, in 1948, 69% of Americans considered themselves Protestant. In 2012, Protestant affiliation was down to 41%.

One particular part I wish I could write in the sky for all to see is that in the same Pew-PBS survey already cited, 58% of the respondents say they "often feel a deep connection with nature and the earth." It's the most important aspect of alternative spirituality and connection and the greatest opening for modern society since organized religion closed its door on spirituality and equality, choosing fundamentalism over freedom.

An organized religious group's politics can reveal murderous cruelty at its heart. A church that would get in the way of a pregnant woman whose life is in danger — as the Catholic Church has done several times in recent years, refusing a woman lifesaving surgery in Colorado and also Ireland — has lost its moral center, not to mention its sacredness. No religious organization has the right to let a woman die because of church doctrine. Holding religious institutions accountable for these policies is the job of modern society.

During the conclave that selected Pope Francis I, an interesting article popped up in the *Washington Post*. Ashley E. McGuire, a senior fellow with the Catholic Association, authored the piece, in which she argued that she didn't know "of a single man being 'sent' to Rome" for the conclave. Then in an effort to rehabilitate the Vatican's image with women, a herculean task, McGuire offered her best defense of the male hierarchy, saying its "workforce is approximately forty percent female [and] has a very progressive maternity leave policy, allowing women paid leave beginning two months before their due date and allowing them a year of paid leave after birth. When the women return." McGuire writes, "They are allowed to create a 'milk schedule' so that they can structure their hours around their nursing needs."

This policy obviously reflects the respect the church has for women as mothers, which is absolutely deserved, but also happens to be the primary role the Catholic Church sees for women. It in no way addresses the continued second-class status of women's leadership in matters of spirituality that still exists inside the Catholic Church, and the refusal of the Vatican to respect and support the social justice work of American nuns.

It's these types of decisions and outcomes that have people running from church buildings, preferring to find solace in nature through the peace and calm of God's outdoors.

It's amazing what kind of conversations you can have with your partner while hiking or walking in nature. Taking the time to breathe, to take in the quiet and hear the life around you, while convening with the source of life itself — nature and the earth — proves God is indeed outdoors. When children are involved, what better teaching is there than to appreciate and protect our planet and all of its creatures? This has a vast spiritual and practical meaning.

In the midst of all this change, megachurches are faring better than traditional churches, even staying aloft in troubled economic times. In 2011, the top ten U.S.

megachurches reportedly brought in $8.5 billion. Joel Osteen is considered the "rock star of Christianity," through his non-denominational ministry that draws forty thousand in attendance each week, with Jumbotrons to view the service, while reaching seven million on television. The annual budget for his Lakewood Church is more than seventy million dollars, according to reports.

Osteen is out of a new mold. When asked in an interview on Beliefnet.com whether his advice is like cognitive therapy, because he encourages a way of thinking to be happy and optimistic, Osteen replied, "I think a lot of it is." The emphasis on positivity jumps out from Osteen's message. The guilt and damnation that have been the central focus of organized religion, the "Repent, sinners" shout, is not only missing but has been replaced by inclusivity. The message is very much about the power of positive thinking, straight out of Norman Vincent Peale, a man my mother read religiously. We fought her cancer together for more than a decade, and it's unlikely she'd have lived and I'd be where I am today if she hadn't read Peale.

Positive thinking even has its own place on MayoClinic.com, which devotes a full page to it from the Mayo Clinic staff. What are the benefits? "Increased life span; lower rates of depression; lower levels of distress; greater resistance to the common cold; better psychological and physical well-being; reduced risk of death from cardiovascular disease; [and] better coping skills during hardships and times of stress."

The staff of the famed and respected clinic write that it's unclear why people benefit from positive thinking, but the fact is, people do.

It's the same with meditation.

Osteen's positive messaging is also seen on gay marriage. In an interview with Oprah Winfrey, Osteen responded to questions about gay marriage quite differently from most religious leaders, which made headlines on TheBlaze.com, Glenn Beck's website. Osteen said, "I believe that homosexuality is shown as a sin in the scripture. Oprah, it's a hard thing in a sense, because I'm for everybody. I'm not against anybody. I don't think anybody's second class." Osteen is obviously putting scripture in the lead and not confronting gospel, because no preacher wants that fight, while continually making it clear he's not here to judge or condemn *anyone*. His humility is revealed through his words, as is his humanity.

The notion that homosexuality is a sin makes no sense when you think about the creation of life itself. Homosexuality is simply how someone is born.

It's the bright side of religiosity, and what's most important for people, that Osteen represents. The joy he exudes from his preaching is fundamental to his message. Osteen wants faith exploration to be a happy journey that happens right now, even in the midst of challenges or life's perils. The size of his ministry proves its relevancy.

Osteen leaves a lot of the journey to the individual to find on her or his own. There is something profound in this message, because that's the job of each of us that no community church or its meetings and clubs can do. Eventually, we've each got to answer the question of God and religion or spirituality for ourselves. At least Osteen seems to be making it a little more joyful. That he also stays well away from politics is not by accident but by design.

Most of us are curious or involved in our own personal quest to learn about the meaning and purpose of life. This question applies to our primary relationship, when we are privileged enough to create it with someone. We ask what we are going to do together. You may say start a family, which is a natural and primary motivator. However, then what?

We are living longer lives, busier lives, with more coming at us to involve us and take us away from what once was quiet family living. What else are you going to create with your partner, as well as your family and children, that binds you?

Seeing the Grand Canyon was a holy experience for me. The crowds can rob us all of a meditative moment, but nothing can deny the magnitude and majesty of what we're seeing. A magnificent forest like Yosemite can do the same thing. The natural wonders list inside America alone is limitless, especially if you've enjoyed the gift of travel. That six in ten people who are religiously unaffiliated feel a deep connection with nature and the earth is telling us something profound. If only we would harness these feelings to save the planet we profess to love.

Without human judgment and morality dictated from on high by a religious hierarchy, our connection to God is only as powerful as the openness of our mind allows it to be, with the personal empowerment of individual faith exploration shifting what religion means to people and our society today.

The biggest reason this isn't a wider topic of discussion, with modern women declaring their religious freedom and a spiritual break from organized religion that no longer serves us, is that the American media is still run by people who won't challenge the traditional religious hierarchy, which continues to be honored in ways that never include women.

This whole trend toward lack of religious affiliation also bridges generations, again according to Pew Research: "In 2012, 21% of Gen Xers and 15% of Baby Boomers describe themselves as religiously unaffiliated, up slightly (but by statistically significant margins) from 18% and 12%, respectively, since 2007."

If you're thinking of marrying, with spirituality important to you or at least something you want to discuss, because having children is your intent, a conversation on the subject begins with the God factor. You can start the conversation after suggesting a walk outside, where there's plenty of room for you both. A philosophical discussion will let you know a lot about a man. In a modern marriage, however, two people do not become one, so differences in how you both relate to spirituality shouldn't be the end of the world, even if children are involved. Being exposed to different points of view will only make you richer.

Learning your own philosophy about religion and spirituality is a lifelong quest. It's very personal and it doesn't require us to be "God-fearing," because fear has nothing to do with spirituality or God. When I think of the Old Testament, that phrase certainly has meaning to me. I visualize Michelangelo's white man with a beard, an image that rendered me awestruck when I first saw it in the Sistine Chapel. But what I've come to know through meditation and the teachings of modern leaders of spirituality has made the scary, malevolent-sounding God a fictional character to me. The irony that Michelangelo got into trouble with the church for his Last Judgment fresco, which dares to suggest Jesus and others communicated directly with God, isn't lost on me.

"We originated in a field of energy that has no boundaries," Dr. Wayne Dyer writes in his book *Inspiration*. "Before entering the world of form, we were in-Spirit — a piece of God, if you will."

In the sense that God lies within, as New Age gurus teach, this reinforces that the primary relationship of life is with yourself. This primary relationship matters most in life, because if you're not centered on the path to your own bliss, it really doesn't matter whom you love; at some point, you're headed for an awakening, which could shake the foundation of your partnership.

This modern-day shift toward self-actualization and away from the church's dominance over our lives has had a dramatic effect on relationships, most of it for the better, especially for women. Breaking free of the structural cave of organized religion has freed women to explore spirituality in a much more personal and unique way, with no guilt trips, no political agenda and no scandals to sift through that make a mockery of everything being heard. In addition, there's zero bigotry and prejudice to overlook in the comfort of a meditative *om-m-m*. I do sometimes miss singing the hymns in a cathedral, and that's why when we do go, I get such joy.

Meditating in a beautiful cathedral, well, there's just nothing like it. When we first moved to the Washington, D.C. area, the first thing I did was get tickets for Easter service at the National Cathedral. It was packed, politicians running down the aisle to take their seat up front, where the price was higher as you got closer to the pulpit. It wasn't the same as taking a tour in the church, when stealing a moment in a pew to just shut my eyes and connect was far more private. Wherever I travel, I always seek out the great churches, the architectural splendor still seductive to me.

Beyond our spiritual excavation, the traditionalism enforced through religious norms, which, no matter the religion, is shared across the world, remains an impediment to women's advancement and leadership. It is also counterproductive to include it in relationship advice today, with stereotypical gender roles no longer serving women or our families.

"No matter how society changes or how many responsibilities men take on in the household, the bottom line is that everyone still expects the woman to turn a house into a home — a clean home," Steve Harvey writes. But it's Harvey's follow-up that unmasks perfectly and succinctly the dilemma for women in the modern era: "Now if we're both working and you don't have time to keep it up, and I don't want to keep it up..." *Full. Stop.* So, women can get too busy to clean the house, but men may just not *want* to clean it. Harvey suggests in this case that "the house simply cannot be dirty," and that couples may need to "carve out some cash to get a housekeeper." But what if there's no cash to carve out of the monthly budget? After all, men don't want to do it. Oh, if only women had that choice.

Steve Harvey, regardless of the many excellent points he makes for women to consider, represents traditional religious views on relationships. Even in his punchlines: "We're still in a jam right now because of Eve."

Harvey does know the story of Adam and Eve is fiction, right? I refer him to the mapping of the human genome.

Common relationship advice, including from *The Rules'* authors Ellen Fein and Sherrie Schneider, adheres to a traditional path, representing people who know their fan base and cater to it, but are missing the modern era's liberated reality. While they do speak for a certain contingent, they do not demand enough of men at a time when women are needed to take the world the next step forward and can't do so without men stepping up.

Rigidly defined roles for men and women today are becoming obsolete, but not soon enough. Take a traditional Jewish prayer, which Betty Friedan utilizes in *The Feminine Mystique*. Men say: "I thank Thee, Lord, that Thou hast not created me a woman." Women respond: "I thank Thee, Lord, that Thou has created me according to Thy will." Perhaps we should really blame the Greeks, with Socrates and Plato supposedly believing thanks should be given openly "that I was born a human and not a beast; a man and not a woman; a Greek and not a Barbarian."

When you stop and look beyond the United States, it becomes even more apparent what religion and culture continue to do to women, especially in countries that promote fundamentalist stereotypes. Honor killings, acid poured in the faces of girls and women trying to learn, and stoning for women who are victims of rape, all prove that fundamentalist misogyny is still rampant outside the U.S., led by countries that are guided by religious fanatics. When fourteen-year-old Malala Yousafzai of Pakistan was shot in the head and neck by the Taliban, almost dying because she dared to speak out against them and speak up for girls to be educated, the event became a battle cry for girls and women around the world.

The message this now sixteen-year-old heroine is sending to American women, who met with President Obama in the White House, and Queen Elizabeth II at Buckingham Palace, should steel us all for the important work that is still left for us to do, because what we face pales in comparison.

Modern women are still trying to break out economically in a country that continues to support equal pay for equal work in theory, but not through laws. This unequal pay status was set up by traditional religion through the foundational societal belief that the man is the sole provider, which is still supported by traditional capitalism. However, it no longer serves our purposes. When a woman's income matches or exceeds her husband's there is an automatic shift in the dynamics of family. Equal pay enforcement must catch up.

If organized religion doesn't recognize women's leadership role in its own hierarchy, how will its leaders support the changes in the family, which include child-rearing duties and domestic chores? They won't.

There is no way to get policies changed, from government to corporations, to support women in leadership, if our most vaunted institutions, which includes organized religion, don't embrace the modern reality of twenty-first century living.

The independent individualism that permeates modern living now and applies to women and men offers the opportunity to live freer and fuller lives, but also more separate ones, too, which often breathe easier outside the church's traditional strictures. Each of us is uniquely suited to finding her own codes. For more and more people, fighting against organized religion's rules and dictates are a waste of time. The power of the church today is too entrenched, stubborn and male-dominated to allow the reforms that would bring it the new vibrancy and relevance that so many people would welcome. Change begins with opening *all* doors to women.

It's why nature has become the choice of more and more people searching for solitude and a place to think and convene with whatever might be there in the beyond. For those of us who know that God is outdoors, not just inside a church, nature offers Holy Communion, if of a different sense.

"As a single footstep will not make a path on the earth," Henry David Thoreau wrote in one of his journals, "so a single thought will not make a pathway in the mind. To make a deep physical path, we walk again and again. To make a deep mental path, we must think over and over the kind of thoughts we wish to dominate our lives."

The reason our environment has fallen apart from neglect, man's arrogance and marauding self-indulgence and corporate greed, is that we have taken God inside a building and forgotten our connection to the beauty that was created so we might live. That we are part of God, the Force that creates all of life, that moves the seas, that allows our precious earth to house us and sustain our lives, has been all but forgotten. Supporting the church has replaced protecting that which actually sustains us. This natural connection to the earth doesn't require a church or a religious man or woman, it only requires our attention back to the fundamental life of nature all around us.

As the fourteenth Dalai Lama said, "The earth is not only the common heritage of all humankind but also the ultimate source of life."

Aligning with something greater than ourselves, believing there is something else, even if we can't define it, is the majority view of Americans. This belief, the notion of faith itself, can't always be understood. It certainly doesn't require separate rules for men and women that are different, or roles that are pre-defined. It also doesn't originate from inside a church.

For the moderns, we all define our own beliefs well outside of organized religion, which includes our own roles that will fit our relationships and our families, as well as how children should be introduced to the modern world in which they will live. Definitions get filled in as life is experienced.

In this context of living your life, finding that person you are at your core, as well as finding a life partner, the notion of waiting three seconds or thirty before you reply to a text message from someone you're interested in seems silly. The idea that you should ever choose to reduce a potential romantic connection to such trivial communication sounds absurd. The games we choose to play through our daily lives with one another reveal how far from our own heart centers we have strayed. That we can't trust ourselves on any road we choose unless we're playing by someone else's rules, or a societal role from another era, puts us in a box we chose to construct around ourselves.

Being the individual you know you are at your core in every moment is the only way you'll ever find your own place in the world, let alone someone to share it with. This takes you beyond a post-dating construct, or waiting thirty seconds to text, or believing you have to limit yourself and your own enjoyment because the man needs to have space to play protector. It gives each individual the opportunity to fulfill his or her own personal adventure, while honoring the person's private journey inside a relationship that in the modern era must have more elastic boundaries to thrive.

To fulfill your own dreams of being the individual you can be, you must above all things find that thing inside you that makes you who you are. We must each find inside ourselves that thing that inspires us. You may want a relationship and children, but there are years before that time manifests when you owe it to yourself, as well as your potential mate, not to mention the children you dream of creating, to find your personal uniqueness.

Creating a life together means many things. The philosophy of life you both bring to the relationship is foundational to its possibility of working long-term. Perhaps the dreams you both have for what lies beyond working to pay the bills can weave into a relationship of mutual support in helping each other reach personal goals.

If neither of you are religiously affiliated, which is happening increasingly today, what is that cohesive philosophy that helps you make sense of life and the partnership you hope to create? What are you here to do, experience and share with the world, as well as each other? What's your contribution? What type of life will you build together, and what effect do you hope to have in your little corner of the world? If children are in the picture or you hope they will be, what will you teach them about the world and how it works?

A belief in God today has a wider, freer meaning. Liberated individuals have the opportunity to redefine what it means to be spiritual and believe in some sort of connection, beyond what religious institutions used to force down on people, who had little choice but to embrace the societal fence of structured faith or be cast out and branded unfit.

Holy books and texts will always remain a guide for people. However, as has been proven through Deepak Chopra, as well as Wayne Dyer, Gary Zukav, Marianne Williamson and even the Dalai Lama, there is much more to be explored beyond organized religion.

No one has been more influential in the New Age spirituality revolution than

Oprah Winfrey. Her influence, backing and promotion, including her Soul Series webcast, as she has offered introductions to alternatives to organized religion, cannot be overstated. Ms. Winfrey's independent thought and curiosity are an American tradition.

"How many ages and generations have brooded and wept and agonized over this book!" wrote Walt Whitman in *The Bible as Poetry*, which is online through the University of Chicago website.

Ralph Waldo Emerson took that thought a step further: "Make your own Bible," he wrote. "Select and collect all the words and sentences that in all your readings have been to you like the blast of a trumpet."

Women can certainly relate to Emerson's suggestion. Thomas Jefferson obliged, while anyone having studied or even passed time through reading the Bible can agree with Whitman. To ponder the words attributed to the man called Jesus of Nazareth, quoted by Dr. Wayne Dyer in *The Power of Intention*, is to be on the threshold of changing your life and the possibilities of your relationship, because of the attention to your own purpose.

> If you bring forth what is inside you,
> what you bring forth will save you.
> If you don't bring forth what is inside you,
> what you don't bring forth will destroy you.

If that is true of self, it is surely true of our most important relationship, which can't possibly thrive unless the choices we make resonate with our most profound selves, which we are on this planet to know first, above all. Whatever we find in life, including God, is found through this self-discovery.

Carlos Castaneda said, "In the universe there is an immeasurable, indescribable force which shamans call intent, and absolutely everything that exists in the entire cosmos is attached to intent by a connecting link."

"May the force be with you" had such power in the legacy of *Star Wars* that the cult status the film attained could be appreciated even by those who simply enjoyed the film. Yoda says to Luke Skywalker, "You must feel the force around you," and to anyone who has ever connected in a moment of life, or endeavored to, we can understand the intent here, the manifestation of purpose through these words.

The intent we each have to manifest the life we want has nothing to do with calculated rules for dating, the notion that a relationship can be forged through traditional roles alone. In a modern era, where we're mining human potential through

New Age thinking, study and application, the thought that any connection can manifest through manipulation, fakery and role-playing makes no sense. It certainly won't lead to happiness.

Isn't that what this is all about?

Dr. Howard Cutler writes extensively on "the art of happiness," including in a book of the same title he co-authored with the Dalai Lama. Sharing his views on Huffington Post, he talked about the benefits of happiness, but also about the notion that being happy is selfish or frivolous: "One of the fundamental principles of *The Art of Happiness* is that cultivating greater happiness not only benefits oneself but also one's family, community and society. There is new scientific evidence supporting this principle as well. Such evidence helps dispel our common cultural biases and myths, such as perceiving happiness as a somewhat 'soft' or frivolous subject, or considering the pursuit of happiness to be self-centered or self-indulgent."

Cutler, a psychiatrist, goes on to emphasize the importance for us to recognize the value of happiness in our lives, and how people in the harsh economic times since the great recession of 2007-2009 are finding paths back to what's really important in life.

Nothing is more underrated than happiness and what it can do for your life, but I want to stress here the importance of happiness to finding a partner and building a relationship that will last.

We experience many challenges throughout life, sometimes falling into the dark despair of self-destruction that can threaten your very life. Sometimes choosing happiness in a single moment is a way of navigating and surviving, a profound tool on which life can depend. Your relationship cannot survive without happiness. Dr. Wayne Dyer says that when you change the way you look at things, the things you look at change. Even in bad times, one thought that emphasizes that *you want to feel good* can make the difference.

We feel it in a fleeting moment, but often don't take the time to nurture it. That pure lift of joy we get when we experience something, an event, a task or a person that sparks that energy pulse from inside ourselves that breaks out into physical reaction, joy. The contagion felt as a result of that moment, a lift in life that can wipe out whatever calamity you've experienced for a split second. To feel happiness, let alone sustain it, you have to be doing the excavating of your own life's purpose as well.

Where do you go to feel happy, what do you do to replicate the feeling? Can you manifest happiness in your daily life? Who makes you happy? Are you authentically happy when you're on an adventure such as a date? If you believe we're in a post-dating era, also choosing group events, is it a happy experience?

There has to be time in your life for laughter and having a blast with the one you love, with whom you hope to share a lifetime. This is made possible through living your own version of happiness in your own life, no matter what's going on around you.

Life's too short to do a job you hate. To live somewhere that doesn't fit your nature. To kowtow to other peoples' rules to make *them* happy. To wish you looked like someone else or had your girlfriend's talent or body, while disrespecting the unique person you are and the talent you have inside that no one else can match.

Again, if you don't know who you are and what makes you happy, you'll never be able to have a great relationship with someone else. Finding that thing that makes life sing for you, that you're good at and love to do, is a start, the happiness it brings you is the beginning.

Every day you must find time to disconnect from the noise, unplug from technology, and invest in something that thrills you and takes you away from all the negative energy around you. Take a yoga class or learn to meditate. Walk in God's outdoors to remind yourself of the beauty outside your office cubicle. Choose to be happy for a little while each day. Find something that inspires this feeling inside yourself. It may only last for five minutes the first time, but eventually it will expand.

Stop depending on other people's guidelines that follow along a path that puts the power outside of yourself.

Stop the tape in your head. When the words come blathering through, push the off button, then mentally throw the tape out of your psychic window. More enlightened people than myself have written this many times before, but the words you're listening to in your head are the quotes you've picked up, for bad and for worse, that hit you hard and likely stopped you cold. Some may have lodged in your mind that are worth keeping, so edit the tape, which should only have those things that inspire you on it and make you feel good.

What makes you happy? What in your life right now gives you joy? If you don't have an answer, it's the first place you need to start. Because if you don't know what makes you happy and how to experience it for yourself, on your own, no one else can give it to you or make you happy. Your own life, as well as any relationship you hope to sustain, not to mention your children's lives, depend on your involvement in your own happiness.

If you can't find it, take a walk. The answer might not be found in God's outdoors, but the path to it could be.

8

The Perfect Relationship

Is there such a thing as the perfect relationship? Absolutely, it's just that it doesn't come in one-size-fits-all. It's something each woman designs for herself. Smooth sailing is not part of the package. Just be careful what you ask for, because you most certainly can attract it.

There are components that put any relationship on the road to perfection. But in the end you get the relationship you set up and inspire the man to deliver, because believe me, that's exactly what men want to do.

The sole goal of a man ready for a relationship is to make a woman happy. He lives for it and feeds off of it. The world will be yours if you let him know when he's done it. But in order for him to have a chance of delivering you have to know what will make you happy, which begins with being happy by yourself.

If you don't know who you are and what you want from your life as you stand there a solitary person, no man can give you what you can't find yourself. If you don't know what makes you happy in the confines of your own life, a relationship, family, or children aren't the answers or the solutions.

No man can complete you.

No man can make you happy.

A man can add to your life. He can widen your experiences. He can be a magnificent co-adventurer in escapades of personal and professional grandeur, as well as a playmate in life. One thing he most surely must be is an erotic adventurer who delights in thrilling you sexually.

Intimacy is the beginning of it all, which is emotional, intellectual and physical. It's a connection with someone that you can sense with your heart. It's not brain-centered. Hopefully, you know yourself well enough to judge the difference between lust and what happens in that mystical instant when someone potentially important has crossed your path. But we're often fooled more than once before we learn the difference.

The first thing a smart woman accepts when constructing a perfect relationship is that having sex with the man before you decide "he's the one" is something you owe yourself. Waiting until you're married to have sex is not only an antiquated notion, but should be seen by any smart man as a warning that you're not remotely ready for marriage. Having sex with a man before you decide to marry him is mandatory.

Slut-shaming women into believing that abstinence before marriage will make your union last is counterproductive, worse still is telling a woman that if she has sex with a man before marriage, he'll leave. A virgin wedding night was rarely anything but a bragging right, which in the twenty-first century just sounds stupid. How can you marry and pledge to spend the rest of your life with a man you haven't had sex with?

We're not living in a magical fairy tale, with women tied to a make-believe world where the princess bride has to hold out or her prince will think she's a slut. Once bedded, the conquest done, he'd be forever bored. Sex is an elemental part of modern marriage, which is why you have it with your husband and no one else. If you didn't, you'd just be friends. Friendship is another critical component in any relationship meant to last a lifetime, one that gets you through the worst of all possible moments in life that sometimes hit like a nor'easter without a warning. However, what sets a romantic relationship apart from friendship is sex.

Only 5% of unintended pregnancies are represented by those who used contraception correctly (and every time). That's me. So, yes, it happens, but *very* rarely, and today there's also the morning-after pill. Responsibility is important for women and men who are having sex but don't want to get pregnant. But the fear of pregnancy is no excuse for waiting until you're married to have sex. The abstinence message usually comes from traditionally rigid people, whose strict rules have absolutely nothing to do with what actually makes a successful modern marriage and a happy, healthy life.

According to the Guttmacher Institute, the "U.S. unintended pregnancy rate is significantly higher than the rate in many other developed countries." When broken down into ethnic groups, a 2006 study relied on by Guttmacher reported that "black women had the highest unintended pregnancy rate of any racial or ethnic groups. At 91 per 1000 women aged 15-44, it was more than double that of non-Hispanic white women (36 per 1,000)."

One thing premarital sex might also do is slow down marriages, because the longer you wait to marry, the more likely it is you'll find the right partner, and have a better chance of making your relationship work.

Creating the perfect relationship requires that, from the beginning, you never surrender what it is you want for yourself. You only get one chance to set this up. So, if you don't know the details of the relationship you want, simply consider having fun and enjoying yourself, postponing anything serious. Being single is delectable, as long as you take maximum precautions, so until you're sure, have fun and learn.

The perfect relationship is an equal-power prospect. The only control over you a man has is the power you give him. In that surrendered power is the failure of most relationships.

Sharing power in a relationship is what has a better chance of making you and your partner happy. Then he can step up to do what he does best and that is to add to your happiness by delivering the part of life that's possible for him to offer. It may consist of working every day and delivering a paycheck that, added to yours, amounts to a step up for you both. It could mean lobster dinners and champagne, or a truck ride to a campground. But if you make clear what you want and is required of him by setting it up in a way that he can understand, the world that's his to give will be yours.

This means that when you go to your first meeting or date, if you like wine, or perhaps prefer one coffee shop over another, let him know. The good news for him is that this is easily deliverable for him. The good news for you is that if he can't pass this test, you can cross him off your list early. This is a common-sense tactic that works and saves a lot of time that might be wasted on losers.

Even if the guy who's asked you out doesn't really do it for you, practicing this doesn't hurt, because you have a full life and it's not worth wasting your time on low-expectation relationships. Attachments can be costly and not get us what we want. The time we waste in loser relationships can exact an emotional toll. The bad habits you form and the destruction a loser can have on your confidence can end up being explosive.

If the man takes you to your favorite coffee house, or you meet there, or your date with him leads to you enjoying a glass of wine and great conversation, his reward is your happiness that he can easily see, because he delivered what you asked of him. You rewarded him by smiling, laughing and simply enjoying yourself.

On the flip side, if you meet him and he botches this simple task, he doesn't deserve your energy or your time. He likely knows he's not come through, unless he's stupid, but is either being stubborn or allowing his ego to run the show. Forget these types of guys and move on.

The next move after the first date is his. However, it might not come immediately, which can mean several things. If you have a great first date, but he never calls, it's because he's not ready and his own life isn't in order for you to walk in. It has absolutely nothing to do with you, unless you show up and dump your problems in his lap, act like a crazy person by interrogating him, or talk about an ex-boyfriend. If he doesn't call soon after the first date, keep living your life, and by all means keep dating. If you haven't heard from him after a month, let him go.

When your girlfriend asks about the date, unless she's one of your most trusted and loyal confidantes, keep your thoughts to yourself. The stories of our romantic encounters tend to take on a life of their own and can become oversized very quickly. Do not check his Facebook page. Do not make any public notations in your social media network about the meeting, unless you want to talk about the restaurant or coffee shop you went to. That's a completely neutral comment, and if you enjoyed the place it can be fun to let them know it.

Whatever you do, never hold any days open for any new guy you've just met. It doesn't matter what he's promised. Some guys will promise anything quickly, but never deliver. These drive-by guys will create a lot of emotional carnage if you let them.

If you're on a date with someone who has boyfriend potential, you need to decide beforehand if you expect unplugging, turning off the technology so you can spend time together. You don't need to ask him. Just unplug yourself, if that's what you expect; then tell him offhandedly that you're doing it. If you have a job that demands you stay connected, this is the moment he needs to know. Then see what happens and whether he reacts to your demanding life.

You may find out he's on call all the time, too, just like you. If his job is as demanding as yours, that needs to be discussed at some point, though it's not necessary until you're clearly dating. That conversation will center on how you'll eventually carve out quiet time to be together. His job demands will directly impact whether you can have what you want.

What do you want, and is your career important to you? If it is, then part of setting up your perfect relationship is to attract a man who respects that your career is equal to his. You may make more money than he does, too. Can his ego handle it? You aren't going to apologize for it. You may be building to something seriously stratospheric in your career, and whoever you choose to share your life with needs to be on board. This might be creating and managing your local town farmers' market or running your own business, but if it's the center of who you are and what makes you happy, it's something your partner needs to support enthusiastically. If your career is demanding, this means any future partner will have to share in household chores.

You'll get a clue if this is possible when you finally are invited in to see how the guy you're dating lives. "How often does the maid come?" you might ask him, if everything is spotless. If it's a disaster and he doesn't mention it, you've got a problem.

The relationship must be set up on your terms, and you must know your deal-breakers. Do you want your door held open? If it's a deal-breaker, don't budge. It doesn't matter how much you like him, how cute he is, how much money he makes. If this doesn't matter, then open your own door and tell him it doesn't matter.

If you've gotten yourself out of debt, and financial responsibility and being debt-free is important, the man you're dating cannot be neck-deep in debt. You don't talk about this on a first date, but before you're a month in, you need to find out where he stands financially. If being debt-free is important, at the very least he's got to be digging himself out of his challenges by not overextending himself. If, like a lot of people, he never pays for anything with cash, you'd be smart to wonder how much debt he's accumulated, especially if he pays with a different credit card every time.

Other than sex, finances are a predictor of relationship success or failure, especially if financial fights become a weekly occurrence. This has been reported in multiple studies to be the number one beef with men, while women cite finances and sex as strong predictors of divorce.

The truth is, in the first month, depending on what you're sensing from the guy, you'll have to play date detective most of the time, while making sure nothing gets too heavy at the beginning. Nothing is a potential relationship killer more than a person who actually wants a therapist as a dating partner, or even worse, can't stop complaining and just enjoy meeting someone.

Notice his body language, but most of all listen to what he's saying. Get him talking and pay attention, because sometimes what he doesn't talk about is where trouble lies. When he talks about his life, watch for that happiness quotient. If he's a plumber, does he enjoy his work? Is his job drudgery? If he hates it, what is he doing to change his situation? If he's not doing anything and has no plans to make a move, the guy is a loser.

The first eight weeks of dating someone, you know nothing, including when lightning strikes, which can happen to anyone.

It hit me out of the blue. It was 2002 and I'd just moved to Las Vegas to co-produce a radio show after my options dried up in Los Angeles, my co-producer buying time on a local station when few liberals were on the air. I'd been in my new apart-ment for twelve hours, when I heard a knock on the door. It was the gas man. The guy came in to turn on my gas and ended up lighting up my whole world.

By the time he left my apartment I thought, now there's a guy who should call. But I really couldn't be bothered thinking about it. I had business to take care of and my ass was on the line, because all the odds were stacked against me. The show was short-lived, even if well received, and it helped fuel my political writing, keeping me inching forward.

Two weeks later, he called and asked me out to dinner. We were both in our forties, experienced, and neither of us wanted any drama or at least any more drama than a relationship can be with a headstrong writer determined to change her corner of the world, who'd just met a blue-collar man who didn't have a clue what he was getting himself into.

I told him I'd be thrilled to have dinner. He knew I didn't know the town, so having a near-native show me around held promise.

When he arrived at my door the night of our first date he was color-coordinated from head to toe, wearing nice cologne, but when I got down to his feet I saw that not only were his shoes shined, but his socks were a patterned fabric that matched his shirt and accented his entire ensemble. It was damn impressive, and the detail meant something. When we got outside and turned toward the parking lot, he was taking me toward a big truck. I laughed out loud as he opened my door. "What's so funny?" I told him I just knew he'd own a truck.

The men I'd dated for decades were corporate honchos, lawyers, entrepreneurs, all of whom drove high-end cars, not a truck in sight. A single soul, even when I was hooked up with a man, I didn't look for a certain income bracket, though I made it clear I liked to go out to dinner, to movies, shows, have fun, and party on my day off, though nothing extravagant was demanded. I loved fancy cars and have driven my share of them, but I haven't owned anything close. However, none of these men had turned my head enough for me to stay around, especially since I was so focused professionally.

There was just something different about this guy.

On our first date, he couldn't get through his entree. We both knew something was happening between us. It was seismic. By the time we got back out to his truck after dinner, he took me in his arms and said, "I'm going to marry you." I told him he was out of his mind, as his lips enveloped mine and my stomach did a flip from which I've never recovered and hope I never do.

The next week, he started bringing me gifts. The first was a copier and fax machine, because I didn't have one in my office and he knew I needed one, but also that my work was my center of gravity. The guy learned quickly what drove me and was determined to help however he could.

I rejected his marriage proposal three times before finally saying yes. Then, after we were engaged, we had a massive fight one night and I told him he had to take care of something or it was over. It doesn't matter what it was; the point is that up until you make the commitment, the work to get what you want and make sure it's delivered never stops. Marriage is a serious thing for any woman, which starts with the guy being able to handle who you are, deliver what you want, and understand the life path you are on as well. For someone whose career had always been the center of my universe, a man's understanding of this priority is rare.

The reason I told him no is that I didn't think he could handle the life I had been living and intended to keep on living. The details are my story, just like your details are yours. The specifics that matter are that I warned him that my kind of life was hard, uncompromising and the riskiest thing he'd ever do in his life, especially since he had six children, most grown, two not yet in their teens. I was on the path to *do* something through writing and political analysis, which meant taking on the world, telling truth to power, and taking on people above my pay grade. I also told him I didn't think he was up to it, because no man I'd ever met was, and they'd proved me right every time.

That's when my entire life changed. He sat me down and looked into my eyes and said he knew exactly who I was and what I was made of, and he was ready to go on that ride and make sure, as far as he could, that I'd have whatever I needed to make it happen. He believed in me and my work, and he was willing to place a bet with his whole life, because he knew I'd deliver or die trying. It was clear he not only was ready for a big adventure, but hungered for one.

The day he said these words to me I knew I had to give marriage with this man a try. I still knew he didn't know what he was in for, but it wasn't like I hadn't warned him and laid it all out. There are innumerable other details, but what threads through this story is setting up for him what it would mean to be with me, as I continued on a career path that was volatile, filled with unknowns, but also bursting with excitement, adventure and potential for a real partnership if we could commit to sharing this life and jumping into the adventure together. My husband is the bravest man I know, and he's never delivered anything less than what he promised. Neither have I.

As one of the pioneers of new media, which I can easily claim because I was part of the first wave of writers on the web when I began in 1996, the early dot-com era was a time when being a content provider and working in start-ups was a way to make a decent living. After the dot-com bomb in 2000, making money on the web pretty much dried up for freelance writers and got increasingly difficult for independent web content providers. Blogs were born later, with new media exploding on a platform that had no revenue model whatsoever, with all content free.

Today, as newspapers are sold off, legendary newspapers like the *Washington Post* being bought by Amazon mogul Jeff Bezos, and magazines are folding, the web remains a titan-take-all medium, with the biggest companies gobbling up the advertising, while one by one, new-media sites begin to move to pay models, which the *New York Times* began and other sites are now following in order stay alive financially. Many other sites and organizations, including blogs, are dependent on fundraisers. So, after making money and supporting myself all of my life, the 2000s brought big financial challenges and blocks for me, which my husband had to also face, as we kept inching forward.

Huffington Post was put on the map through people like Alec Baldwin writing for the site, but also by people like myself, with my articles regularly featured on the Politics page as well as on the front page. It was great branding for me as a political writer, especially in the run-up to the 2008 election cycle. The writing I did covering Hillary Clinton's presidential campaign put me on the political map and led to my being featured in a *Washington Post* interview, as well as one in the *New Republic*, with my website deemed a central hub where Hillary supporters hung out.

The Huffington Post model, prior to the AOL purchase, was called working for exposure, which I have also done by writing for sites like *U.S. News & World Report* and *The Hill*, a very popular political news hub out of Washington, D.C., while also being paid for articles, including non-political stories like the one I wrote for Zócalo Public Square. There's also advertising on my new-media site. It's writers who are often eking out a living that are making the biggest changes in our media landscape, especially politically and on women's issues, as Internet new media continues to struggle to find an economic model that works. This includes partnerships with digital, independent and small publishers who provide platforms for determined writers, as the traditional book world buckles under economic forces and new-media reality.

I'm telling you this story, because it's part of the creative pulse of our marriage on my side, even if our passion, love and the fun we have is the foundation. Following my bliss is how I met this remarkable man, who not only loves me, but whose sole intent is to help fuel the work I'm doing by being an integral part of it. We do this together, sometimes against great odds, though we've got plenty of company. People who are working new media, like myself, because you can't beat it, and others who feel burned by the technical revolution.

In November 2013, *The Wrap* reported that outgoing editor of The Daily Beast, Tina Brown, former editor of the *New Yorker, Vanity Fair* and *Newsweek*, was basically done with journalism. Her new company is named Tina Brown Live Media, which will focus exclusively on "live conversations" and "going back to oral culture where the written word will be less relevant." Brown is quoted telling the THiNK conference in Goa, India, "The digital explosion has been so explosive. There isn't a single place where the digital thing is a profit thing. The disruption hasn't brought a business model."

An example came in March 2013 from Nate Thayer, a professional freelance journalist who was contacted by the *Atlantic*, a vibrant publication. They wanted him to adapt a story for them, but there was a catch, which Thayer recounted in a blog post on his site (natethayer.wordpess.com), beginning with this communication from the *Atlantic*: "Thanks for responding. Maybe by the end of the week? 1,200 words? We unfortunately can't pay you for it, but we do reach 13 million readers a month. I understand if that's not a workable arrangement for you, I just wanted to see if you were interested." Thayer responded that he was a professional journalist who had to pay his bills, but also that he knew people at the *Atlantic* who got paid, and that writing for free after twenty-five years of making a living writing was not something he was going to do. The *Atlantic* responded that some writers "use our platform as a way to gain more exposure for whatever professional goals they might have."

Medium.com pays freelance rates for writers, with Gawker doing one of the first stories covering it in the spring of 2013. Twitter co-founder Evan Williams launched it and also co-founded Blogger, which he sold to Google, so he's no novice.

The startup Tinypass is one of the new pay-wall enterprises working with new-media publishers to make the web pay, the best known being Andrew Sullivan, who partnered with them in 2013. Readers get some free access and are encouraged to become paying subscribers, with Tinypass providing the software, the publisher deciding what works best for his or her readership. I began partnering with Tinypass in January 2014.

So, as you see, the industry in which I work made my husband's investment even more of a gamble. This is why when I talk about a woman who values her career as part of who she is and how important it is to find a partner who understands this, I know what I'm talking about.

On our anniversary just after the 2008 presidential election, after we had taken trips across the Southwest and Pacific Northwest to decide where to live next, because Las Vegas was always only a springboard for me, not a final destination, Mark walked into the living room to announce, out of nowhere, that we needed to be in Washington, D.C., because that's where the action was for the writing I was doing. I was floored — thunderstruck, actually — and elated, because I'd been traveling to Washington, D.C. regularly for conferences and events but had only dreamed about moving there. Like the first time he asked me to marry him and I said no, I knew he didn't understand what was in store for him, but what hit at the same time is that he didn't care. It became instantly clear this was an adventure he desperately wanted for himself, too. As Mark likes to say, "Mountain climbers don't climb hills."

If that doesn't signal to you the beginning of a great love story, nothing will.

This was all a stark shift from what he'd experienced before, when Mark's first marriage ended badly, leaving him with a deep sense of betrayal, because he had gone all in and expected the same in return, but didn't get half of what he put into it. Now he'd met and married a woman who was delivering everything he'd always wanted and deserved, but never had. He had loyalty, was worshiped and appreciated like never before and was recognized for the amazing man he is, the provider, the great lover, the hilarious human, who embraces a spirituality that has absolutely nothing to do with organized religion.

Mark cashed out all he had, and off we went, betting everything on the adventure he had joined when lightning struck and we fell madly in love and got married. Creating a partnership where I was in the lead, he would have my back, as we endeavored to make a difference in our little corner of the world. I'd never had a partner, someone who not only understood that my life revolved around my work, which now was the crazy world of thinking and writing, but who respected and believed in me so much he wanted to help me thrive while doing it. Mark proved to me that this was possible; he taught me that it could work. It's hard to describe the synchronicity that followed us. It's something you have to experience to understand and appreciate.

The shock of what Mark left behind and where he now found himself didn't hit until much later. The separation from his kids was a killer, something I always knew would register at some point. Our goal to get him back to visit them regularly soon evaporated, partly due to his work schedule requiring longer hours. I was headed into writing *The Hillary Effect* which meant a significant amount of overtime for him at his new job, while I excavated recent history that wasn't all that easy to chronicle. I worked double-time throughout, to keep my new-media site going, because without my readers I would never have had the chance to get published. Through it all, Mark has been not only a sounding board, but an adviser and a consummate debater, sharing his common-sense, no-bullshit opinions that are invaluable. Not only does he tell me when he thinks I'm wrong and why, but he encouraged me to take the leap into writing books, insisted on it, even though it meant more stress for him.

The partnership we have entered into is revolutionary. Mark doesn't need to read Sheryl Sandberg's book *Lean In*, because he invented it through his actions before she wrote about it. Because he was a career gas technician in Las Vegas, a consummate professional, his skill-set meant he believed he could get a job anywhere. The first year in the Washington, D.C. area was hell, and it almost all fell apart. Then in the middle of the economic downturn, Mark's talent helped him land a good job. It required a complete retooling and learning a new type of technical trade that included electronics, to fix appliances of all types for a leading company. Not many men are brave enough to leave a great job, move across the country and learn a new trade, while backing a woman on the belief that her work will pay off.

When we met, Mark was a man of the desert who had never left Las Vegas. I was a gypsy artist who'd lived from Missouri to New York to California, now making a living writing in new media that had evolved into a free content model, a long way from where I began. It's still a crapshoot, but this is my third book, and we keep remembering the one thing that sustains us, our purpose together, which has the foundation of deep connection, loyalty, abiding love and unflagging knowledge that we are in this together, *forever*.

There is no ejection lever in our agreement, our marriage, our partnership, or our madcap adventure. We just keep going, never giving up, never giving in, never stopping. Being committed to each other and on an adventure that makes you both feel alive, because you're creating something together no matter what happens, is not a consolation prize if you get your shot and live the life you both choose to live together. It's been over eleven years and we're happy, having the time of our lives and still as committed and on purpose as when we started.

What it takes to create a perfect relationship begins with both people dedicated to the same thing, being on the same page, working for the same vision. When you're on a high wire like we are, it also takes total focus on communication and complete, unvarnished honesty, no bullshit. It gets rough in the economic trenches when your current reality hangs over a cliff, which it does when the bottom falls out of the American economy and you're part of the working and middle class, which takes the biggest hit. Add to that moving thousands of miles, plus needing to get a new job at fifty-something, as my husband did, and you've got the biggest gamble you can make at mid-life. It shows what two people can do together, no matter the odds, if they are totally committed to the same thing. My husband is fond of the saying, "I'm the pig at the ham and egg breakfast," and believe me, I am, too.

The average guy would walk one hundred miles barefoot in the desert to provide for the woman he loves. This is the organic nature of a man. Every day, a man works hard, and when he comes home he wants to know he's appreciated for doing what comes naturally to him, which is providing for his family, whether or not he and his partner have children. Sometimes, the "children" can be a project the husband and wife both believe in. Mark and I don't have children together, but we are creating something that is just as important to us, because we're both invested in changing our part of the world through the work I do.

Women must understand what it means to be a man. The things that make him who he is don't change just because a woman makes as much as he does. Feminism doesn't change what makes a man who he is.

A man needs to know he's appreciated for being the provider whether he's good at it or not, because that's the heart of his manhood. A woman making equal or more money than a man doesn't change this fact.

A man who can't protect those he loves in battle will still die trying.

Whenever Mark takes me out or we're shopping at the market, I take the time to stop, look in his eyes and tell him "thank you." It's something I don't have to do, because we're partners, but it tells him he is appreciated every moment we're together. It is impossible to stress how important this is to a man. It validates the man he is and is something only the woman he loves can do.

This is not to downplay that a woman today often works equal hours to a man, including that she has domestic chores he often doesn't have. We share those duties fifty-fifty. I have twelve-hour days and work six to seven days a week, sometimes into the wee hours of the morning when he's asleep and the world is quiet. My husband acknowledges this by having my back, allowing me not to get distracted, as well as dealing with the bullshit that bombards us all. We've negotiated the contract and we both have specified our needs, with my blue-collar, working class hero husband more than willing to clear the stage for me, because he knows I couldn't do it as effectively without him.

Equality can't be accompanied by ego. It is about balance. The give and take between lovers, giving grace to the man when you know he needs it, him returning the feeling through respect, while you both remain vigilant about the tender pendulum you guard and on which your love depends.

Personal self-knowledge is what it takes to attract and then mold a perfect relationship. The discipline required continually to risk it all to have it all is overwhelming at times. Each of you, especially at first, has to keep reminding the other when something doesn't jibe with what you promised each other. You cannot be afraid to have a fight over something that matters. The security of commitment and marriage means that you have the safety, but it requires that you never get lazy. If one of you screws up on something big, you've got to have it out. Discussions, arguments, even fights are healthy, as long as you both have been doing the work all along.

You can't come out of the blue and blame your partner for something, throw an event in his face. Respect and love have to stay at the heart of all discussions. But you can't be afraid to be honest with one another. You also have to be big enough to say you're sorry when you're wrong. It matters a lot more than you may think.

I'm not talking about disloyalty, which is something altogether different. Men can get over many things, but very few can get over being shown up through another man bedding his wife. This is a betrayal that hits men so deeply that the relationship is often unsalvageable.

Before we got married, one of the hottest discussions we ever had was the conversation about forgiveness. I said a marriage that is meant to last forever means you must forgive me if I screw up, including if I have an affair. That's just not the way he felt, and I've talked to enough men to know this is a view of most men. Some women feel exactly the same, but there are many others who would forgive. However, the more financially secure the woman, the less likely this is to be the case. Physical disloyalty is such an intimacy assault, such a breach of trust, that financially independent women just aren't as forgiving as the feminine mystique generation.

If you travel or have a job that puts you into situations where you meet a lot of people, temptation will rise as will the opportunity to be unfaithful. Men often think of sex quite differently from females. It's just sex. It didn't mean anything. But when you're in a partnership or marriage, if the man knows it means something to the woman he's involved with, then he's wrong — it means more than sex, because it hurts her and damages her ability to be happy. Once a woman no longer associates a man with making her happy, it's over. She may stay, but it's over, and if she's smart and has taken care of herself first, which is always the priority, it's only a matter of time before she gets out. A man won't hesitate to pack up and leave. For someone who tries to convince us that an affair is "just sex" and "doesn't mean anything," if you play that game with him you'll find out just how much disloyalty can cost. Nothing is more important to a man than loyalty. The more he's invested in the relationship, the wider the fallout if you betray him.

So, if a tall and handsome stranger turns your head and you feel something stirring, you have to have the guts to take that experience home and replay it for your partner, admitting the feelings and everything else, before anything ignites. Never allow the notion of an illicit affair to percolate, stoking the drama and excitement of a secret sex life and giving it oxygen on the whim of it being "harmless" flirting. Carelessness can lead to calamity quickly. You both have to agree on this plan from the start, no matter how hard it is or how small you might think a connection that hits you from out of the blue is. Lance the lust.

Nothing I've experienced personally is more rewarding than marriage, which has been the surprise of my life. My husband gave me this and taught me more about love than all the conversations I've had with people. It's a love at the highest level of any partnership, with the unconditional support of someone who's in it all the way with you, no matter what happens. All that's required is that we both give our all and put the marriage first. There's nothing each person won't do for the other, with no job too dirty for either person. A total partnership.

But you've got to set it up from the start and demand it all the way down the line. There will be fits and starts and eruptions, but the bottom-line agreement and understanding must never be broken. Trust, loyalty and love, the whole commitment to the partnership and what you're creating is the entire focus of both of your lives. Nothing is more thrilling or exhilarating and fulfilling.

Then there's the sex, the one thing a friendship doesn't have, which is why marriage or a long-term partnership must have sex in it to thrive, regularly quenching sex.

I'm going to get into trouble here, but there are few times to justify saying no to sex. Obviously, serious illness and life traumas happen and there are bad days and exceptions, but few really worthy ones. During pregnancy, if she's not in constant morning sickness, a woman can at the very least sit next to her man and make sure he gets his. I've given this advice to quite a few women and not one has told me it doesn't work. It won't take him long and he'll be very happy. Watch an adult movie with him, touch him, whatever it takes. Service sex has its virtues. When couples get really busy, service sex can also be a real stress reliever and there's no reason women can't get into it, especially with toys.

Sex is also something the two of you can only do with each other, so it's necessary, because it's vital to our lives, no matter your age. That's because it's good for our bodies, mind and spirit. It's a mood elevator. Sex sends signals across all avenues and intersections of our bodies. It's the one act that separates your relationship from all others, so sex can't go missing for very long without the partnership suffering.

Using sex as a weapon is always a bad idea. Just as sleeping on the couch should be considered a major statement, because sleeping together is a time of peace and calm between two people. Your bedroom is a place of sensuousness, a physical, mental and emotional sanctuary. It's not a place to talk finances. If you have kids, they're going to invade and that can be a lovely sharing time. But when they're not around, the atmosphere must change. The bedroom must remain a place of physical communion for just the two of you.

The sexual connection between you and your partner must be respected, with the added pleasure of intimacy and hugging part of it. It's a vital component of partnership, the intimate connection it engenders precious. Sometimes it can involve flowers and romance, wine and seduction. On a stressful workday, it can be a scratch to an itch, where the only thing desired is release. Sex comes in innumerable measures of pleasure. Just do it.

Modern life is crazy. Having a partnership to navigate it is a gift you give yourself. Once you've created it, don't blow it.

Women's roles continue to grow, even as the financial floor has shifted underneath men, which came to a tipping point in the 2007-2009 great recession. From the Economix blog in the *New York Times*: "As of June 2009 (the latest month for which these figures are available), women held 49.83% of all nonfarm payroll jobs. That's up from around 30% for women in 1940. Men were 50.17% of the workforce in 2009."

But a similar situation developed after the 2001 recession, which subsequently saw men gain back again what they had lost in the previous years. Since the government started keeping tabs on women and men's unemployment in 1948 through the Bureau of Labor Statistics, women have had a higher unemployment rate. But for thirty-two consecutive months leading up to the 2009 figures, men have surpassed us, which was laid out by Dr. Mark J. Perry at the Carpe Diem blog, as well as in his testimony before Congress when he was the first to invoke the term *mancession*.

This can translate to a big relationship surprise, a societal shift that takes place that wasn't expected when you first created your partnership. For women, this can translate to the inability to get our due, no matter how hard we work, which can cause equal stress in a marriage. For modern career-women, economic inequality hits as hard as it would for any man, which still isn't fully appreciated. The conversation is beginning to turn toward this very real element of women's lives that is impacting partnerships in ways that resonate and are finally getting covered publicly. Even considering women still do not make equal pay for equal work, which impacts families in serious ways, there has been a disparity in how these things are judged, but also covered.

Have you looked at Congress lately, where laws impacting work and family are made? Even starker is the composition of Fortune 500 companies and the numbers of women in top management. According to a Fortune 500 2011 annual report on the "gender diversity gap," focusing on women in business, the numbers are even more sobering for females: "In 2011, women held 16.1% of board seats at Fortune 500 companies. In both 2010 and 2011, less than one-fifth of companies had 25% or more women directors, while about one-tenth had no women serving on their boards. In both 2010 and 2011, women of color held 3.0% of all board seats."

In February 2013, *The Nation* magazine's Bryce Covert quoted more statistics from Catalyst, which also did the research for the *Fortune* study:

> Women make up about half of middle management, an impressive statistic when one considers that they made up about a third of the entire workforce just sixty years ago. Yet they only count for 14% of executive officers in Fortune 500 companies, 16% of board seats in those companies and just a measly 3.6% of CEOs. On top of this, only 7.5% can be counted among the top earners at these companies. Research does not suggest that women are dropping out of the race for these higher-earning jobs. As Ilene Lang, president and CEO of Catalyst, put it to me, "Often women get stuck having to prove themselves over and over again. That's a block; they're not going up."

Covert's *Nation* article "One Mancession Later, Are Women Really Victors in the New Economy?" also pointed out what's happened since the recovery in 2009:

> Women gained less than 8% of the 1.9 million jobs added, and now men's and women's unemployment rates have converged at 7.7%. Public sector layoffs have hit women particularly hard. Across the country, women have lost 414,000 government jobs, many due to teacher layoffs. As of October, 300,000 educator jobs had been lost, accounting for over half of those lost at the local government level.

This is one of those instances when you have to hold two opposing thoughts in your head at the same time. Women aren't achieving paycheck equality to men, but there can be little doubt that women's importance to countries and the economic future of nations is being appreciated more, because when women rise, nations become more stable. So you'd think it would be in everyone's best interest to make sure women are promoted to leadership positions equally and paid equally, too. When we are, our families benefit, and our marriages do, too.

A central theme of Secretary Clinton's State Department legacy was implemented at the Clinton Foundation in 2013, through her "No Ceilings" project: "When women participate in peacemaking and peacekeeping, we are all safer and more secure. And when women participate in politics, the effects ripple across the entire society. [...] We need to help our girls see they are capable of doing anything, and stand behind our women as they break through the doors that are still closed — to overcome any obstacle, to crack any ceiling."

Rosin in her article, "The End of Men," illustrated the Secretary Clinton model she would apply at the State Department:

> In 2006, the Organization for Economic Cooperation and Development devised the Gender, Institutions and Development Database, which measures the economic and political power of women in 162 countries. With few exceptions, the greater the power of women, the greater the country's economic success. Aid agencies have started to recognize this relationship and have pushed to institute political quotas in about one hundred countries, essentially forcing women into power in an effort to improve those countries' fortunes.

So, even as women aren't at economic parity, our presence in the economic engine of our country is not going to decline, because many families need the second paycheck, and modern women want to have a husband, family, children and a good job, too.

Rosin cites statistics showing that "about a third of America's physicians are now women, as are 45% of associates in law firms — and both those percentages are rising fast." Before the feminist revolution got going, women's incomes were only 2-6% of the family finances. According to Rosin's data:

> Now the typical working wife brings home 42.2%, and four in 10 mothers — many of them single mothers — are the primary breadwinners in their families. The whole question of whether mothers should work is moot, argues Heather Boushey of the Center for American Progress, "because

they just do. This idealized family — he works, she stays home — hardly exists anymore."

Traditional relationships no longer resemble reality in twenty-first century America. There are stay-at-home moms, but they are not the norm anymore, often for practical reasons, but also because women want more. There's no reason why we shouldn't expect more.

However, the notion that the ambitious, go-after-what-you-want thinking can translate to online dating is wrong. On the way to creating the perfect relationship, attracting a guy takes patience, discipline and having a full life to live while you're dating. It's the full life you're leading, which could actually lead you to attracting the right man.

If you've connected with someone online and have exchanged a few emails, maybe even a couple of texts, if that's what you choose to do, at some point you have to step back to see what happens next. Like it or not, the nature of the beast is that if a man wants you, nothing will deter him from pursuing you, as long as the time is right for him. Whatever instant intimacy you're conjuring up online before you meet means absolutely nothing. At some point, the man has to ask you out, and the two of you must set up a first rendezvous to see if there's anything more between you. Until you meet, nothing is real, so keep your fantasies in check.

But while you're doing the online dating dance, don't be surprised if after a few flirtatious emails or texts you get radio silence. He's only seen a picture and a profile, whether on Facebook or an online dating site, so if he backs off, then you mustn't take it personally, something I've been saying since the mid-'90s. Christian Carter of eHarmony says it perfectly: "There is no rhyme or reason for why a man will do this, and trying to figure it out will only drive you crazy." Don't get into your head.

Carter gives advice through his website, all geared for women and how to "catch him and keep him." His focus is teaching women the signals men give, understanding them, but also learning the secrets so that he is pursuing you, instead of you pursuing him, which is the wrong position for any woman to be in.

You will only have success in creating the perfect relationship, however you choose to define it, by attracting the man to you. Men react strongly when a woman catches their attention. But a connection is just that and means nothing more if the man doesn't make a move. Pushing the response yourself by moving in first is certainly something an independent woman can choose to do, and can work in the short term to jump-start something, but closing the space further with a man until he's had a chance to make his own move is seldom the best choice. Trusting who you are and your own value includes letting things come to you, while trusting that a man will respond if he's ready.

A confident, secure woman knows she's ultimately in control of any relationship that she creates with a man, so allowing him the space he needs to perform his own mating ritual doesn't make her less of a feminist. It reveals her as a smart woman.

Nothing is sexier to a good man than a secure woman who knows herself, what she wants, and is happy and fulfilled in her life, even while she wants more. She also makes the man earn the right to be with her.

No man wants a needy woman whose life is filled with drama and emotional noise.

The object is for two whole people to come together to create a larger world in which they both can thrive, as well as create something together. A partnership based on wanting the same things.

At the foundation of it all is the courage to be honest with each other, no matter what. It means hearing things from your best friend that you'd rather not hear, but they're what he thinks, so it's important for you to listen. What he says must be of value to you, because without mutual respect, the relationship isn't going to last very long. You're coming together as equals, even if one of you makes more money, which as the modern era progresses could just as easily be the woman as the man.

Women's work is now man's work, and a man's world is now a woman's world.

What hasn't changed is that our human desires and fondest dreams remain the magic carpet ride that exposes our most fundamental and basic human needs. To love and be loved in a relationship of meaning, maybe even some definition of permanence, if we choose, is a gift we give ourselves that requires space, patience and tenacity.

A perfect relationship has to have joy in it, which takes root from the start.

A marriage cannot last without happiness. Find it every day. When you're furious, find a way to forgive. If you're committed, almost nothing is unpardonable. Grudges are petty and for the weak. Getting even is for enemies. You must always be kind and each other's best friend.

Above all things, don't let anyone else in. It doesn't matter what your mother or sister thinks, or your girlfriends. They shouldn't know the details of your relationship. If you've had a knockdown, drag-out fight, it's your fight and no one else's business. Smolder in silence until you figure it out. Protect the privacy of your relationship. If it blows over and you've told the dirty details, which always sound worse than they were, it taints what you actually have built. Hold your tongue, unless the conflict is of breakup proportions and you need help. If you can afford it, find outside help.

Most of all, keep investing in yourself. Your relationship can only be as perfect as the relationship you have to your own life and the things you do that are important to you.

Don't be afraid to set standards that you expect, things you want, then make sure you get them, because you deserve them. He does, too.

Then keep referring back to make sure you're both delivering to one another and be mature enough to make an honest assessment. That's the only way to be happy, which is the only state of mind that will attract the right partner to you in the first place.

Enjoy yourself. Do what makes you happy and fulfilled. In the middle of living your life, you just might shock yourself by what you'll attract on your own.

And guard against letting your ego get involved. To have a perfect relationship, both individuals must be humble toward one another. This means you are always working together to make each other feel valued, loved and supported, at all times. Your problem isn't more important than his, and vice versa. But sometimes it will seem that way. Take turns giving in. Trade off, when it's time for one of you to bitch about something. Putting ego aside to make peace must be more important than proving you are right.

The perfect relationship is also vulnerable. Everything can be going great, then a life-altering catastrophe hits it and the bottom falls out suddenly. In a marriage this can happen. No matter how you've both prepared, and even when what you both created is exactly what you both signed on for, sometimes what life delivers is a lot different from what was imagined. There are times when you just can't push a resolution. You have to wait for it. Let turbulence blow over so you can see the combustion from a distance, because if you push things at certain moments, it can make matters worse.

No matter how perfect a relationship, you remain two individual people. Two do not become one. The magic is what each person brings to the party. The outcome is seldom the picture you've been given to hang in your head.

It's extraordinary when you find someone. It heightens the adventure you're already living. It can even change you.

In 1943, a federal judge named J. Waties Waring met Elizabeth Avery Hoffman. You've likely never heard of either person. Waring was an eighth-generation Charleston man, with segregationist beliefs in South Carolina, a state where this wasn't at all shocking. Elizabeth Avery Hoffman was a staunch liberal from a wealthy family in Detroit, Michigan. President Franklin D. Roosevelt nominated Waring for a U.S. district judgeship in 1942, and he was confirmed without objection.

When Waring met Hoffman, they were both married to other people. But by 1945, he had divorced his wife, to whom he was married for thirty-two years, going to Florida to get it done, because South Carolina didn't allow divorce. Hoffman divorced her second husband. They then married each other.

A former bigot, Judge Waring would eventually end the segregation of white and black jurors in his South Carolina courtroom. In October 1948, according to Charlestonmag.com and other reports, he appointed an African-American man, John Fleming, as his bailiff. In 1948, a time when the Democratic Party was segregationist, Waring ordered the party's rolls opened for everyone, regardless of race, "with all deliberate speed," as was the saying at the time. *Time* magazine wrote about Waring in 1948, headlining their story about him "The Man They Love to Hate."

Waring's famous dissent would become a part of American civil rights history. "His most dramatic ruling," wrote James Hutchisson for Charlestonmag.com, "was the 1951 *Briggs v. Elliot* case, for which he declared the Clarendon County school board's separate but equal doctrine unconstitutional, laying the groundwork for the historic 1954 *Brown v. Board of Education* school desegregation decision."

J. Waties Waring and Elizabeth Hoffman Waring became outcasts, pariahs of white society, with African-American civil rights activists often invited into their home. The Warings had a cross burned on their lawn. They received hate mail and telephone calls that "began and ended with slurs and condemnations." Elizabeth was called "the witch of Meeting Street," named for the street on which the couple lived. The new Mrs. Waring was blamed for her husband's turn against segregation, her liberal politics the scourge responsible for changing his stance.

Elizabeth Waring appeared on NBC's *Meet the Press* on February 11, 1950, which you likely now recognize as the crescendo before the feminine mystique era, when women's activism was hardly appreciated. When she said that states were making progress on civil rights, but South Carolina remained "an exact replica of Russia," all hell broke loose at home. According to an article posted on CharlestonRevisisted. blogspot in 2012, "On February 12, 1950, the South Carolina House of Representatives introduced a resolution to appropriate funds to purchase one-way tickets for Judge Waring and his wife, Elizabeth, to 'any place they desired, provided that they never return to the state.'"

Waties and Elizabeth Waring would eventually settle in New York City. Activists today are working to get a memorial for J. Waties Waring, the South Carolinian who became a civil rights hero, influenced, no doubt, by the great love of his life, Elizabeth.

The right partner can make all the difference.

It's a gamble, a great adventure you're in together.

The perfect relationship requires you do the work to keep it that way, which means you spend time together. If you both have careers, make dates if you must, but see each other. Schedule the time and don't break it.

Have a good time often.

Laugh.

Enjoy delicious food.

See a great movie; take turns picking them if one of you likes action and the other likes comedy.

Talk.

Have sex.

Nurture the attraction you first felt. The moments when you're first starting a relationship are times you'll celebrate forever. Fill them with fun and never stop.

We can be inspired by tales of great love in books, and through the movies. *Casablanca* is one of the most famous and most cited. People in history we romanticize, like John F. Kennedy and Jacqueline Bouvier Kennedy, impact us, even though their real stories hardly match the myth, bringing them down to mere mortals in size. Ronald Reagan's confessions to Nancy that he was "the most married man in the world and would be totally lost and desolate without you" remind us of love's intensity. The adventure of Hillary and Bill is an epic tale of undaunted commitment lived beyond the blaring headlines. Then there are those ordinary people we know, deciding to create a life together, who simply make their own corner of the world a better place, sometimes through civic accomplishment, or having a family, maybe by having children who go on to move the world forward.

A perfect relationship is the one you create and live yourself with someone who has joined with you to see what you can discover and share together. It starts with attraction, then a bond of friendship that explodes into passion, lust and then love. If you're ready and willing to do the work that comes with anything in life that's worth having, you just might be able to make it work.

Whether you can make it last is another matter entirely.

That depends on how you each ride the ravages of life's events, personally and together, which can only happen if you remain strong as individuals as you stand alone. Nothing can divide two people who know who they are and what they've got, and are determined and committed to protect it for life. It's a decision you make no matter what the act of living throws at you, which is often unfair and at times overwhelming, but inevitably thrilling, if you never give up.

As a beauty queen who dreamed as a kid of working on Broadway, I never thought stage fright would hit me out of nowhere at the end of those heady days and jettison me to Los Angeles, California, where I found my calling as a writer, leading me to excavate the worlds of love, politics and sex. From Beverly Hills, the very last place on earth I thought I'd land was in Las Vegas, Nevada. And if anyone had ever suggested it was here I'd meet a blue-collar, truck-loving, gun-toting gas technician, a man who would walk through my front door 12 hours after I arrived in Sin City, whom I would marry five months later… Well, I'd have said you were nuts!

It's not like I mapped it out.

"If They Could See Me Now" has a whole new meaning from when I sang it at the Miss America Pageant.

One thing I never planned to have was the perfect relationship. But I've got it. Life happens when you're busy fulfilling your own dreams. It comes when you least expect it, whether you think you want it or not. However your perfect relationship is defined, it doesn't mean it will be easy.

Life is wet and messy.

I actually attracted the perfect man for me simply by surviving and thriving through the battles of life that made me who I am, however wild things might have gotten on the road that led me to his city and he to my front door.

It happened by making room for a man as he shows up, not as you think he should be.

On paper, my husband and I couldn't have been a more unlikely match. But that's the thing about being unafraid to live your life as it's presented to you. It honors the mysteries of life's adventures that blow us onto an unplanned course, dropping wildly fascinating people in our path. The moments that arrive out of nowhere that dare you to be brave and choose the risk.

Just make sure you know what you want and don't be afraid to ask for it. You just might meet someone who's prepared to deliver his half, leaving the rest up to you.

Epilogue

So, what did I learn in the trenches?

That relationships depend on answering the question *What do you want?* The answer is different for every woman, every individual.

Sofia Vergara was the highest-paid TV actor (of either gender) during the fiscal year of 2012-2013, according to *Forbes* magazine. The gorgeous and talented star of ABC's *Modern Family* is crafting her own modern family. She and her fiancé Nick Loeb want to eventually have a child together. Vergara confessed she intends to use a gestational surrogate; Vergara's eggs, Loeb's sperm. The rumor started spreading, Vergara believes, because she had her eggs frozen, which required going to her "doctor's office a hundred million times to do injections," as she put it to *Cosmopolitan* magazine in June 2013. "A friend will carry the baby for them. They have been planning this for a while," said an unnamed source. Vergara explained she had had "thyroid cancer and lots of radiation," making the surrogate a necessity for the couple.

This is not your average decision, but there's no reason it couldn't be, because women can choose whatever they can afford. Women of means can throw money at their challenges to create the exact life they want. Vergara's option is one prior generations of wealthy women couldn't have dreamed of doing.

If a poll were conducted of women who have children, how many of them would prefer for someone else to carry and deliver a child for them, especially at forty-something?

Such conversations are important, not because women will all start making these choices, but to widen the discussion of what women can do for themselves if they have the support group and means. Financially independent women blowing out a few norms makes it easier for other women to customize their own lives without worrying what people will say, though how other people see your life shouldn't matter. It's your life.

Vergara's fierce independence blows the doors off of traditional stereotypes and rules that we don't need anymore. Anything that expands options for women is a positive advancement.

One thing we're all facing is the possibility of a second-chance relationship or marriage. The first try at love doesn't always stick or last. Some people marry young when they're not ready and by forty are ready for another try. This means luggage. Some parts of it are harder to handle than others.

When it became public that Tiger Woods, the famed golfer, and Lindsey Vonn, World Cup champion skier, were a couple, the tabloid world went crazy. "Dangerous Romance," screamed the *US Weekly* April 2013 headline. "She was warned!"

The stories exploded on March 18, 2013, when Woods and Vonn admitted they were dating, then posted four photos of themselves together on the Internet.

It was about the same time Woods reclaimed his number one golfer in the world status. When it happened, Vonn tweeted simply, "Number 1!"

Of course, Ms. Vonn felt compelled to also make a statement, where else but on Facebook: "I guess it wasn't a well-kept secret but yes, I am dating Tiger Woods. Our relationship evolved from a friendship into something more over these past few months and it has made me very happy. I don't plan on addressing this further as I would like to keep that part of my life between us, my family and close friends. Thank you for understanding and your continued support! xo LV."

The chattering classless predictably bombarded the comments section, warning Vonn of the inevitable to come. It does no good to be cynical about love, because people often beat the odds.

The sports megastars met at a 2012 Tiger Jam charity fundraiser in Las Vegas. At the time, Lindsey Vonn was going through what's been described in the press as a brutal divorce. Woods and Vonn started dating off the radar, meeting clandestinely.

When Vonn had her epic skiing crash in February 2013, Woods sent his jet for her, so she could quickly travel to get what everyone hopes was the career-saving operation. The speculation about their romance started churning immediately, with TMZ getting the photo of Vonn boarding the jet.

Tiger Woods told Vonn everything, the whole sordid story of his so-called sexual addiction, which brought personal and professional humiliation, as well as the complete collapse of his marriage. The event shook Woods' golf standing, as well as his allies, the conflicts ravaging his concentration and professional prowess. The Associated Press in 2012 estimated Woods had dropped $22 million, or 30% of his revenue, by losing several key endorsements, but he was still at the top of golf's earning elite.

Does anyone believe a woman as worldly as Lindsey Vonn wasn't aware of most of the dirty details? The salaciousness of the events was front-page, television and Internet news for months. Nothing is so deliciously seductive for the American public as a mighty sports hero being taken down to size through his own actions. The women involved were all too eager to help, jumping in to reveal the dirty details and sordid secrets of their sexual romps with Tiger Woods, so they could bask in their fifteen minutes of fame.

There is no reason for Vonn to think that Woods would risk another worldwide sex scandal. For one thing, his kids are old enough to be close witnesses this time. People can change after being humbled. When they're humiliated publicly, it's even worse. That Woods won't get another chance to remake himself is obvious.

Vonn's own marriage is also part of this story. It was making her miserable, even if on the outside everything looked great. The tabloids detailed a "controlling husband," a man who was her manager and coach, whom she wanted to get away from for "months, years." Vonn herself simply told *People* magazine in 2012 that "Nothing bad happened, but there was just unhappiness." She recounted to *People* the debilitating depression she had suffered because of the troubles in her marriage, but which had also been an issue since she was a teenager.

When you peel back the notoriety of the two people involved, Woods and Vonn dating makes perfect sense. Who could possibly understand the intense training and dedication more than a person who has to do it herself? However, the number one golfer in the world paired with the number one skier in the world makes for significant time apart, which will likely be as much of a challenge as the luggage Tiger Woods brings to the relationship. Maybe the seasonal differences in their careers will allow them to fit their professional lives together.

This is an extreme relationship case, obviously, but the faith Lindsey Vonn has placed in Tiger Woods, as they attempt to be together and make their relationship work, is something every woman must do when she meets a man with a complicated past. Vonn's public embrace of Woods takes even more courage, because of the involvement of the international press. It didn't take any time before media outlets were jumping on how the relationship could affect *her* endorsements with Under Armour and Red Bull, in addition to Rolex, which they both represent. There's no reason her endorsement deals should suffer at all.

Businessweek talked to an athletic branding expert, Anthony Fernandez, who offered this assessment: "I don't think her price tag will go up. But she'll definitely become more valuable to her existing sponsors. She was a name to begin with, but now that she's dating Woods, she's entered another league."

Woods and Vonn have a lot in common. They're also older — he's thirty-eight at this writing; she's twenty-nine. They've been through the ringer, which goes double for Woods. She's already been introduced to his kids, so it's obvious it's serious. After their pasts have been shared and digested, which it has by now, the rest is simply up to them. It's now about who they are with one another, the value they place on the relationship and the commitment of each person to keep working on themselves. We all have demons, and if we ignore them they won't go away, they just get bigger.

When Tiger Woods first faced the media after his sex scandal humiliation, he handled it very, very poorly. It's obvious he learned from that mistake or, at the very least, got good advice, so he and Lindsey Vonn are ahead at this point. Together, they also pulled off beating the tabloids, by conspiring as a couple to release their own photos when they made their relationship public. Tiger Woods told the *New York Times*: "We wanted to limit the stalk-a-razzi and all those sleazy websites that are out there following us. I've had situations where it's been very dangerous for my kids.... We basically devalued the first photos."

It was a stroke of genius. There can be little doubt that effort alone made Woods and Vonn closer, bonding them as a power-couple that has decided to go on the offense, thoughtfully presenting their own public image together. Relationships are difficult enough in private, but the pressure on Woods and Vonn is incalculable. If they can steal some normalcy amid their high-flying careers they just might enjoy themselves and get a chance to see what's really between them.

With more people having second marriages and serial monogamous relationships, the possibility you'll meet up with the perfect guy who has no past is between slim and nil. What matters is the full honesty with which he describes his past failures, including moral lapses. When he's telling you his story, perhaps about a prior marriage, does he accept blame? Does he admit getting help for an addiction? Does she say she works daily on her depression?

Lindsey Vonn, if the relationship progresses, will also face what many women do today, which is taking on the role of the second female in the life of her new man's children, maybe eventually the duties of a stepmother. Few responsibilities are more complex.

Some women come into a relationship with a man who has children after the kids are grown, so their involvement is minimal. It can be tricky, especially when the divorce is bad, which I've seen close up. It's not a situation for the young or inexperienced. There are countless books on how to handle the situation, which comes in all forms, but nothing quite prepares you, especially when you fall in love with a man who is also wounded. Read up and make sure you're ready. Spend time with the children involved, but also know what will be expected of you. Marrying someone divorced with children requires a mature person who is fully secure and knows how to set boundaries. Nothing quite prepares you for the hell-on-wheels ex-wife or ex-husband, who hasn't let go and has issues to burn. It's as serious as it gets, and you shouldn't go into it lightly.

It doesn't matter your age; relationships are the dessert of life, with the urge to find a spectacular connection always on our minds. Martha Stewart proved in April of 2013 that if you're healthy, vibrant and single, even famous women find using online dating sites a way to meet men. In an interview with Matt Lauer on the *Today* show, Stewart said she's looking for someone "youngish..., tallish..., really smart," and successful, because "that would be important to him." She's exactly right, because men can have very sensitive egos about money, which must be respected.

Martha Stewart's profile on Match.com states, "Yes, it's really me." She is looking for a man between the ages of fifty and seventy. At seventy-one, she looks fantastic, with her economic status allowing many options, especially if a man is secure. This is part of her terrific page, which Match.com chief executive Sam Yagan helped her compile: "Someone who's intelligent, established and curious; and who relishes adventure and new experiences as much as I do. Someone who can teach me new things. A lover of animals, grandchildren and the outdoors. Young at heart." Oh, and Martha wants someone "spiritual, but not religious." Amen to that.

One other thing in Ms. Stewart's profile is something I can confirm because I've seen it myself: "I've always been a big believer that technology, if used well, can enhance one's life. So here I am, looking to enhance my dating life." Online dating can work and trying it beats sitting around and wondering.

There is a lot of advice on the web that has gone from "girls should never say yes to sex on the first date" to "never say no to sex, ever, if you're in a relationship." Other columns talk about what a man goes through when he hears no to sex. In a relationship there is one reaction, while before the relationship it all depends on the situation and the development between the two people. Sometimes on the first date, sex just comes naturally. Sometimes sex on the first date means you never hear from the person again. Connection between the people and circumstances of the sexual encounter are what matter. But detailed sex news still assaults us all daily, reminding us that even in the best marriages things can go off course.

When former Democratic Representative Anthony Weiner started sexting provocative pictures of himself to women, it ended with his secret sex life being exposed, which is what anyone faces today. The risks Weiner took, weighed against what he had to lose, made his reckless exhibitionism look even more extreme once it was featured on *The Daily Show* by his friend Jon Stewart, a situation that embarrassed them both. Lisa Weiss, one of the women who received Weiner's sexy photos and then chose to expose him publicly, ended up apologizing to him on Facebook in September 2012. Weiner's wife Huma Abedin has forgiven him. His run for mayor of New York City was to be his rehabilitation tour.

It began through slowly building his approval rating with voters, with it looking like he just might be able to make a comeback. Then his sexting with Sydney Leathers hit the tabloid press and went viral, a dalliance that happened after he was forced to resign from Congress. Dragging New Yorkers and everyone else back into the tawdry details of yet another X-rated Weiner show. Only this time, the woman he'd chosen had her eyes on cashing in on the notoriety her virtual tryst had brought her, quickly accepting an offer to star in a hard-core XXX-rated Vivid movie titled *Weiner and Me*.

In an interview with *GQ*, published in November 2013, Anthony Weiner talks about what his wife Huma Abedin has had to go through and how she doesn't deserve it. That Abedin has been a trusted aide of Hillary Clinton for years, and considered family by the Clintons, made the coverage even more intense.

Even knowing his wife is "more sensitive" about these things, Weiner still couldn't stop himself. "I'm just an empty, soulless vessel, so it doesn't hurt me as much," Weiner told *GQ*, which was described as being delivered with "an utter lack of humor." The masochistic persona revealed through this statement seems to come from an exhibitionist who's content to wallow in humiliation, otherwise why continue to give interviews? The self-destructive behavior of Weiner's alter ego, Carlos Danger, provided an outlet for his fetish. Where's that release to go now? Reading his rhetorical self-flagellation in *GQ*, there's no evidence that he's healed or that Carlos Danger has been put down, only that he's now speaking through Weiner publicly. A woman choosing to stay in the vortex of this tortured inferno is in a very precarious place.

When Gawker.com caught very married Republican Representative Chris Lee sending a shirtless photo of himself to Craigslist's "Women Seeking Men" forum, and then uncovered embarrassing emails he'd sent to a girl who answered his ad, Lee ended up losing his seat in Congress.

Neither of these episodes involved actual sex, unlike former New York Governor Eliot Spitzer, who also tried a political comeback running for New York City comptroller in 2013, but was turned away by voters, too. Spitzer's marriage came to an end soon afterward.

When a woman gets caught sending naked selfies, it's seen as something even more scandalous, even in these liberated times. It's also dangerous. It's just that we rarely hear of this happening to a professional woman, let alone one in politics, which is actually unthinkable.

The self-destructing-photo program Snapchat had an estimated 5 million active monthly users in April 2013, according to the *Guardian*, who in November 2013 estimated that Snapchat likely had "around 26 million U.S. users." That number was based on the Pew Internet and American Life Project, which reported in October 2013: "This is the first time we have measured Snapchat use. Some 9% of cell phone owners use the app. It is especially popular among cell owners ages 18-29, 26% of whom use the app. Among all smartphone owners, 12% use Snapchat."

Snapchat deletes photos ten seconds after you send them, with the evidence deleted from the servers once the photos are opened. Or maybe not. Snaphack, a new app available through iTunes, allows you to save a photo or video, without the sender knowing it. The details from Huffington Post, who tried it and found it worked, from October 2013: "You download Snaphack app and log in with your Snapchat name and password. When someone sends you a photo or video via Snapchat, open it through Snaphack rather than through Snapchat and you'll have it permanently in Snaphack." Facebook made an offer of $3 billion for Snapchat, but were rebuffed, which the *Wall Street Journal* reported in November 2013. Facebook hoped to utilize Snapchat to attract teens, but founders Evan Spiegel and Bobby Murphy held out for a higher offer.

We're bound to get bored with this stuff eventually and ricochet back to being satisfied with a little less risk in our communications, right? It's already happened with teens and twenty-somethings, who are turning to messenger apps. It would be a good start if people didn't use social media as a confessional, with the hard rule and discipline to never drink and sext, post on Facebook, or blast out racy selfies when you're bombed.

America still hasn't quite grown up.

As far as our culture is concerned, even as we enter the second decade of the twenty-first century, age is the arbitrary measure of maturity. We look to a number that jettisons every girl into womanhood, instead of her own internal signals, which go off long before society wants to acknowledge. Parents are too petrified to consider that girls become sexualized before puberty, involuntarily. The thought of mommy's or daddy's little girl getting it about sex all on her own just as she enters her teens, even if the mechanics and complications still mystify, is too horrifying to contemplate, even if it's true. So, it's no wonder parents find themselves scared to death about the virtual and social media world that confronts a girl's independence and confidence daily, just as her body starts screaming at her.

Today's generation of girls is different, even if parents don't want to admit or accept it. The important thing to make clear is that you're always there. Giving girls more respect, inside boundaries, might make them more willing to come to you before things go horribly off course.

Marie Osmond, a Mormon and multitalented singer and actress, wrote about her lesbian daughter in her memoir, *The Key Is Love: My Mother's Wisdom, A Daughter's Gratitude*. Huffington Post covered the story in late March 2013, and on same-sex marriage, Osmond is quoted saying to ABC's Diane Sawyer: "I believe in [my daughter's] civil rights, as a mother. I think that my daughter deserves everything that she desires in life. She's a good girl. She's a wonderful child. I don't think God made one color flower. I think he made many."

I didn't wake up one day and choose to be heterosexual, so I have never understood why people think gays and lesbians get to determine their own sexuality. A person is born gay. It's not a choice. When you know someone who is gay, and I know many, it educates you. Whether it's Marie Osmond realizing her daughter is gay, or you making that realization about your own child, maybe even yourself, it becomes obvious very quickly that we are who we are, because we're born a unique individual from the start.

Everyone in America has the legal right to love, marry and pursue happiness. We also have the right to choose to simply live together for all eternity.

Marriages and relationships come in every form.

Goldie Hawn and Kurt Russell have been together since 1983, have raised four kids, and remain unmarried.

Jon Hamm, of *Mad Men* and the movies, and Jennifer Westfeldt, an actress and writer/director, have been happily unmarried since 1997. Hollywood.com quotes Hamm as telling *Parade* magazine in 2012, "I don't have the marriage chip, and neither of us have the greatest examples of marriages in our families. But Jen is the love of my life, and we've already been together four times longer than my parents were married."

I can so relate on the missing "marriage chip" thing. I absolutely didn't have it either. When I met my husband, I told him so. Marriage was never for me. I never wanted it. The thing is, Mark demanded it. He gave me a very straightforward ultimatum. His case was that we were in love, he knew who I was and the course I was on, and that marriage was the only way he'd sign on. I had to take the jump and marry him, or it was over. It was that simple for him.

It blew me away. The ultimatum didn't come off harsh, because the case he made was very convincing. He was willing to risk it all, fight the fight with me, protect and love me, but that it had to be an all-in proposition. Knowing I had always been just passing through Las Vegas from the start, while he had never lived anywhere else in his adult life, he knew he'd have to live in another city, away from where his family lived, to be with me. Women are asked to do this all the time. Men rarely are.

It was all or nothing for him, and it needed to be for me, too, which for Mark meant marriage.

I could have committed to living with him forever, but marriage? It's the last thing I wanted from him, something I didn't need from him either. We loved each other madly and that was enough for me.

I'll never forget looking into Mark's eyes the day he proposed the final time, laying it on the line one last time. I'd never seen such intensity, such fierce love and understanding coming from a man. In that instant, I simply knew he'd deliver and stand tough in the turbulence I knew he'd face. I'd had many an adventure, but sure didn't want to hurt this wonderful man, so I'd told him how difficult it would be. We weren't kids and we both knew ourselves, and what we wanted from a life together. Then I asked myself, what's the worst thing that can happen? There was no other decision to make but to go for it.

We had met in July and were married in December of the same year. None of my friends believed me when I said I was engaged. When I asked my sister Susie to be my maid of honor she said, call me in a month and if it's still on I'll do it. Marrying Mark is the most important decision I've made in my life and the best one, too.

If my sexual education in the trenches proves anything, especially in my own life, it's what Victor Hugo said: "There's nothing more powerful than an idea whose time has come."

I'm talking about the idea that a woman can expect a man to be an equal partner in a relationship, but also in a marriage, which can include signing on for a career adventure that doesn't come with a net. A man can choose to believe in a woman's purpose, creativity and vision, knowing it doesn't devalue his own contributions in any way. When he truly believes that what she's exploring is worth betting on, a man can feel pride sharing in her success, which validates the choice he made to take the leap with her.

It means marriage can survive redefinition from the traditionalist model and work at least as well as an equal partnership that includes two careers, because there are no tasks defined strictly by gender anymore. We're carving out a revolutionary way to think about marriage that empowers women and gives us a shot at leading, which was once only experienced by men. The men in turn get a chance to enjoy home life, including being an equal partner in raising children, if the couple chooses.

Facebook COO Sheryl Sandberg put it succinctly in her book *Lean In*: "A truly equal world would be one where women ran half our countries and companies and men ran half our homes. I believe that this would be a better world."

Smart women also know, as Sandberg wrote, that one of the most important decisions a woman makes is about the man whom she decides to date and commit to.

Committing to someone, often through marriage, is the most difficult adventure in life. It's one of the most rewarding, too. But if it works, you will still be living a solitary life, too, having an adventure on your own, outside the one you're having with your mate.

We each live in our own world, so if you want a healthy life, you will also maintain your own privacy, while giving him his. You will have solitary experiences that don't include your partner, though not ones that should threaten your relationship. These are the personal moments you can choose to bring back to him to discuss over cocktail hour or dinner at night, sharing the amazing things you learned during your day away from one another. Separate experiences that matter to you both, if in different ways. They expand you as a person, while transmitting to your partner that you're engaged in your own life, excited and fulfilled by your own journey.

Modern people need downtime to take a breath, to be alone. It can be as simple as time to read a book, go to the gym, catch up on paperwork, even watch television. The battle of the sexes is over, but we haven't yet replaced it with a modern deal between the sexes, an all-for-me-means-all-for-you-too grace. It can be a replica inside our relationship that mimics the distance we had when we first started dating that creates space for longing and appreciation that reminds us of when we met, before convenience took hold — part of the alchemy of your love.

The magic that ignites the potential of the modern relationship that starts with a physical whiff. The scent of someone who ignites the sexual chemistry that immediately hits you, even if you can't explain it. The moment we meet someone unique that could come down to an involuntary reaction to the way he or she smells. Our nose may tell us how we feel before our heart or head engages. But when it happens, we sense it first.

The rest is about timing...

...and believing you deserve it. It's trusting that you are worthy of finding delicious, sexually thrilling, life-altering love. That it can happen to you and that someone would be fortunate to be loved by you. It's that meeting of minds, body and energy that allows two people to form an alliance to take on the world.

Meeting someone who ignites that mysterious part of you, who can inspire you to be more than you are by yourself. A partnership that challenges your notion of the life you want, including what's possible to experience with someone else. Attracting a partner who excites you to add the adventure of being part of a team. All for whatever you desire, both for each other and forever together.

Of all of the things I've learned in the trenches, talking to more men and women that I can accurately count, there is one constant. Everyone desires an electric connection, a person that sets your life aflame. Someone who inspires you to get naked and risk living out loud in front of them and with them every day. From there it can be further defined, sometimes fitting sublimely into marriage, sometimes not. It's not the delineation that matters. It's the agreement between you on what it is that you've got and that what you've discovered is worth protecting.

If you're living an authentic life of your own design and imagination, someone can fly into your life and force you to make room so they fit.

Prepare to be surprised.

Then say yes.

Acknowledgments

The first political writing I ever did was on November 23, 1963, after President John F. Kennedy was assassinated. It wasn't until 2011 that I was handed the index cards I wrote on that day by my big brother Larry, the scribbling on them by a little girl chronicling what she saw on television. This was the instant politics became real to me, which was cemented years later when Gloria Steinem kicked off the modern feminist revolution that changed my world forever. Little did I know it would all end up where it has, including writing this book.

There aren't words to express how grateful I am to my creative counsel and great friend Judith Proffer, and everyone at Padaro Press. Judy and I have been on this road together for twenty years now, as plotters and dreamers, separately, but always together, no matter how many miles may separate us. I learned what it's like to have an engaged publisher, someone who loves books and nurtures the vision by extracting all a writer has to give, then asks for a little bit more.

Applause for designSimple, and art director Dave Shulman, who are responsible for the cover to cover creative packaging in which this writing is nestled.

Thanks to Premier Digital Publishing who published my second book, *The Hillary Effect*, which was instrumental in making this book possible. When everyone thought Hillary Clinton's 2008 campaign was old news, Thomas Ellsworth of Premier Digital Publishing knew they were wrong, with Barnes & Noble picking it as the first political book in their Nook "featured authors" launch. PDP continues to stand behind *The Hillary Effect*, and now the title is available online and in paperback in 2014 through Open Road Media.

Eric Estrin has been my editor on two books now, fact-checking material, challenging me on content, for which I am grateful. Additional proofreading by Frank Culbertson was invaluable.

I've bugged my older brother Larry my entire adult life to keep adding morsels to our family history so I could one day put it all together. If he hadn't been so diligent, I'd never have made sense of the puzzle. It was my sister Susie who produced the final corner piece at our sibling reunion in 2011.

About my big sister... It was Susie and her late husband Steve who provided the first healthy relationship I ever saw between a man and a woman, an epic love affair by every measure. Oh, and did they know how to party! I will be forever grateful for their generosity. I idolized Susie as a kid, hung on her every action, and will never forget her taking me to Our Lady of Fatima, my first introduction into Catholicism that eventually led me to the Episcopal Church that changed my journey of faith. My relationship with Susie was one of the casualties of our father Floyd, her forgiveness and our reconnection becoming part of the private chapter in this story that made for a happy ending.

I'm indebted to both Larry and Susie for respecting my creative journey, even if the artistic path I am on is difficult to understand. They each made sure their children got autographed copies of *The Hillary Effect*, so my nephew and nieces might better understand what the hell is up with their aunt, who lives in another universe.

Continued gratitude goes to Lorie Miller, Vice President, Web Services of AgoraNet Inc., who has been indispensable to me over many years. There aren't enough superlatives to heap on Lorie to express all she's done for me, from expertise to her professional graciousness, while keeping my new-media site humming and continually on the cutting edge. Lorie and the AgoraNet team are the best in the business, and I can say that with some authority.

To the readers of TaylorMarsh.com over many years now, I am blessed to have such loyal followers, as well as haters. If it weren't for my readers, I wouldn't be able to get my books published.

A very special shout-out is deserved to the people who support my new-media site through subscriptions and donations. You make all the difference, as do my advertisers. It's the way independent writers like myself survive in the brutally competitive new-media world, where mega-sites gobble up the advertising dollars and the traffic, too.

The love of my life, my husband Mark, makes everything in my life more joyful, with every second I spend with him a gift. Nothing could have kept me off the path I have forged, which started long before we met, but meeting him and becoming true partners has added immeasurably to my work, not to mention my life, and understanding of love and marriage. He's the strongest feminist male I know, for which I have his late mother Joanne to thank. Having a courageous partner has made me a more uncompromising thinker and writer in every way.

Mom, wherever you are, and I hope you are finally at peace, thank you. My mother not only gave me life, but refused to accept when it was time to leave, because she knew I still needed her. Because of her unflinching fearlessness, her ability to withstand everything that was thrown at her, I was able to do the same. Every tiny success I have is hers to share with Mark, whom I wish she could have met.

I've had a lot of creative dreams in my life, but being able to write what I'd learned about relationships and sex in the trenches always seemed a bridge too far. There was so much I had to face myself before I could write this story, so I needed a lot more than a room of my own to get it done. The timing was finally perfect, thirteen years after 9/11 hit and blew me onto the course that's become a seminal chapter in my life. It's just one reason I can relate to Hillary Clinton saying, "Never give in, never give up on your dreams," just keep on going.

Thanks for buying this book.

Maybe it will help my husband get more time off. Though for him it really boils down to what he wants for me. Witnessing the endless hours watching me work, he believes in what I'm doing and wants for me the full rewards that he thinks I've earned. I've got so much, because what was once my work is now our passion and a joint adventure that revolves around changing our corner of the universe, while having fun doing it.

The ultimate lesson I've learned by living it is that it's possible for a female artist, thinker and writer to find a partner and create a wildly unpredictable and lively relationship of love, lust and purpose, which doesn't require sacrificing that thing that drives you. It didn't happen through searching for it or forcing it to happen. It manifested while I was doing what I love, that thing that makes me tick.

Taylor Marsh is best known for being a "die hard Clintonite," as the Washington Post described her in a 2008 profile, "For Clinton, a Following of 'Marshans.' " The New Republic profile of Clinton in 2008, "The Hugh Hefner of Politics," chronicles Marsh from her artistic career into politics. A contributor to the *Huffington Post* as well as other sites, Marsh's blog (www.taylormarsh.com) was on the front lines during the 2008 election season.

Marsh grew up in St. Louis, Missouri, where she was Miss Teenage St. Louis and was crowned Miss Missouri. She attended Stephens College in Columbia, Missouri, where she was born, graduating with a BFA. Next stop was Broadway, where Jerry Herman cast her after her very first audition. Marsh has produced her own one-woman show on JFK and her life growing up in the midst of the feminist revolution, and has done national television commercials.

In the early 1990s, Marsh worked at the alternative news source *LA Weekly* in the personal ad department as "relationship consultant" with her column "What Do You Want?" dispensing relationship advice mixed with a little politics. In 1997, she jumped to become managing editor of one of the first outlets online to make money, a soft-core site covered on the front page of the *Wall Street Journal, U.S. News & World Report*, and *USA Today*. Marsh took her long-established new-media career to blogging during the Kerry campaign of 2004. But it was the 2008 election and Marsh's fearless coverage of the campaign that catapulted her.

Marsh has been interviewed by the BBC, CNN, MSNBC, C-SPAN's *Washington Journal*, Al Jazeera Arabic, and Al Jazeera English, among others, including radio from coast to coast. Marsh has been featured in the *Hill*, the *Washington Scene, National Journal's Hotline On Call*, the *Los Angeles Times*, the *New York Times* online, and many other new-media and traditional news venues.

OPEN ROAD
INTEGRATED MEDIA

Open Road Integrated Media is a digital publisher and multimedia content company. Open Road creates connections between authors and their audiences by marketing its ebooks through a new proprietary online platform, which uses premium video content and social media.

Videos, Archival Documents, and New Releases

Sign up for the Open Road Media newsletter and get news delivered straight to your inbox.

Sign up now at
www.openroadmedia.com/newsletters

CPSIA information can be obtained at www.ICGtesting.com
Printed in the USA
LVOW11s2142280914

406297LV00001B/151/P